ASPECTS OF ROTHERHAM 3

ASPECTS OF ROTHERHAM

3 Discovering Local History

Edited by
Melvyn Jones

Series Editor
Brian Elliott

Wharncliffe Publishing

First Published in 1998 by
Wharncliffe Publishing
an imprint of
Pen and Sword Books Limited,
47 Church Street, Barnsley,
South Yorkshire. S70 2AS

For up-to-date information on other titles produced under the
Wharncliffe imprint, please telephone or write to:

    Wharncliffe Publishing
    FREEPOST
    47 Church Street
    Barnsley
    South Yorkshire S70 2BR
    Telephone (24 hours): 01226 - 734555

ISBN: 1-871647-44-4

A CIP catalogue record of this book is available from the
British Library

Cover illustration: *Interior of Rotherham Parish Church 1846* by William Cowen.
Courtesy of Rotherham Metropolitan Borough Council, Department of Libraries, Museum and Arts.

Printed in Great Britain by
St. Edmundsbury Press, Bury St. Edmunds, Suffolk.

CONTENTS

INTRODUCTION

by Melvyn Jones

The publication of this third volume in the *Aspects of Rotherham* series marks a further important stage in the development of the *Aspects* series as a whole. From its beginnings in 1993, with the publication of *Aspects of Barnsley*, it has now grown to a series of eleven volumes: five volumes on Barnsley, three volumes on Rotherham, and single volumes on Sheffield, Doncaster and Leeds, with more to come. So far this represents more than 160 articles by local authors on every aspect of local history: economic history, social history, popular culture, historical biography, environmental history, landscape history, medical history, transport history, military history, the history of religion, oral history, architectural history... The list of subjects is almost endless.

The present volume continues the tradition of bringing a wide variety of studies in local history to the attention of the general reader. They are all written by local experts with long experience of researching their subjects, with an intimate knowledge of the sources that will give up the secrets of their chosen topic, and illustrated with a bewildering variety of maps, diagrams, photographs and other illustrations, many never before published. The articles should have a strong appeal to long-established Rotherham residents and newcomers alike.

Not surprisingly, industrial topics loom large. There are three articles on the local coal mining industry. Ian Medlicott charts the development of coal mining on the Wentworth estate during a critical 100 years spanning the eighteenth and nineteenth centuries; Graham Hague investigates the landscape remains of the network of colliery tramroads that once criss-crossed the north-western part of the Borough; and Trevor Lodge demonstrates the long inter-relationship between the coal and steel industries and shows that history is as recent as yesterday, with this particular alliance still affecting communities in the local region. Continuing the industrial theme, Chris Morley shows the national significance of Rotherham's stove grate, range and decorative cast iron industry.

It is not surprising, either, that the extensive Wentworth estate, with the largest collection of archives accessible to the public (in Sheffield Archives), should attract the attention of local historians. Mention has already been made of Ian Medlicott's article on coal mining on the Wentworth estate; in addition Melvyn Jones shows how successive heads of the Wentworth family enlarged the estate in the eighteenth century through purchase, enclosure and marriage; and Marjorie Bloy discusses the complexities of managing an army of indoor and outdoor servants on the Wentworth estate in the second half of the eighteenth century.

Landscape and architectural history are also well represented in this volume. Alice Rodgers makes extensive use of archival and landscape evidence to uncover the history of deer parks in the Maltby area; Howard Smith examines the development of a number of ancient highways linking Rotherham with the surrounding region and beyond; Alan Whitworth investigates the history of local windmills; Brian Elliott surveys the careers of members of the Platt family, important mason-architects; and Simeon Bennett and Tony Dodsworth demonstrate the richness and variety of pre-eighteenth century church monuments in the Rotherham area.

Finally, there are articles on military, and electoral history. John Goodchild describes the role and organisation of the Wath Wood Volunteers, a home guard corps in the Napoleonic wars; and finally Alex Fleming uses contemporary accounts and reports to reconstruct the details of the riotous behaviour and its aftermath at Wath during the General Election of 1865.

The book could not have been produced without the help and support of a number of key individuals. I would like to thank Charles Hewitt of Wharncliffe Publishing for his continued support for the *Aspects* series and to Barbara Bramall, Roni Wilkinson, Paul Wilkinson, Mike Parsons and Paula Brennan at Wharncliffe for their sterling efforts. I also acknowledge the help of Hazel Proctor with word processing and Neil Donovan for technical help with discs. I also wish to thank Bob Warburton who has produced a number of key maps and Eric Leslie who has contributed superb line drawings. The help given to contributors by staff in the Archives and Local Studies Section of Rotherham Central Library and at Sheffield Archives is also gratefully acknowledged. Finally, I would like to acknowledge the wise advice of Brian Elliott, overall series editor.

The book is dedicated to the memory of Robert Chesman of Thorpe Hesley (1909 -1998), gentleman, and historian of Thorpe.

1. DEER PARKS IN THE MALTBY AREA

by Alice Rodgers

PARKS OF WHATEVER DATE HAVE, in recent years, become the obsession of students of the landscape. To a local historian, intent on the study of large scale maps and plans, the pursuit of them soon becomes addictive. They combine two rather attractive features. The first is that, because they are relatively large, long after they have fallen out of use, they are capable of remaining visible as names or as outlines on maps. The second is that earlier students, who relied mostly on national or regional sources have tended to underestimate the numbers of parks in particular areas, so that it remains possible for a parish historian to uncover significant but previously unknown examples.

Those who use local sources must base at least some of their conclusions on the rather flimsy foundations of place-name evidence. The name *park* on a modern map can mean a variety of things. Derived from the Old English *pearroc* (an enclosed piece of land) the term park was, in medieval England, used specifically to denote a private enclosure where deer or other wild animals were kept. In the seventeenth century, the meaning broadened to embrace a formal landscape compatible with the keeping of deer, whilst in the eighteenth, the contrived informality of the landscape park, complete with lakes, serpentine walks and ornamental buildings, was in its heyday. The municipal parks of the nineteenth century brought another shade of meaning, whilst the twentieth century has seen the word distorted to embrace forest parks, country parks, theme parks, science parks and even car parks. That places witnessed some of these uses sequentially or even discontinuously successively can be a trap for the unwary.

Deer used to be regarded as the property of the Crown so, in theory, from the medieval period to that of the later Stuarts it was necessary to obtain a Royal Licence before a park could be created. Susan Neave, in a recent study of medieval parks in East Yorkshire[1], suggests that this was not always done and that even if a licence were sought, evidence of this does not always survive. Reliance on early county maps can also prove misleading. Saxton's 1577 map of Yorkshire, for example, records in the Rotherham area, only Thrybergh Park and two parks near Aston. This map was made after the decline of some parks of the medieval period and before the spate of park creation under the Stuarts, so for Saxton, the area embraced by this study was a parkless landscape.

My aim here has been to record systematically all pre-nineteenth century park names and associated references within the chosen area and to relate these to the modern landscape. The opportunity has also been taken to examine the creation and early history of Sandbeck deer park, licenced in 1637. The boundaries of this study are essentially those of the ancient parish of Maltby, but there is one foray into that part of Laughton near to Roche Abbey where this casts light on or shows influences of features described.

Domesday and later woodland

Very few parks existed prior to the Norman Conquest but, as essentially woodland features, they were most likely to be created in well-wooded areas. The Domesday survey records the extent of local woodland. Based on a form factor of 0.7, there were an estimated 784 acres of *silva pastilis* (wood pasture) in Laughton and 560 acres of the same in Maltby.[2] This gives a general impression of abundant pasturable woodland in the area considered below compared with settlements immediately to the west. This picture is confirmed by large grants of woodland in the parishes of Maltby and Laughton made to Roche Abbey at, or shortly after, its foundation in 1147.

Of particular interest is Henry II's grant of 100 acres of wood in Lindric near the abbey(see Roche Abbey, below). *Lindric* means limewood and its common occurrence as a place-name on the Yorkshire/Nottinghamshire boundary is suggestive of once extensive limewoods there. (Lime here refers to those small and large leaved species of ancient woodland, which are both still found near Roche, rather than to the more modern hybrid lime planted in parks.)

Medieval parks associated with Maltby Manor

MALTBY PARK alias THE OLD PARK, *Grid reference: SK 5292 and 5392.*
Location: in Maltby to the north of the A631. It includes part of the grounds of Maltby Comprehensive School, the sites of Manor Infant and Junior Schools and the Manor and 'Little London' Estates.
Designation: Medieval park associated with Maltby Manor.
Probable area: about 110 acres.

The earliest reference to Maltby Park is found in a charter of Roche Abbey made shortly after 1215.[3] Maltby Park is referred to in the definition of the boundaries of a piece of titheable land:

In campo de Malteby a fossato quod capitat super parcum de Maltbye in longum usque ad divisas de Steynton, et in latum a semita quae ducit ad grangiam de Lambecotes usque ad fossatum ipsius grangiae versus Le West (In Maltby it extended from the ditch which abuts on Maltby Park to the boundaries of Steynton in length and in breadth from a path which leads to the grange of Lambcotes to the ditch of the said grange to the west.)

At this time the Manor of Maltby was held by Idonea de Veteri Ponte (Vipont) descendant of a cadet branch of the de Builli family.[4] She also held Kimberworth with its park[5] and in 1242/3 is recorded as holding a park at Austerfield in the parish of Blyth.[6]

That Maltby Park continued in use for a considerable time is confirmed by a reference in Dodsworth's Church Notes.[7] Dodsworth, who visited on 24 July, 1627, reports a conversation with Mr Perkins, Vicar of Maltby. (John Parkins, instituted 23 December, 1602). Following his description of Stone Park (see below), Mr Perkins adds: 'Ther is another parke called The Old Park which is not past 12 score broad'. If by '12 score broad' Mr Perkins was thinking in the basic unit of the land surveyor, the $5\frac{1}{2}$ yard linear perch, this would suggest a maximum width of threequarters of a mile ($12 \times 20 \times 5\frac{1}{2} = 1320$ yards).

Figure 1. The known and conjectured boundaries of Maltby Park superimposed as solid and dotted lines on the Six Inch O.S. map of 1854. Field-names are taken from a sale catalogue of 1869 but they are almost identical with those found on an estate plan of 1791.

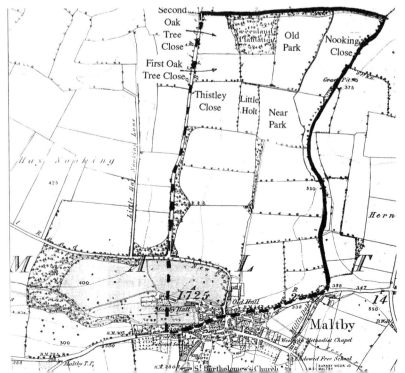

This coincides quite closely with the distance from the seventeenth century Maltby Old Hall to the parish boundary.

Further light is cast on Maltby Park by Joseph Young's plan of 1791 of the Estate of Richard Acklom at Maltby[8], (this being the land associated with Maltby Hall) particularly when this is considered in conjunction with the Roche Charter above. The field-names *Far Old Park*, *Old Park* and *Near Park* locate the feature to the north of the Old Hall (see Figure 1), the site of which is now occupied by Maltby Civic Centre. The Young map shows a long boundary on which the park field-names abut and this can still be traced on the ground as a culverted watercourse (marked by manhole covers) and as an old

Figure 2. An aerial view of 1971 showing the northern and eastern boundaries of Maltby Park (emphasised in white). Note how the post 1940s housing abuts upon boundaries which have been identified from a charter of 1215. *Rotherham Archives*

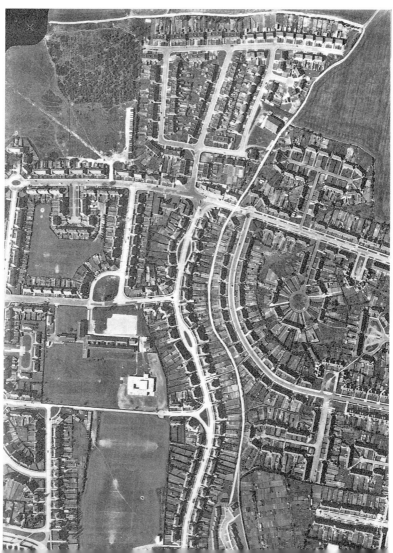

hedge and a ditch (see Figure 2). This line continues unbroken to form the Maltby/Stainton parish boundary and later that between Stainton and Braithwell parishes. The titheable land of the charter clearly lay to the east of the ditch (watercourse line), in what was later known as the Hern Field and would have been conveniently farmed from Roche Abbey's grange (outlying farm) of Lambcotes in Stainton parish. The northern boundary of Maltby Park, as identified by field-names, is that of the parish, which kinks to accommodate it (Figure 2). Its southern boundary would logically be placed on approximately the line of the present A631 (the pre-turnpike route from Rotherham to Tickhill.) It seems likely that its western boundary defined or was defined by the Braithwell to Maltby road, traces of which the Young map shows continuing south,without diversion, down the steep hill in the direction of the parish church. Park names continued in use until at least 1869 when they appeared in a sale catalogue.[9]

STOAN (STONE) PARK, *Grid reference SK 5492 and 5592.*

Location: In Maltby, north of A631, mostly beneath Maltby Colliery and spoil heap and Highfield Park housing and allotments. Small pockets of woodland survive to the west and south of its site.
Designation: Probable medieval park associated with Maltby Manor.
Area: 205 acres in 1622.

No medieval reference to Stoan Park has yet been traced but late sixteenth and early seventeenth century documents bear witness to its antiquity.

In 1585/6, George Clifford, third Earl of Cumberland, whose family had inherited the Manor of Maltby from the descendants of the cadet branch of the de Builli family (see Maltby Park above), sold the Manor and his extensive landholdings in Maltby.[10] The holding was divided with the manor house and nearby land being sold to Anthony Wright Esquire to form the core of the later Maltby Hall Estate. The manorial rights together with cottages and a large acreage of woodland including *Stoan Park* were sold to Sir Edward Stanhope, whose son Edward, in 1622, sold this portion to Sir Nicholas Saunderson (of Sandbeck).[11] Robert Oliver of Gainsborough was commissioned to survey the woods in June 1622 and the plan he drew survives at Sandbeck[12] (Figure 3). This clearly shows the boundaries of Stoan Park set amongst a larger area of woodland. Adjoining Stoan Park, to the south-east, (on a damaged portion of the map) is the small wood, *Diet* (later Dike) *Hagg.* This, together with the oddly shaped south-

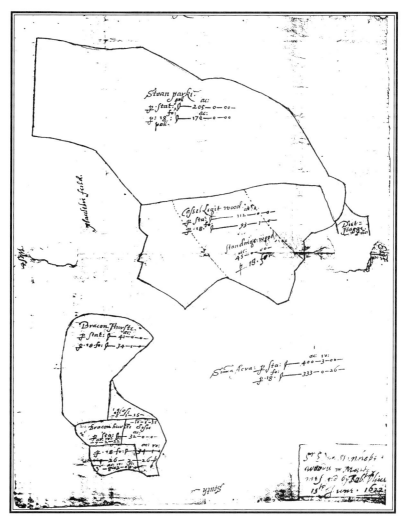

Figure 3. Robert Oliver's 1622 plan of Sir Edward Stanhope's woods in Maltby. Note the clearly defined Stoan Park and compare with Figure 4. *Lumley Archive*

eastern extension of the park, is well situated to have served as a place (holly hag) where holly could have been encouraged. Unbarbed leaves, which grow high on holly trees, were valuable winter fodder which could be cut and fed to deer when required.

Five years after the making of the map, in 1627, Dodsworth (see above) made reference to the park in his church notes on Maltby. He quoted the vicar, Mr Perkins, as telling him 'Ther is a park some 3

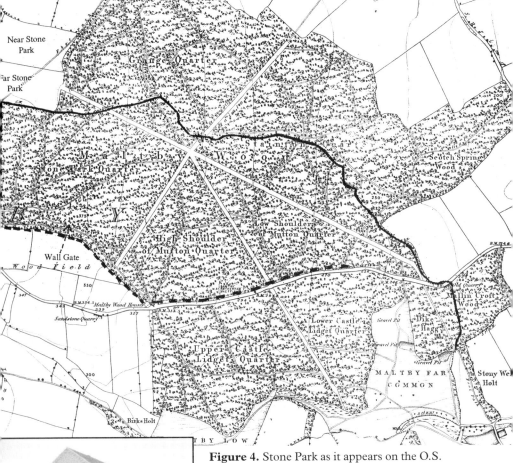

Figure 4. Stone Park as it appears on the O.S. map of 1854. The Maltby/Stainton parish boundary (emphasised with solid line) follows its northern limit whilst almost all of the rest of its former boundaries can be traced (dotted line). Neighbouring park-related field-names have been superimposed.

mile compasse called Stone Park and hath formerly been walled with stone'. This reference clearly looks back to the Cliffords and perhaps to earlier medieval manorial lords.

Stone Park was by 1686[13] subsumed into a greater Maltby Wood and gave its name to one of its quarters (subdivisions, of which there were more than four). The Stainton Tithe Map[14] records two fields on the parish boundary adjacent to its site as *Near* and *Far Stone Park*. Its western

Figure 5. The name of a medieval park lives on! This 1990s housing development has been given the neighbouring field-name Stone Park Close. *The Author*

boundary gave the name *Wall Gate* (*gate*: road) to a woodland track which, along with *Stoan Park Quarter*, survived to be mapped by the Ordnance Survey (Figure 4). Another adjacent field-name has been given to a mid-1990s Housing Association development near to Maltby Progressive Club called Stone Park Close (Figure 5).

Although the exact southern boundary of the park had disappeared by the 1850s its northern boundary continued as a civil parish boundary until 1974. It remains the boundary of the ecclesiatical parish of Maltby winding undefined over the barren landscape of Maltby Colliery spoil heap.

Was there ever a medieval park at Roche Abbey?

Anyone could have a park who could afford it. It was the status symbol of the whole upper class, of gentry and ecclesiastics as well as nobility. Oliver Rackham.

A thorough search of Roche Abbey charters, of extensive title deeds of the site and of estate surveys and plans has revealed not a single reference to a park or park name of any antiquity. A lone field-name may, however, provide a tiny clue.

In a Particular of Grant of 1545/6 of the Roche Abbey site is to be found:

Of one little close called the Launde, with the waste there, containing by estimation 6 acres of arable land.[15]

This field is noted next to an eight acre close called *Grange Wood*. *Laund* is a unique field-name in the area and it is used, elsewhere, specifically to denote an open grassy area within a deer park. Its later form lawn is to be found in just such a situation on the 1724 Dickinson map of the Sandbeck Estate suggesting that it was a technical term in local usage. The same map, the earliest of this area, shows a group of Grange Wood Close names set within the characteristically oval shape of an economical wood bank or park pale (see also Figure 6). The possibility that this, (58 acres on the Ordnance Survey First Edition 25 Inch map), was, at some stage, used as a park cannot be totally ignored.

Was there a Royal Forest close to Roche?

Throughout our Middle Ages a Forest was a place of deer, not necessarily a place of trees. Oliver Rackham *Trees and Woodland in the British Landscape,* Dent, 2nd Ed., 1990, p.165.

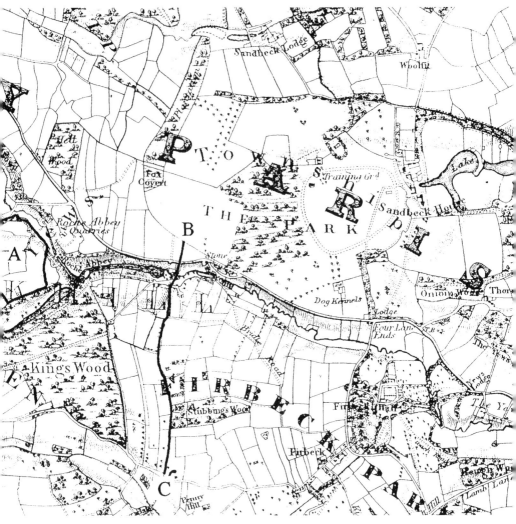

Figure 6. Section of Sanderson's map of *Twenty Miles Round Mansfield*, 1830-34, showing the extent of Grange Wood (A), the boundary of 'Le Foresterbalke' (B-C), and Sandbeck Park including Sandbeck Lodge (Bugthorpe) ponds and avenues of trees and vistas (surviving seventeenth century features).

To the south of Roche Abbey lie some 160 acres of predominantly semi-natural ancient woodland now called Kings Wood which Aveling, by process of elimination, identified with Henry II's grant of 100 acres of woodland 'in Lindric' *juxta predictam abbathiam* (beside the aforesaid abbey).[16] The original grant does not survive but we know about it from later deeds of confirmation, the earliest of which was made by Pope Urban in 1186. (This implies that the grant was made between 1154 and 86.) Later confirmations of the grant were made by Adelicia Countess of Eu in 1219 and by Edward III in 1342/3. Lindric's location in or near to the Manor of Laughton and its association with both Henry II and the Countess of Eu suggest a link with the Castle and Honour of Tickhill (*Honour*: large feudal territory centred on a castle)which both held at the appropriate time. (The Honour was ultimately to became part of the Duchy of Lancaster.)

One unusual feature of the grant is its definition of such a remarkably round-figured acreage which perhaps indicates that the wood was part of something bigger. Credence is lent to this notion by the description, in 1402[17], of a piece of disputed land near to the abbey. It is defined by a boundary called *Le Foresterbalke* (*balk*: boundary bank) which runs south as a continuation of the way which leads *ad molendinum de Ston* (to the mill of Stone). This mill has been identified with the modern Roche Abbey Mill.[18] This long boundary, which can be traced on Sanderson's Map of 1830-34 (see Figure 6), runs almost parallel to the present eastern boundary of Kings Wood and makes a very logical former eastern limit of it. Part forms the Laughton/Firbeck parish boundary and further south, abutting upon it is a field named , as early as 1609, *The Wrenparks* and later *Rein Park* (*rein* : boundary bank).[19] This boundary would imply an area for King's Wood/Lindric of some 260 acres. (Even allowing for large local medieval acres, more than twice the Lindric grant to Roche.) Title deeds of 43 Elizabeth I (1601) of nearby fields in Firbeck make reference to their proximity to the *Quenes Wodd* and *Regiam silvam*[20] literally 'the royal woodland'), a description alluding to tenure rather than a mere wood name. That nearby Firbeck was once more extensively wooded is attested by the 1487[21] place-name *Northmanstubbing* (*stubbing* : clearing from woodland) which may be identified with the oddly named modern Stubbings Wood.

Was there ever a Royal Forest near Roche? The site identified with Lindric lay four miles from Tickhill Castle and whereas Conisbrough castle and Sheffield castle had parks, none has ever been convincingly traced in association with that of Tickhill.[22] Perhaps a nearby forest meant that Tickhill did not need a park in the early medieval period.[23]

The idea of a Royal Forest in Laughton, associated with the Honour of Tickhill is rather tempting but the evidence is far too fragmentary to be conclusive. It merely makes the case for further research.

The parks of Sandbeck

EVIDENCE FOR A MEDIEVAL PARK AT SANDBECK *Grid reference SK 5690 and 5790.*

Location: South and east of the present house at Sandbeck.
Designation: In all probability, a small monastic park associated with Roche Abbey.
Area: Unknown but probably less than 50 acres.

The name *lytle pke* was first recorded in a 1596 survey of oaks and ashes in Sandbeck.[24] Early seventeenth century Sandbeck field surveys note *Great Parke Meadow, Parkefield* and *Little Parke Meadow.* In addition a document of between 1622 and 1630 records *Parke close* and *Pingle* together with *Parke Close beside the wood grounds*, this in association with *Lords Meadow* and *Shepe Coate Closes.*[25]

In 1241 Sandbeck had been granted to Roche Abbey and it was apparently worked as a grange (outlying farm). In view of the rela-

Figure 7. A section of the Dickinson Survey of Sandbeck of 1724 showing (bottom right) the isolated field-name 'Park Meadow' which may indicate the site of a medieval park probably associated with Roche Abbey. Possible boundaries of this park are indicated by white dots. This also shows detail of the 1637 park-related Lawn and North and South Paddocks. *Lumley Archive and T. W. Beastall*

tively early date at which park names are applied to fields, it seems probable that the park was a monastic development. After the Dissolution, the manor of Sandbeck, together with associated land, was purchased by Robert Saunderson of Fillingham in Lincolnshire for whose descendants it became the core of a large estate. Robert's son, Sir Nicholas, inherited the estate in 1582 and continued his father's sheeprearing interest. The way in which the park is recorded suggests that in the hands of the Saundersons, if not before, it had reverted to agricultural use.

Clues to the location of the park are found in its association with the still surviving names Lord's Meadow and Sheepcote closes. This suggests a site to the south or east of the present house. This view is confirmed by the Dickinson survey of 1724[26] whose map (Figure 7) places a Park Meadow immediately to the south of Lord's Meadow and well to the east of the site of the deer park of 1637 (see below).

Dickinson's long boundaries may give some indication of the extent of the park suggesting something in the region of fifty acres. (This compares with thirty-one acres, the maximum total area of 'park' field-names in any single survey.) These 50 acres make sense in terms of access to water and convenience for winter foddering of deer.

SANDBECK DEER PARK OF 1637 *Grid Reference SK 5589 and 5590 and 5591*

Location: West of Sandbeck.
Ancient Parish: Maltby.
Designation: Deer park licenced 1637.
Acreage in 1724: Park 392 acres, Lawn 81a 2r 00p, North Paddock 34a 3r 00p, South Paddock 38a 2r 00p, Triangle 12a 1r 00p. Total of park-related landscaping, 568 acres.

The redistribution of vast former monastic acreages, following the Dissolution, had seen the rise of men of enterprise intent on the establishment of large consolidated holdings of land. In Maltby, the declining fortunes of the Clifford family (Earls of Cumberland and descendants in title of the de Buillis) contributed further to that process. By 1627, the Saundersons of Sandbeck held by far the largest acreage in the parish and, about 1626, work began on a substantial new house at Sandbeck. Its builder, Sir Nicholas Saunderson, was created Viscount Castleton in 1627.[27] Sir Nicholas had inherited Sandbeck in 1582 (see above). He had added to his inheritance by purchase, notably in 1622, of the Manor of Maltby with woods, cottages and a mill (see Stoan Park above) and, in 1627, the site of

Figure 8. Detail of Royal Licence to Empark and Grant of Free Warren of 1637. *Lumley Archive; Photograph Brian Elliott*

Roche Abbey together with some 600 acres.[28] Viscount Castleton died in 1630, before the creation of the deer park.

In 1637, Charles I granted by letters patent, to the Second Viscount and his heirs, right of *free warren* (the sole right to hunt certain beasts or fowls) in the Manors of Sandbeck, Roche Abbey, Maltby and Stainton and in Bagley, Marris and Spital (in Tickhill Parish) (Figure 8). He also gave licence to inclose and

> make separate with pales, banks, walls or hedges 500 acres or there-abouts of land, meadow, pasture, gorse, heath, wood, underwood, wooded land tenements and hereditaments lying and being within the said manors or one of them.... to make a park where deer and other wild animals might be grazed and kept.

The greater part of the land in the manors listed was said to be 'wooded, stony, rocky and otherwise infit for cultivation' and thus appropriate for emparkment.[29]

The choice of site for Sandbeck Park

The early seventeenth century activities of the Saundersons have left valuable documentary evidence and this has been employed to seek to test the veracity of the description of the condition of the land as well as to examine the process and the social and economic impact of the making of the park. Detailed study of title deeds, where land is often described in relation to that which abuts upon it, and of surveys and rentals, has provided names, acreages and approximate locations of features 'lost' beneath the park.[30] The information has been mapped (see Figure 9) and conclusions checked by fieldwork. Such a reconstruction, based on context and size rather than defined boundaries will always be incomplete but it has informed understanding of the emparkment.

The site chosen for the park and for the landscape relating to it lay entirely to the west of the house of 1626 and included land in the Manors of Sandbeck and Maltby together with parts of the Roche Abbey estate.

The land in the Manor of Sandbeck lay in enclosures of varying size whose names, at first glance suggest a mixture of arable and pasture, with large acreages of *field* and *flat* elements suggesting common field cultivation. That common field cultivation had ceased is evidenced by a plan of Maltby Field (in Sandbeck) of 1617 which shows clear subdivisions into arable, pasture and *woodground* (the local name for wood pasture) and by a particular of 1628 where parts of Maltby Field and Otefield are subdivided and let to tenants with various uses indicated including pasture and meadow. Whinny Flatt, on higher land adjacent to Sandbeck Common, suggests a reversion to pasture in the hands of those concerned with sheep rearing and the wool trade. No major parcels of woodland have been traced in Sandbeck Manor beneath the park but hedgerow trees and small wooded areas seem to have been abundant.[31]

The 1622 purchase of the Manor of Maltby with associated mill, cottages, woodland and common contributed some 63 acres to the north-west of the park. This area was called Brackenhurst Wood and Brackenhurst Closes (formerly wood). (Its name survived until the late eighteenth century both inside and just outside the park so its general location is confirmed.) The north-eastern boundary of the park followed a tongue of land which stretched from Maltby Field[32] (in Sandbeck Manor) to the outlying settlement of Bugthorpe (now Sandbeck Lodge) which was apparently in the Manor of Maltby. Between and beyond these lay a southern extension of Maltby Common known as Sandbeck Nooke and a small holding, perhaps in origin an encroachment, called Saugh Spring. In 1632 Saugh Spring was held by George Parkins 'natural son' of the Vicar of Maltby (That same John Parkins who was helpful to Dodsworth, see Maltby Park above).

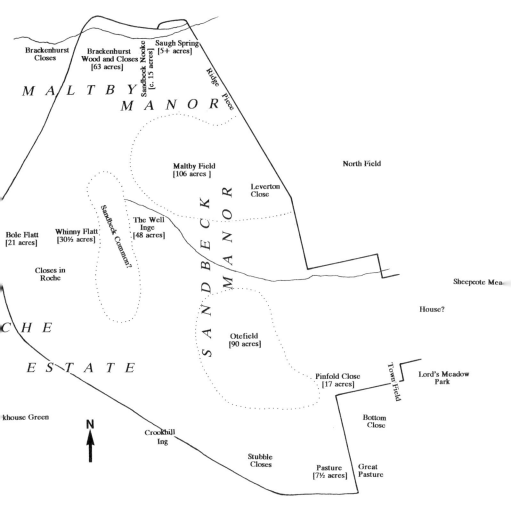

Figure 9. Sketch map of Sandbeck Park showing the approximate location of pre-emparkment acreages.

Both Saugh Spring and Sandbeck Nooke were needed to round off the northern boundary of the park. The former was rather expensively purchased.[33] The latter, though the soil was owned by Viscount Castleton, was subject to rights of common. Clearly these rights had to be extinguished if Sandbeck Nooke was to be emparked.

The freeholders who possessed them were local men of substance including John Wright 'gent', a descendant of the 1585/6 purchaser of Maltby Manor House and land, the two Ralph Fretwells (grandfather

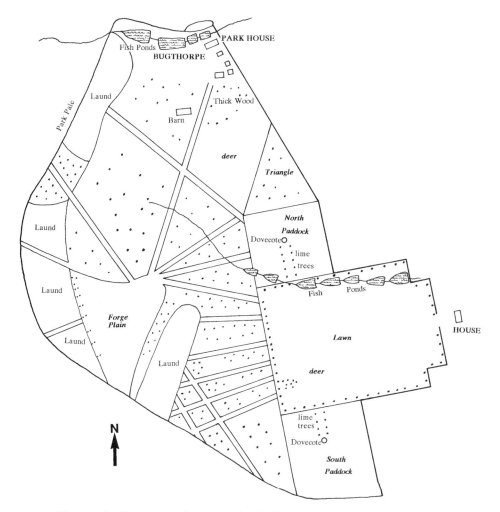

Figure 10. Sketch map (based on the Dickinson Survey of 1724) showing the main features of Sandbeck deer park. See Figure 7 for details of the House, Lawn and Paddocks.

and grandson) of Hellaby, John Parkins (Vicar of Maltby) and Thos. Spencer (almost certainly of Newhall Grange). They proved more than capable of negotiating a mutually beneficial arrangement.

In 1636 the rights of common over Sandbeck Nooke were transferred to another piece of land which had come to the Saundersons with the Roche estate. *Parte of Norwood next Woodlea* was at the limit of the Sandbeck estate but was much closer to Maltby than Sandbeck

Nooke so was more convenient for many of the freeholders.[34] The agreement was duly recorded in the Parish Register and Viscount Castleton was thus able to enclose within his park the Bugthorpe watercourse which was dammed to make fishponds and to provide a watering place for his deer.

The Roche estate purchase contributed more directly to the park whose south-western boundary was made to sweep through 'great' closes acquired in 1637. An earlier (1612)[35] purchase of Bole Flatt (part of the Roche Abbey estate) contributed further woodland to the west of the park.

It seems fair to deduce that the emparkment's description of the land to be enclosed is not too fanciful. Much of it was already woodland, wood pasture or rough grazing which would have needed little encouragement to be transformed into the predominantly wooded park landscape mapped by Dickinson in 1724[36] (see Figure 10).

Although the Saundersons had acquired the 'Clifford' *Stoan Park*, they did not see fit to include it in their emparkment. To do so would have required the transfer of commoners' rights from Far Common to the ample area of land they held near Woodlea. This was no bar: they had in 1626 demonstrated their capacity to negotiate such an arrangement. What militated against such emparkment was, almost certainly, the regionally important trade route between Sheffield and the port of Bawtry, which ran immediately to the south of Stoan Park and which separated it from the remainder of the estate. The wider interests of the estate were better served by road than park.

The economic and social impact of the Sandbeck emparkment

The acreage of the Park recorded in the Dickinson Survey is 392 acres. If the related landscape of the Lawn, Triangle and North and South Paddocks is added to this it totals 659. We have seen that, prior to the 1637 emparkment, much of this was divided into enclosures of varying sizes not all of which were in hand. It is reasonable to ask by what process the tenanted land was taken in and what impact the creation of the park had on the wider management of the estate.

The surviving Sandbeck rentals for 1633 and 1635-40, although only providing sparse information about individual holdings, do cast light on the process of change.[37] In 1633 twenty-two tenants are listed (some in pairs) paying one or more rents. Of these three were from Firbeck, one from Oldcotes, three from Styrup and two from Tickhill. Succeeding rentals show a steady decline in both tenant numbers and in rental income. In 1635 there were 17 tenants and in 1640 there were nine. The annual rental income of £99 18s 4d in 1633 declined to a low of £56 12s 8d in 1639. Where individual rents can be traced throughout the period, the evidence is that they remained stable so that the decline in rental income is attributable to land being taken in hand. All but one of the tenants from neighbouring parishes fell out of the rental before 1635 as did a number of smaller holdings between 1635 and 1640.

There remained a core of tenants with larger holdings whose rents varied but who stayed throughout the period. James Barlow, for example, who occupied a farm in 1628 (some of which was later emparked), was still in the rental in 1640 with an increased holding. In 1640 there were four holdings worth between £8 and £14 6s 8d per annum, and there were three smaller holdings worth between £2 6s 8d and £5 4s 0d. Beside the park was emerging a pattern of consolidated tenant farms.

Sandbeck Park 1637–1750

There is very little documentary evidence about the early park although a possible indication of the nature of its pale is found in an unused draft of the Sandbeck Nooke exchange.[38] The land in question was to extend

> *so farre to the west in the grounds lying next without the pales and props and stays and leaps thereof as may secure for a reasonable ditch or wall as need shall require.*

Much labour must have been expended on the creation of such a complex barrier and in the digging of the Bugthorpe ponds.

A comparison of the conjectural reconstruction of the landscape lost beneath the park and the first plan of it (Dickinson) shows that at least some of the pasture evolved into launds. The enclosed Roche closes become Forge Plain, a *plain,* like a laund being a technical term for a grassy area where deer gathered. In the area of the Lawn and paddocks, traces of former field boundaries appear to be visible (see Figure 7). Whilst Dickinson shows much woodland divided by ridings, nothing is immediately recognisable as coppice despite the proximity of the Stone (Roche) Forge with its enormous appetite for charcoal.

The presence of known master's names in the account books suggests that the forge was established in the mid-1630s, at about the same time as the making of the park. An agreement for the nine year lease of the forge, together with the sale of a large quantity of wood,was made in 1681 between the then Viscount Castleton and the partnership of Sheffield forgemasters William Simpson, Francis Barlow and Dionis Heyford. This makes reference to the park. The sale includes 'two thousand one hundred and seventy timber trees standing or being in Sandbeck Park and Bole Flatt.... [being] marked or figured with iron marks' together with other trees and springwood, and one hundred yews in Sandbeck Park and also 'all or soe many of the dead roots in Sandbeck Park as in other woods' as the forgemaster or his assigns 'shall please to take stubb and carrie away'. The agreement contains provision to allow access over a nine year period and also to 'cutt coal cord' and dig sods and dust for the purpose of making charcoal as well as to make sawpits. For all this the forgemasters paid four thousand pounds.[39]

The Park timber is visible here, and in the 1686 valuation[40], as an estate asset but it is tempting also to see the removal of dead roots and the selective extraction of timber trees as contributing to the process of landscaping the Park. The Dickinson map of 1724 shows that by then a system of ridings had been made through the park woodland and that five vistas had been cut into the park from the west end of the Lawn along radii whose origin was the house. These would have created visual links between the house and its formal setting and the wilder area of the Park.

Sandbeck deer park in the eighteenth century

To the general picture of the Park provided by the Dickinson survey of 1724 can be added information from timber valuations[41] of the early eighteenth century. These confirm that the Park was essentially a landscape of native trees with ash, oak, yew, elm and maple predominating and with some areas of (large or small leaved) lime and of syrup (wild service tree?). Still surviving today, however, are vestiges of the 'park' lime avenues leading to ornamental features in the centre of the Paddocks and of those of Spanish chestnut deeper in the park.

When, in 1723, James the first Earl of Castleton (and the last of the Saundersons) died, his estates were willed to Thomas Lumley who subsequently became third Earl of Scarbrough. It was Thomas Lumley's son Richard, the fourth Earl, who oversaw the major mid- and late-eighteenth century improvements at Sandbeck.[42]

A picture of the deer park at the beginning of this period of improvement is revealed in a 1750 account book.[43] *The Garden, Nursery and Planting Disbursments* show trees from the nursery being taken up and planted in 'the seven acres in the Park'. Later comes the 'levilling' of a bank in the new plantation, the cutting up of dead trees and the weeding and 'howing' of the area followed by further winter planting in the Park. (An estate map of the early 1770s shows that the former launds to the west of the Park had been replaced by Long Plantation.[44]) In the *Park and Woods Disbursements* Mary Robinson is paid at a rate of eight shillings per month for 'foddering deer' and George Elsom receives expenses for 'Carrying out Venison' and for repairing fences whilst William Dodworth is paid for 'Stubbing Whins ith Park'. William Smeaton is paid for new keys for the park gates and for mending the locks, John Fisher for 'Repairing the Park Gates, Pails and Stiles' and for repairing the 'flaggs about the trees in the Park' and William Eastwood for 8 days 'Repairing the Park and Paddock Walls'. Finally the account for wood sales reveals that cordwood from a large area including the Park, Paddocks and Triangle was being sold in quantity to the forgemasters, Mr Fell and Partners.

References in the account book to the Paddocks and to the Triangle suggest that the Park in 1750 was essentially similar in layout to that of 1724 although by 1750 there appear to have been parcels of coppice as well as new plantations.

A comparison of the Dickinson survey with Jefferys' map of 1772 (Figure 11) and with Sanderson's of about 1830 (Figure 6) shows the extent to which the third quarter of the century brought changes to Sandbeck. Some 86 acres, formerly within the Pale to the north of the deer park, were enclosed for agriculture and this area was cut off from the rest of the park by a new boundary bank. Surviving account books suggest this happened between 1762 and 1765.[45]

As the new house was built and a new landscaped park, complete with lakes and plantations was created to the east of it, so the deer park became a source of stone and a provider of mature trees for trans-

Figure 11. Sandbeck Park as it appears on Jefferys' map of 1772. Bugthorpe Lodge (marked inaccurately) and the fields nearby are, by then, outside the park. Avenues of trees recall the seventeenth century landscape of the deer park. *Rotherham Archives*

ure 12. Ancient Spanish chestnuts, photographed r Stone in 1998, evoke the atmosphere of the :nteenth century Sandbeck deer park. *The Author*

planting. The ponds to the west of the house were filled in and the formal seventeenth century landscape was softened into something more naturalistic. Sunk fences (ha-has) superseded park pales and the ordered divisions of the park woodland were not kept up. There are references in the account books to the setting up of 'fleaks' (hurdles) to contain deer whilst all this was going on.

Following the fourth Earl's death in 1782 more of the deer park (particularly that out of sight of the house) was finding agricultural use and by 1800[46] the area formerly the closes in Roche was being farmed again. Today the seventeenth century park remains in the shape of its surviving boundary and in the lines of venerable Spanish chestnuts with their distinctive corkscrew trunks (Figure 12).

Summary and conclusions

There is good documentary evidence for two parks associated with the Manor of Maltby and some evidence for a medieval park at Sandbeck, possibly associated with Roche Abbey. A park nearer to Roche has not been convincingly identified although it remains possible that Grange Wood, at some point, fulfilled that function. Further research is needed to confirm the presence, close to Roche, in the early medieval period, of a forest probably within the Honour of Tickhill.

Of the parks, Stoan Park is the only one whose extent is known with any certainty. At rather more than 200 acres, its size was modest. What evidence there is suggests that Maltby Park and Sandbeck Park were smaller. Parks of small size add credence to Oliver Rackham's view that the medieval park was much more a deer farm than a place set aside for the chase. The two parks associated with Maltby Manor were made on marginal land abutting on the parish and manorial boundary. The use of such land to provide fresh winter meat in response to, what may have been, the unpredictable demands of a high status household, represents productive and sustainable management.

In shape the parks varied. Stoan Park is the most oval but is still pretty irregular. This may be explained by its having suffered selective disparkment before it was mapped. Maltby Park and Sandbeck Park seem rectangular. As Maltby Park is an absolutely certain medieval park, this suggests that park hunters need to look wider than (so-called) classic park shapes. Stoan Park ultimately evolved into managed woodland whilst Maltby Park and most of Sandbeck medieval Park fell to pasture. It seems that parks should be sought amongst fields as well as woods.

That the park-free landscape of Saxton's map of 1577 almost certainly contained three medieval parks and that none of these was noticed by Hunter, confirms Susan Neave's view that parks have previously been under-recorded. Their conclusive rediscovery depends not only on a close study of minor place-names but also on the corroborative evidence of early maps, plans, estate surveys and title deeds, documents with which parts of Maltby are singularly well endowed.

The post-medieval Sandbeck deer park, licensed in 1637, marks the culmination of a long process of estate development and consolidation which had followed the Dissolution of the Monasteries. Significantly, it was created away from previously emparked areas and it needs to be understood in relation to the new Sandbeck Hall. Built in 1626, this house, together with its extensive landscaping, both recognised and asserted the significance of the Saundersons' Yorkshire holdings. Equally, it provided a model to which nearby high-status houses and grounds could aspire.

Notes and References

Unless otherwise stated, document reference codes relate to items in the Lumley Archive at Sandbeck Park.
1. Susan Neave, *Medieval Parks in East Yorkshire*. University of Hull and Hutton Press Ltd., 1991.
2. For a study of local Domesday woodland, see Melvyn Jones, *Rotherham's Woodland Heritage*. Rotherwood Press, 1995.
3. S.O.Addy 'Roche Abbey Charters', *Transactions of the Hunter Archaeological Society*, Vol 4, (1937).
4. See pedigree in *A Cartulary of Blyth Priory*, Ed. R.T. Timson, HMSO 1973.
5. See Melvyn Jones, 'The Medieval Park at Kimberworth' in M. Jones (Ed.) *Aspects of Rotherham 2*, Wharncliffe Publishing, 1996, p.79.

6. Joseph Hunter, *South Yorkshire*, 1828-31.
7. Dodsworth (ed. Clay) 'Yorkshire Church Notes 1619-1631', *Yorkshire Archaeological Society Record Series*, Vol 34.
8. Sheffield Archives LD 1094.
9. 17/50b.
10. MTD/B51 etc.
11. MTD/B50 etc.
12. EMS/1/1.
13. ETP/1/2.
14. Lumley map cat.
15. J. Aveling, *The History of Roche Abbey*, Robert White, 1870, p.128.
16. *Ibid*, p.120 (See also Addy above).
17. Addy, 'Roche Abbey Charters', p.243.
18. See Alice Rodgers 'Water-powered Mills in Maltby' in M. Jones (Ed.) *Aspects of Rotherham*, Wharncliffe Publishing, 1995.
19. MTD/B33/11 and EMS/4.
20. MTD/B33/8&9.
21. MTD/B33/3.
22. Information kindly provided by Tom Beastall.
23. David Hey in *Yorkshire Archaeological Journal*, Vol 47, 1975, p.109, cites a single reference in Dodsworth which has not yet been traced.
24. ETP/16.
25. EMS/1/4-6 and MTD/B79.
26. EMS/4.
27. See T.W.Beastall, *A North Country Estate*, Phillimore 1975.
28. MTD/B30 etc.
29. MTD/B79/12 (Translated by A.P.Munford).
30. Including many quoted above. See also MTD/B52 and 53 and MTD/B79, etc.
31. See ETP/16.
32. EMP/1/1.
33. MTD/B52/14.
34. EMC/76 and see also Yorkshire Parish Register Society 1926, *Maltby Register*.
35. MTD/B79/8.
36. EMS/4 (map uncat.).
37. MR/SA/1 and MTD/B30/40.
38. MTD/B/54.
39. MTD/B8/4.
40. ETP/1/2.
41. ETP/27, ETP/1/3, ETP/17, ETP/18.
42. See T.W. Beastall, *A North Country Estate* and 'Sandbeck Hall and Park' in M. Jones (Ed.) *Aspects of Rotherham*, Wharncliffe Publishing, 1995.
43. EMA/10.
44. ETP/1/3.
45. EMA/15 and EMA/249/1&2 and EMR/8 (located at EMA15).
46. Lumley map cat.

Acknowledgements

I should like to thank the Rt. Hon. The Earl of Scarbrough for allowing access to the Lumley Archive and for permission to reproduce items from it. Both to Lord Scarbrough and to Tom Beastall, I owe a particular debt of gratitude for sharing with me their detailed knowledge of Sandbeck. Warm appreciation is also expressed to the following, who have offered general advice or specific expertise : Brian Elliott, Sally Shepard, Melvyn Jones, Tony Munford, and Bill Ely. Final thanks are owed to my family, to Stuart and Eleanor for putting up with my near obsession with invisible park boundaries.

2. THE ANCIENT HIGHWAYS THROUGH ROTHERHAM

by Howard Smith

PRESENT DAY ROTHERHAM'S CORE is the small area between the parish church and the former market place round Bridgegate running downhill towards the ancient crossing point of the Don – for centuries a ford, and from the fifteenth century onwards the still-existing masonry bridge. The town began as a village surrounded by large fields which provided its inhabitants with subsistence, but even before the Conquest it had developed into a small market town with a church, mill, market and fair. This must have been a consequence of its geographical position, as it was never a castle-borough like its neighbours Sheffield and Tickhill. The river Don was a considerable barrier to communication in those days, and Rotherham possessed one of the few reliable fording points and an important north-south road sought out this nodal point, as did a trans-Pennine route from Cheshire and Lancashire via Woodhead. The latter continued east-

Figure 1. Rotherham's ancient highways.

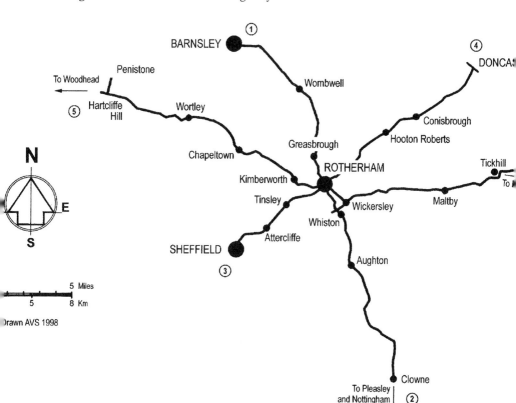

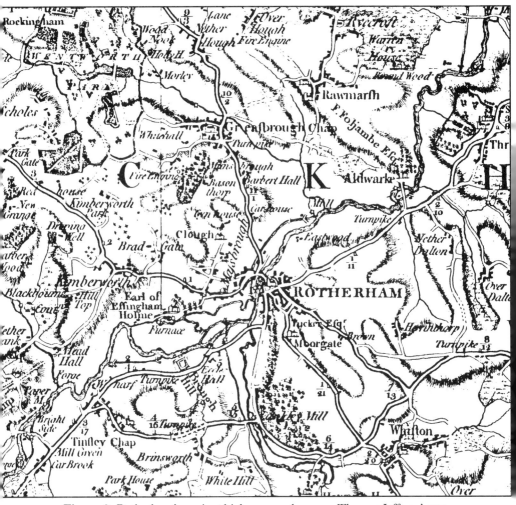

Figure 2. Rotherham's ancient highways as shown on Thomas Jefferys' map of Yorkshire, 1767-72.

wards to the important inland ports of Bawtry and Gainsborough. Another road passing through the town linked Sheffield with Doncaster and the Great North Road.

These six highways – for most of their history little better than trackways which were mainly used by strings of packhorses before the turnpike age, though there was often local two-wheeled cart traffic especially on the Bawtry road – are still in use to this day (see Figures 1 and 2). However, their relative importance has fluctuated over the centuries. The travellers of old would not recognise the modern roads, as such, but the routes laid down by trial and error in the earliest days of Rotherham's history have persisted with remarkably little deviation over the long period since the town's foundation. Each of these will be examined in turn, leading out from the town centre, and their history described briefly. The routes taken by these old highways are described in detail at the end of this article using their current road names.

The roads in pre-turnpike times were made by trial and error over many years. They were not planned or engineered, or given drains, foundations or a hard surface. In winter they would be turned into quagmires and, at times, were impassable, whilst in summer they would be dusty, deeply rutted and pot-holed. It was accepted practice to by-pass the worst hazards so that in some places the highways were very wide, with parallel tracks, though where confined by walls, hedges or houses, they often became deep, sunken tracks known as holloways. On busy packhorse ways flat stones, or causeways, were laid to ease the passage of horses and men.

Roads were first improved in the Rotherham area in the mid-eighteenth century when turnpike trusts were given parliamentary permission to take over particular highways. Each trust usually ran just one or two roads, and to cover their costs could set up tollgates (or turnpikes) to charge road users set fees laid down by Parliament. The Rotherham to Hartcliffe Hill road was a very early turnpike – 1740: other main roads were completed between 1759-64.

The prime purpose for turnpiking the roads was to create carriageways capable of carrying wheeled vehicles, especially waggons to move heavy, bulky materials such as coal, iron, stone and timber much more conveniently and cost-effectively than by packhorse. By our standards the early turnpikes were very crude, and it was not until about 1815 that more sophisticated roads were designed by Telford, McAdam and their followers Nonetheless, the web of turnpikes round Rotherham did enable the town to expand industrially before the railways age – the increase in population alone shows this – from *c*.2,800 in 1740 to over 14,000 in 1841. The improved roads also encouraged greatly increased passenger traffic in both private vehicles and public stage-coaches, and gradually helped Rotherham – and dozens of similar types of town – to become less narrow and provincial. The turnpike roads of the Rotherham area, with dates, are shown in Figure 3. They are virtually the same as the ancient highways shown in Figure 1.

Trade on the Don Navigation was essential to Rotherham's industrial expansion, but was generally fed by the local roads, as were the

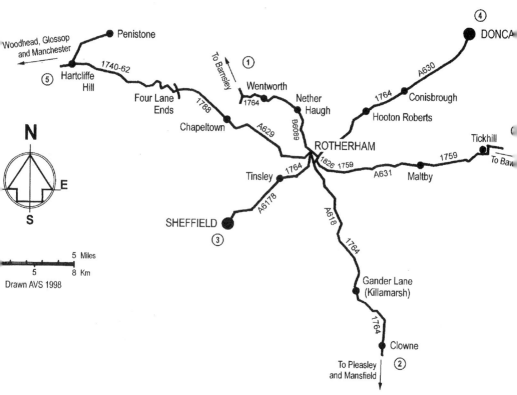

Figure 3. Rotherham and District Turnpike Roads, with dates of Turnpike Acts and modern road classifications.

railways that first came to the town in 1838. The railways rapidly won most long-distance freight and passenger traffic during their astonishingly rapid expansion in early- and mid-Victorian Britain. The turnpike roads lost business, which reduced their income, forcing them to cut maintenance, making road travel even less attractive. Caught in this vicious circle, many trusts became bankrupt, whilst the public became increasingly irritated with tolls and toll-gates. In common with the national trend, the town's main roads were disturnpiked in the eight years between 1874-1882.

Although long-distance road travel went into a long decline before the rapid development of motor transport, short - and medium-distance traffic was boosted by the new railways, which had to be served by road. As towns expanded, cheap public transportation was provided by the horse omnibus, and, later, the horse tram (thought not in Rotherham). These gave way in turn to the electric tram and trolley bus, and the motor bus in the earlier years of the twentieth century, and in the later years increasingly to the private car.

Rotherham's ancient highways were all affected by these changes, and all have altered in character. Rural roads – as they all were within a few hundred yards of the old town centre – have become industrial arteries or suburban commuter routes. The increase in traffic densities and speeds would have bemused our ancestors. In response to political and economic change, the importance of the six old routes has waxed and waned. The north-south highway from Barnsley to Pleasley, through Rotherham, once an important road, is now insignificant compared with the parallel M1 motorway.

1. The Barnsley Road (12 Miles/19 Km)

This road formed part of an important south-north highway from London to Richmond in north Yorkshire, and from there to Scotland either by the east coast route via Newcastle and Berwick, or to the west via Penrith and Carlisle. From Barnsley, this route proceeded via Huddersfield and on the line now followed by the A629 through Halifax almost to Keighley, and by unclassified roads to Skipton. From here it continued northwards to Grassington (now B6265), and through Kettlewell, Middleham and over a moorland route to Richmond. To us this seems an unlikely route, but it functioned as a higher-level alternative Great North Road to the west and linked numerous medieval boroughs.

To reach Barnsley from Rotherham, before the mid-eighteenth century, a traveller would cross the Don, by ford, or Chantry Bridge, turn right immediately and begin the stiff climb up Car Hill to Greasbrough, and northwards to Brampton, via Nether Haugh, along Packman Road. The road then turned west of north through Wombwell to Ardsley, where it was joined by the Doncaster road (now A635). It was a highway used by merchants, industrialists, gentry, lawyers and members of parliament of the West Riding who had business in the East Midlands and London, and by commercial traffic aiming for navigable water at Bawtry. Charles I, on his forced return to England at the hands of the Scots, was brought down this road, and passed through Rotherham.

It was probably at its busiest in the first half of the eighteenth century when the West Riding woollen area was rapidly growing in importance, as were the iron workings of South Yorkshire, before the Don was made navigable and turnpiking offered a number of good

alternative roads. When the Rotherham-Barnsley road was itself turnpiked in 1764, the ancient route was altered to Nether Haugh, to pass
westwards through the Marquis of Rockingham's estates at
Wentworth, via Cortworth Lane. Although this diversion was unpop-
ular with the locals, the great landowner had the last word. The new
road terminated at Hood Hill, Tankersley, where traffic would join the
important newly-turnpiked (1758) road from Sheffield to Wakefield
and Leeds, via Barnsley. A toll cottage survives at the western end of
Wentworth village.

The road north from Nether Haugh to Brampton and Wombwell
lost status, was never turnpiked and served simply as a local lane -
much of it still called to this day Packman Road (originally Packman
Gate), a reminder of its main function for most of its existence. It is
now the B6089. Traffic movement from Rotherham to Barnsley also
increasingly moved to the parallel route to the east (now A633) with
the development of Parkgate, Rawmarsh, Swinton and Wath in the last
two centuries. In the last three decades freight traffic has largely moved
westwards to the parallel M1. The busiest section of the road has
always been the two miles (3 km) between Rotherham and
Greasbrough, which doubled in size between 1851-81 to just under
4,000 people, owing to industrial development, and there would
always be traffic passing through generated by the Wentworth estates.

The road was disturnpiked in 1874, and in common with the other
main roads out of Rotherham was served by public transport, buses
and – for a period – trolley buses, the main carriers. In recent years
the road has been improved, especially up the much altered Car House
Hill, dualled in 1969-71.

2. The Pleasley Road (20 miles/32 km)

This was the continuation southwards of the ancient alternative to the
Great North Road (see The Barnsley Road). From Rotherham it went
to Mansfield, and from there by the line followed by the present A60
to Nottingham, the A606 to Melton Mowbray and Oakham, and ran
south along the present A6003 to Kettering. It aimed for Bedford and
Luton along what is now the A6 and finally reached St. Albans and
London by the present A1081.

Locally, the old road left town by Wellgate, Hollowgate (= deep,
sunken track), and followed the spine of the Rotherham red sandstone
ridge, rising between Broom Valley and Canklow, over Rotherham
Moor – completely undeveloped land until late Victorian times. From
Hollowgate the original road was not on the route followed by most

of Moorgate Road, but after 220 yards (200 m) or so, where Godstone Road meets it, ran on a route roughly parallel and to the east of the A618 to the junction with Mile Oak Road, where past and present alignments reunite, to continue towards Whiston.

Before the old road was turnpiked, Rotherham Moor was owned by the noble Shrewsbury family, who charged right of passage or 'chymyage' for the privilege of crossing their manorial land. For over 170 years the Feoffees of Rotherham, whose duties included the maintenance of local highways and bridges, paid the Shrewsbury estate £1 6s 8d (£1.33) per annum until the practice ceased in 1786, by which time the road had been turnpiked. From Whiston the road aimed south via Aughton, west of Aston, and to the east of Killamarsh. The long straight runs remind us that this stretch of the route followed part of a Roman road between Templeborough and Chesterfield. Traffic from Sheffield would join this road either at Swallownest (leaving the Worksop road), or at Gander Lane (a name that has disappeared), Norwood, (now the junction of B6058 and A618).

The journey south from here followed a ridgeway route over the western edge of the Magnesian Limestone belt characterised by easy-gradients and well-drained soils offering good progress, and, having passed through Clowne, continued due south for the next seven miles (11 km) to Pleasley. That part of the Pleasley Road between Rotherham and Clowne, as depicted on Ogilby's map of 1675, is shown in Figure 4.

There is a strong possibility that most of this highway follows the alignment of a Roman road between the Trent and the Don, which would account for the long straight stretches, uncommon on old English roads. From Pleasley, the three miles south-east to Mansfield also served as the old highway from Chesterfield (now A617).

The road was usable by carts as well as packhorses, and from 1720 was a post road from London, which meant that letters could be delivered and posted in Rotherham, which saved a special journey having to be made to Doncaster, or Bawtry, on the Great North Road, or to Sheffield. From the seventeenth century this road was plied by stage waggons, mainly carrying freight, but also

Figure 4. A section of the London-Richmond highway (Pleasley to Rotherham and beyond) as depicted on John Ogilby's *Britannia Depicta*, published in 1675. *Courtesy of Rotherham Central Library, Archives and Local Studies Section*

passengers, albeit very slowly – at an average of 15 miles a day, before the road improvement of the later eighteenth century made faster and longer progress possible.

The road was turnpiked in 1764, administered by the Rotherham and Pleasley Trust, and on its way south crossed the Tinsley and Bawtry (1760), the Attercliffe and Worksop (1764), and the Chesterfield and Worksop (1739) turnpike roads, and it terminated at the Chesterfield-Mansfield turnpike (1759). Like most of these toll roads, this turnpike helped Rotherham and surrounding towns to develop industrially and agriculturally before the railways made them temporarily redundant. It was disturnpiked in 1874, after 110 years as a toll road.

After a quiet period the road came back to life, in particular the first two miles from town, as a feeder to the desirable suburbs of Moorgate, first developed in 1845. Several large houses set in considerable grounds were built, including Moorgate Grange, Oakwood Hall and Grange, Red House, Sitwell House and Whiston Grange. In the twentieth century Moorgate was developed for suburban housing, as was Whiston a little further out of town, and as motor transport grew enormously in importance, the former turnpike road became a first class route, the A618, carrying traffic from Rotherham towards Worksop, Chesterfield, Mansfield and Nottingham, before the opening of the M1 in 1968 took away most of its through traffic.

Moorgate Road was much altered in the late1950s when it was widened from 40 to 60 feet (12.4 to 18.6 metres) between Oakwood and Whiston crossroads. It carries heavy commuter traffic at peak periods.

3.The Sheffield Road (6 miles/9.4 km)

It is known that in Roman times well-planned and engineered roads from the fort at Templeborough linked the places which would eventually be the earliest sites of Sheffield and Rotherham, but there is no evidence that the south-westerly road to the former town was used, if it survived physically, by later travellers from Rotherham as the medieval highway followed a different line from the earlier road.

To reach Sheffield from Rotherham in former times, a traveller would leave town by High Street and Westgate. Opposite where Union Lane now lies, the road (now Old Sheffield Road) dropped to cross the Rother just before its confluence with the Don. For centuries this would be a ford, as it was not until 1723 that Bow, or Saddle, Bridge was built (the name describes its appearance from the side).

From here the road, through the villages of Tinsley and Attercliffe, followed the line of the present A6178. It is hard to grasp that until Victorian times that this was a country road – to this day a long stretch of the route is called Attercliffe Common – and the road between the two towns would not be heavily used as there was little interdependence. Both were market towns, industry was very localised, and before the Industrial Revolution both had small populations – in 1500 Sheffield's was around 2000 and Rotherham's less than a thousand. There was little need for the inhabitants of Rotherham to visit Sheffield, whilst the few from the latter town who made the opposite journey were most likely passing through on the way to Doncaster.

The old way kept to the south of the swampy Don on slightly raised land, but had to cross the river at the western edge of Attercliffe Township, by a ford, complete with stepping stones. This was known as the West Ford, now corrupted to Washford. A wooden bridge was erected in the early sixteenth century, being replaced by a stone one, in 1672, which was also known as Attercliffe Bridge. It has been rebuilt three times since.

The old road from here to Sheffield did not follow the line taken by the present Attercliffe Road, but climbed north via Royds Lane, Carlisle Street and Hall Car before entering the Wicker down Spital Hill, and on into Sheffield over the ancient Lady's Bridge – a timber structure dating from the twelfth century, rebuilt in stone in 1485. The busiest part of the route was between Sheffield and Tinsley, as the important road to the river port at Bawtry ran from the latter village. This section of road was turnpiked in 1759, not because of the Bawtry connection alone but because the Don had been made navigable to Tinsley docks in 1751 and the increased traffic had made the worn-out old road even worse. Before this, in 1720, the whole length of road had been designated a post-road along which Royal Mail was carried.

The remainder of the route to Rotherham was turnpiked as part of the Tinsley-Doncaster Trust in 1764, and the road grew in importance as the industrial and commercial activities of the two towns burgeoned, and their populations swelled. At the first Census in 1801, Sheffield had 45,000 inhabitants and Rotherham 6,400, a threefold increase in a century. Industry crept out along the lower Don valley, and Attercliffe was transformed from a rural community to an industrial area. 125,000 travellers passed the tollgate at Tinsley in 1835.

Freight waggons, carts, a variety of commercial vehicles, and stage mail and private coaches in increasing numbers used the road. Washford Bridge was rebuilt several times and the entrance to

Sheffield made easier by the laying out of the present level route along Attercliffe Road and Savile Street in 1806. At a later, but unknown, date the present straight length of Sheffield Road between Bow Bridge and the southern end of Westgate was laid down. Large numbers of curious Sheffielders were conveyed to the Walker Brothers' works at Masbrough to view sections of the great iron bridge to be later erected over the Thames at Southwark. Modified dog-carts were pressed into service to cater for this unexpected trade – and were nicknamed 'Watertoos' as it was 1815 when the bridge parts began to be constructed. Long after the ironwork had been shipped to London, and the bridge completed, these conveyances remained in demand as there was now sufficient traffic between the two towns to warrant the service. They were made redundant by the opening of the Sheffield and Rotherham railway in 1838.

The rural lower Don valley almost disappeared under heavy industry in the later nineteenth century, expanding alongside the canal (extended into Sheffield docks in 1819) and railways, creating enormous traffic. Whilst most of this was moved by rail, the Sheffield and Rotherham road became busier and busier and was freed from tolls in 1873. In the late Victorian era, horse-drawn trams ran from Sheffield to Attercliffe (1873), Carbrook (1874) and later on to Tinsley. Electric trams ran from Rotherham to Tinsley in 1903. Through running between the two towns began in 1905 as a joint venture. Soon motor buses were using the route – and are doing so to this day. Trams were removed in 1948.

For a short period between 1940 and 1949 trolley buses plied between Rotherham and Tinsley. Bow Bridge, even after several widenings, could not cope with the increased traffic, so was replaced by a new bridge in 1927.

The road remained a vital artery throughout the twentieth century, and when road classification was introduced by the new Ministry of Transport immediately after the First World War, it was numbered A630. Some pressure was taken off the road by the construction of Meadow Bank Road in 1933 on the opposite bank of the Don. Later further pressure was taken off the Tinsley-Rotherham section with the opening of the M1 (1968) and M18 (1967), removing most of the through traffic to Doncaster and the Great North Road.

The Sheffield-Tinsley section of the road, the A6178, has been gradually improved in the 1990s as part of the regeneration of the Lower Don Valley following the devastatingly rapid collapse of the steel industry in the 1970s.

4.The Doncaster Road (12 miles/19 km)

It has long been presumed that, in essence, the ancient highway from Rotherham to Doncaster more or less follows the line of the Roman road between Templeborough (possibly *Morbium*) and Doncaster (*Danum*). This ran along High Street and Doncaster Gate and Road, taking the high ground to Aldwarke as Eastwood was a swampy area before being drained in the mid-nineteenth century. It continued through Dalton, Thrybergh and along the Magnesian Limestone ridge south-east of the Don, past Conisbrough and through Warmsworth and Balby. Certainly there are several long, straight stretches of road which are almost certainly following the alignments laid down by Roman surveyors in the sixth decade of the first century AD – a comfortable day's march between the two forts of about 13 miles (21 km). The road kept to higher ground to the south of the Don for its whole journey.

The immediate post-Roman period is largely a mystery in the Rotherham area but it is known that by the tenth century Conisbrough (meaning King's manor or fortified place) was of great regional importance. Doubtless this would generate traffic and travel between Rotherham and Conisbrough, and access to the Great North Road at Doncaster would always be important. The Norman castle at Conisbrough and the growth of the small town (though it was never a commercial centre) in the Middle Ages would keep the old road active and this took the route away from the Roman alignment at Hill Top and into the town along Old Road, West Street and back to the Doncaster road steeply down Old Hill. This was the route turnpiked in 1764, though soon by-passed in 1780 by the road now followed by the A630, which is back on the original Roman line once more.

Even with the eventual redundancy of the great castle, there would always be some traffic, probably primarily passenger, to the important route centre of Doncaster, which was the Royal Mail post town for Rotherham for many years before the latter gained its own post office.

Stage coach travel began along the Great North Road in the seventeenth century, though regular and reliable all year round services were not established until the Hanoverian period. In the early 1700s it would take three to four days to reach London from Doncaster, and Rotherham passengers would have to walk or take a horse to Doncaster to catch a coach, as the first reference to a regular scheduled coach through Rotherham from Sheffield to Hull was not until 1787, whilst another coach did the shorter Sheffield to Doncaster return trip four days a week. Within a few more years there were many more coaches in use, especially on the Rotherham-Doncaster road, which was greatly improved by its turnpiking in 1764. Before the railway age there was always sufficient traffic to pay investors in the turnpike trust a regular five per cent interest, comfortably above general average returns on capital at the time.

However, this was to end with the opening of the railway between Rotherham and Doncaster in 1849. Within a very short time the turnpike trust was in financial difficulties, in spite of an attempt to catch road traffic plying to the new station at Swinton by turnpiking a new stretch of road to link with the main highway. The trust faded away, the road being disturnpiked in 1873.

For a generation the Doncaster Road would have been almost deserted, though horse omnibuses did provide some rivalry to the railway, only gradually reviving with the rapid growth of cycling and the more tentative expansion of early motor vehicles. Following the First World War, though, with motor vehicles becoming more powerful and reliable, the road became busier every year. In 1927 through motor bus services were inaugurated between Sheffield and Doncaster providing competition for the struggling railways, a neat reversal of the situation eight decades previously. After an enforced quieter period during the Second World War (1939-45), the road traffic built up year by year until 1968, when the M18 linked the M1 south of Rotherham with the A1, which had been upgraded to motorway standards in 1959. This immediately took most of the Sheffield and Rotherham through traffic for Doncaster, Hull and the A1(M) off the A630(T), a fact reflected by the latter losing its status as a trunk road.

5. The Wortley Road (9 miles/14.5 km)

A very old highway left Rotherham market, and after crossing the Don, by ford or bridge, aimed north of west for the 1,000 feet (305 m) high ridgeway route between the Little Don and the upper waters of the River Don. At Hartcliffe Hill the old road joined an important highway from Doncaster and Barnsley, via Penistone, on its way to Woodhead via Saltersbrook, where it, too, was joined by a road from Wakefield and Holmfirth. The road descended the Pennine moorlands down the north side of Longdendale, the valley of the River Etherow (whose waters eventually feed the Mersey), to reach the lower and flatter land round Stockport and Manchester, via Tintwistle, Hollingworth and Mottram.

After crossing the Don the local section of this ancient highway climbed up through Kimberworth via the Holmes, Psalters Lane (the 'P' is a clerical error and should not be in the name, which is a reminder that this was the last leg of the 60 mile journey by the salters and their packhorses from Northwich in Cheshire), Church Street, High Street and Old Wortley Road. It then followed the ridgeway high above Blackburn Brook towards Thorpe Hesley, (now called Upper Wortley Road) before descending the steep Cowley Hill, and Cowley Lane to cross the Blackburn Brook at Chapeltown. From here the road climbed on to higher ground via Mortomley, and Howbrook to Four Lane Ends (a little south of Wortley village).

The road continued down Finkle Street Lane, crossed the Don by a ford, still extant at the side of Tin Mill Bridge, and began the climb up to the next big ridgeway, via Holly Hall Lane, to the hamlet of Green Moor. For the next 4¹/₂ miles (7 km) the track ran along the 1000 feet contour. At Hartcliffe Hill the road from Penistone was met, and the highway aimed for the Cheshire border at Saltersbrook, some 6 miles (9.6 km) further west. (The modern road A628 west from the *Dog and Partridge* public house is on a different line from the original route.)

In the reverse direction this route was an important saltway along which packhorse teams carried salt from Northwich in Cheshire to the market towns in the West Riding. This trade had existed since Saxon times as details are recorded in the Domesday Book. The name Saltersbrook speaks for itself, whilst part of the ridgeway road further east carries the name 'Salter Hill Lane'. Other goods carried included cheese and Manchester made items. In the reverse direction packhorses carried hemp, flax, linen yarn, nails from the Chapeltown area, iron from Wortley and coal. Kimberworth had been making iron products from the twelfth century.

So important was this road that it was the first in the region to be turnpiked in 1740. The length up Longdendale from Cheshire (as it was then) had already been made into a carriage road in 1732. However the Hartcliffe Hill to Wortley section, running through largely empty countryside, with a sparse population, never paid its way and the whole road was disturnpiked in 1762. Several of the original milestones remain by the roadside. But in 1788 the Wortley-Rotherham section was revived under a new body (named the 'Rotherham and Four Lane Ends Trust'), which had the advantage of meeting the important, newly-turnpiked 1777 Sheffield-Halifax Road. Not only did the road run past Wortley Forge, a water-powered iron works, which sent its products to many places, it served the nail-making areas of Mortomley, High Green and Chapeltown. Tens of thousands of nails were taken to the Don navigation at Aldwarke and Rotherham, many of them for export to America. The turnpike road was diverted away from Holly Hall Lane at Green Moor, and the new road ran down Well Hill crossing the Don by the masonry Forge Bridge (1782) near Wortley Top Forge, rejoining its original line at Finkle Street Lane.

The disturnpiked road, now controlled by parish authorities, though generally quiet, was used by stockmen driving animals to Rotherham's important beast markets. Some of the farmhouses en route were, for a time, inns catering for this passing trade before railways began transporting farmstock.

Howbrook Lane, from Wortley to Chapeltown, has remained a country lane throughout its existence, but Chapeltown grew from a village to a small town in the nineteenth century with the exploitation of iron and coal reserves, making the road to Rotherham continually busy.

The present Wortley Road from Dropping Well into town via College Road, was, in fact, the last stretch of turnpike road built in the Rotherham area. Opened in 1865, it was constructed to facilitate the movement of coal from pits at Dropping Well, by-passing the difficult bends and gradients of the original route, now Old Wortley Road. It was disturnpiked in 1883, the last to close in the Rotherham area. The New Wortley Road (A629) was constructed to by-pass this road from Bradgate and improve links with Centenary Way in 1984-85.

Upper Wortley Road (for four centuries it had passed through Kimberworth Deer Park) remained a country road, skirting the southern edge of the Wentworth Estate. There has been piecemeal housing development near Keppel's Column, and Wortley Road saw much more intensive building at Dropping Well and Kimberworth, encouraged by the introduction of public transport services from 1904, beginning with trams to Kimberworth, leaving Rotherham town centre via Main Street and following Masbrough Street and Kimberworth Park to the terminus. Both Old Wortley and Wortley roads were busy commercial highways as Masbrough and Kimberworth were heavily industrialised during the Victorian period, their combined populations quadrupling between 1851 and 1901 to just over 26,000.

Upper Wortley Road between Dropping Well and Thorpe Common was improved in the early 1970s as it became an important NW link to junction 35 of the M1 opened to Barnsley and Leeds in 1968.

6. The Bawtry Road (17 miles/27 km)

It must be hard for most people who have visited Bawtry, or perhaps simply passed through it on the way to Gainsborough and beyond, to realise how important the village once was to the economy of South Yorkshire and North Derbyshire throughout the Middle Ages, and indeed well into the eighteenth century. Bawtry had wharves at the side of the navigable River Idle, a tributary of the Trent about 10 miles (16 km) to the east. A variety of goods were sent by packhorse and cart to the port. These included lead, wool and cloth, millstones, coal, grain and metalware (including cutlery). They were taken by small boats to Stockwith on the Trent and transferred to larger vessels for the journey down the major river to the Humber and the port of Hull, whence the goods were transhipped to London, other British ports, or even across the North Sea to the Continent. In reverse, freight such as high-quality bar iron (or steel) from Spain, Germany and Sweden, softwood from Scandinavia, hemp, flax, yarn and hides arrived at Bawtry, and were then distributed over a wide area, including Rotherham.

Bawtry was also on the Great North Road, an important post road carrying the Royal Mail and from 1720 mail was delivered directly from Bawtry to Rotherham.

There was an old-established road between Sheffield and Bawtry, via Tinsley, Canklow and Whiston, Wickersley, Bramley, Hellaby, Maltby and Tickhill, which catered for cart as well as packhorse transport. This route, joined at Whiston or Wickersley by Rotherham traffic, was also used to reach Tickhill, which was an important administrative centre, based on the castle for many years in the Middle Ages. Also, 12 miles (19 km) beyond Bawtry lay Gainsborough, where the Trent was navigable all year round, whereas the River Idle in summer often lacked sufficient depth. Freight thus had to be stockpiled until the Autumn or Winter rain raised the river level.

The road from Tinsley to Bawtry was turnpiked in 1760, ironically at a time when Bawtry was finally losing its importance as a port with the opening of the Chesterfield Canal to the Trent in 1777. This took the North Derbyshire trade, whilst the South Yorkshire trade had already fallen away with the progressive improvements on the Don pushing navigation progressively upriver to Aldwarke in 1731, Rotherham in 1740 and Tinsley in 1751.

Bawtry would probably have faded away into economic insignificance if it had not stood on the Great North Road which saw a great increase in traffic in the later eighteenth century consequent upon road improvements. The little town was the first stage south from Doncaster, where horses were changed, so it had several busy inns which also catered for the crossing trade form west to east and reverse. Many passengers who wanted the fast stage coaches to London and the south, made their way to Bawtry by horse, private carriage or local stage coach to catch them. This practice diminished as more and faster coaches left Sheffield – the 3$^{1}/_{2}$ days' journey to London in 1760 soon falling to 26 hours by 1786, and was killed off in 1826 when a new road was turnpiked between Maltby and Barnby Moor, 5$^{1}/_{2}$ miles (9 km) south of Bawtry, where two inns provided a new staging post on the Great North Road. This new road ran through Firbeck, Oldcotes and Blyth - and is now the A634. To improve connections with Maltby the road from Rotherham to Wickersley through Broom was turnpiked, as part of the same scheme, in 1826. This is now the A6021. It saved coach passengers the longer original route via Moorgate Road and Whiston crossroads. Following a quiet life as a rural lane in the Victorian period, though used at times for outings by waggonettes to Roche Abbey and Maltby Crags, it was disturnpiked in 1878, as was the Tinsley-Bawtry road, gradually becoming more important with the rapid expansion of Maltby from a sleepy country village to a busy little town with the opening of a big coal mine in 1911. Maltby's population increased from 527 in 1901, to 10,000 in 1931. A modified toll cottage survives at the eastern edge of Tickhill.

Figure 5. Milepost on the Rotherham-Pleasley Road at Moorgate Road (A618). *The Author*

The first trolley buses, or 'trackless electric vehicles' were introduced on this road between the tram terminus at *The Stag Inn*, Broom, and Maltby in 1912, and ran for 30 years. (This was only the third such service in the whole country.) Before that there had been private horse-drawn omnibuses to Maltby and Bawtry from the 1880s, and the first motor charabanc plied the road in 1910.

Both Broom Road and Wickersley Road carried increasing commuter traffic, as did West and East Bawtry Roads with the suburbanisation of the area to the south-east of Rotherham. The latter two roads became part of Rotherham's outer ring road, and were a very early example of a dual-carriageway in 1939. Progress on the scheme was delayed by the Second World War and its aftermath, so it was not until 1977 that the whole length of the A631 between Whiston and Bramley was completed. All the above roads became even busier as feeders to junction 1 of the M18, opened in 1967. Bramley itself expanded enormously with housing development (population 1901 - 431, 1991 – 7,973), as did Maltby in the 1970s and 1980s (population in 1991 – 17,110).

Bibliography

Further detailed history of the above roads and the transport along them can be found in:

1.Hall, Charles C., *Rotherham and District Transport, Vol 1 - to 1914*, Rotherword Press, 1996.
2.Hey, David, *Packmen, Carriers and Packhorse Roads*, Leicester University Press, 1980.
3.Hopkinson, G. G., 'Road Development in South Yorkshire and North Derbyshire 1700-1850', *Transactions of the Hunter Archaeological Society*, Vol X, 1971, pp. 14-30.
4.Smith, Howard, *Tinsley and Bawtry Turnpike Trail*, 1988.
5.Smith, Howard, *Saltway Trail: Woodhead to Rotherham*, Rotherham Department of Libraries, Museum and Arts, 1991.
6.Smith, Howard, *A History of Rotherham's Roads and Transport*, Rotherham Department of Libraries, Museum and Arts, 1992.

Appendix

Routes of Old Roads using Modern Roads from Rotherham

1. The Barnsley Road

Before turnpiking in 1764: B6089: Greasbrough Street - Greasbrough Road - Car Hill - (Greasbrough) Potter Hill - Main Street - Cinder Bridge Road - The Whins - (Nether Haugh) Stubbin Road - Packman Road - Rotherham Road - Packman Road - (Brampton) - Brampton Road - Knollbeck Lane - A633 roundabout - 1st exit, Wath Road - (Wombwell) - Park Street - High Street - Barnsley road - A633 roundabout - A633 Barnsley Road - across R. Dove, old line of road now missing to Ardsley - Doncaster Road A635, Stairfoot - BARNSLEY.

After turnpiking in 1764 from Nether Haugh: B6091 - Cortworth Lane - B6090 Cortworth Lane (cont'd) - Hoober Lane - (Wentworth) - Main Street - Barrow Hill - Dike Hill - Harley Road (terminates at junction with A6135 Sheffield Road between Chapeltown and Hoyland. TR A6135 to Birdwell, continue N up A61 to BARNSLEY *c*.6 miles (10 km).

2. The Pleasley Road

From 1764 - Wellgate - Hollowgate - A618 Moorgate Road - Pleasley Road - (Aughton) - Main Street - Aughton Road - High Street - Mansfield Road (line altered by Aston Relief Road A57) - Mansfield Road - Rotherham Road - (Killamarsh) - Mansfield Road - Rotherham Road - (Clowne) - B6417 - (E of Bolsover) - PLEASLEY. (Before 1764 - different line over Moorgate area - see text).

3. The Sheffield Road

Westgate - Canklow Road - Old Sheffield Road - A6021 Sheffield Road - (cross Centenary Way) - A6178 Sheffield Road - (cross under M1 junction 34) - Sheffield Road - Attercliffe Common - Attercliffe Road - Savile Street - Wicker - (Lady's Bridge) - SHEFFIELD CENTRE. (Before 1806 - from Washford/Attercliffe Bridge - WNW to Carlisle Street and Hall Car to Spital Hill - Wicker - Lady's Bridge - SHEFFIELD CENTRE.

4. The Doncaster Road

High Street - Doncaster Gate - Doncaster Road - Aldwarke Roundabout - A630 Doncaster road and on through Thrybergh, Hooton Roberts, Hill Top - (before 1780 Old Road - West Street - Old

Hill - Conisbrough) - Sheffield Road - Doncaster Road, Sheffield Road - (Warmsworth) - High Road - cross over A1(M) - Warmsworth Road - High Road - Balby Road - Cleveland Street - DONCASTER CENTRE.

5. The Wortley Road

Before Enclosure - (approximately only as road lines have been altered by industrialisation)- College Road - Union Street - Holmes Lane - Psalters Lane (now interrupted by A6109 crossing its line) - Kimberworth Road - Church Street - High Street - Old Wortley Road - Upper Wortley Road (A629).

After Enclosure - College Road (approx) - Kimberworth Road (by-passed Psalters Lane).

Post 1865 - College Road - Wortley Road (A629) - Upper Wortley Road (A629) - (cross M1 junction 35) - Cowley Hill - Cowley Lane - (Chapeltown) - cross A6135 Ecclesfield Road/Station Road: former Sheffield-Barnsley turnpike road - Lound Side - Lane End - Mortomley Lane - (Mortomley) - Wortley Road - cross A61 Westwood New Road - Hollinberry Lane - (Howbrook) - Howbrook Lane - the last section of which was truncated by A616 in 1988 - meet A629 Halifax Road at Four Lane Ends (S of Wortley Village) opposite Finkle Street Lane - WORTLEY (for continuation of this road westwards see text).

Post 1984 - College Road and E end of Wortley Road by-passed by A629 New Wortley Road.

6. The Bawtry Road

Wellgate - Broom Road A6021 - Wickersley Road - Brecks Roundabout - A631 Bawtry Road - through Wickersley, Bramley - cross M18 junction 1 - Bawtry Road (Hellaby) - Rotherham Road (Maltby) - High Street - Tickhill Road - Rotherham Road - (Tickhill) West Gate - Castle Gate - Sunderland Street - Bawtry Road - BAWTRY.

7. Continuation of the Barnsley road to Richmond

For those who wish to follow the former alternative London to North road on the map or on the ground the details are as follows:

BARNSLEY, via back roads, Kexbrough, High Hoyland, Skelmanthorpe B6116, Shelley, to Kirkburton, Almondbury, HUDDERSFIELD, A629 Elland, HALIFAX, A629 Denholme, Cullingworth (back road), KEIGHLEY, then parallel to S of present A629 via Utley and Steeton to Kildwick, back roads to Low Bradley and SKIPTON, B6265 Rylstone, Linton, GRASS-INGTON, B6160 through Conistone, KETTLEWELL, then NE through Coverdale, via Bradley, Gammersgill to MIDDLEHAM, over the River Ure to Harmby (SE of Leyburn), then via a lonely moorland route W of Hipswell Moor into RICHMOND. This is not a route any modern surveyor would follow!

3. Corn Windmills of Rotherham and District

by Alan Whitworth

IT IS SAID THAT WINDMILLS were first introduced into Britain by returning crusaders. Possibly this is true, as the earliest written reference to a windmill in England, dated 1185, relates to a windmill at Weedley, in Yorkshire, let at a rental of 8s 0d a year.[1] At that time the mill and manor of Weedley, a small sheep farming community located towards the eastern end of the parish of South Cave in the East Riding, was owned by the Knights Templars, a militant religious order founded at the beginning of the tenth century in Outremer, an arid sandy region on the border of modern Iran and Afghanistan, which was noted for windmills as early as the ninth century – a coincidence which lends credibility to this supposition.

The earliest documented windmill in Rotherham Metropolitan District, however, does not occur for a considerable period after this date, despite the substantial number of early references to windmills in Yorkshire in general which are frequently recorded from the thirteenth century onwards. This may be due to the fact that, in this area, there was possibly a greater leaning towards water-powered mills, and indeed, a number of early steam-powered mills such as Newhill Mill at Wath-upon-Dearne, which was demolished about 1930. This stood on the site of an early medieval corn-mill from which survived a stone carrying a Latin inscription which was set above a doorway at Newhill Mill. There was also a steam mill at Masbrough which outlived the corn windmill which presumably stood in Windmill Yard off Masbrough Street, near to the Wesleyan Chapel, and which had gone by 1851.[2]

Notwithstanding this fact, there were still a significant number of windmills in and around Rotherham, and even where water was plentiful, sufficient to power a watermill, windmills can still be found, such as at Harthill, where a windmill stood in 1591,[3] owned by the lord of the manor, as well as a watermill.

Of slightly earlier date was the windmill at nearby Woodall, owned in 1580 by Lord Dacre, and the windmills recorded at 'Waddermarshe' and Swinton in 1571, in the ownership of Thomas Normanville, esquire.[4] Interestingly, the mill at Swinton, a post-mill

Figure 1. An early post-windmill from a medieval manuscript.

supported on a 'post and cross-tree' buried under a mound 38 feet in diameter, was built on the site of earlier occupation where both Roman and medieval pottery were found.[5] A windmill at Swinton was last mentioned in 1614.[6]

Post-mills (Figure 1) were the earliest type of windmills so named because the wood-framed body of the mill was supported on a massive upright post standing on a horizontal frame of two timbers crossed and jointed at right angles. This constructional arrangement allowed the body of the mill, to which were fixed the sails, to be turned on the post into the wind and so ensure as little interruption to the milling process as possible.

These early medieval post-mills were popular for many centuries, and if the site proved unsatisfactory, it was not uncommon for early windmills to be moved bodily to a new location. One such was that relocated by order of abbot William Meaux from Beeforth to Skipsea in Holderness during the late fourteenth century.[7] Such action demonstrates the versatility of the post-mill over later static smock and tower mills built of brick or stone.

Today, not one single instance of a post-mill exists in the county, and the only example anywhere near to Yorkshire is the finely restored windmill at Wrawby, near Brigg, just across the Humber Bridge in Lincolnshire. However, up until the 1930s, a post-mill stood at North Anston, which was photographed around that time (Figure 2).

This complete free-standing wooden mill raised on the usual arrangement of an open post and braced cross-tree, was powered by four shuttered sails. However, it is possible that two mills stood in the village during the same period, as another post-mill was photographed in ruins around the same date.[8] This second mill stood in Bell's Field, off the Woodsetts Road. In this instance though, the post and cross-tree were enclosed in a roofed roundhouse, a later development which provided greater stability for the working windmill and also dry storage space beneath the mill. Remains of the wands show that it was powered by four common cloth sails, and as a consequence the two windmills must be thought of as separate sites even

Figure 2. North Anston post-mill photographed around 1930. *Rotherham Central Library, Archives & Local Studies Section*

though no documents record two mills there. Moreover, in the eighteenth century, Thomas Jefferys' *Map of Yorkshire* published in 1772, shows only one site at North Anston, which suggests that one windmill was erected after this date, probably the first mentioned, as shuttered sails only came into common usage after being invented about that year.

In 1603 a windmill stood at Aughton, recorded in a document of that date.[9] Unfortunately, few other early windmill sites are so mentioned in the Rotherham district, but a number of place-names suggest sites prior to the eighteenth century. At Greasbrough, *Windmill Hill* is recorded on the 1849 Tithe Award, as is a *Windmill Hill* at Thrybergh in a similar document dated 1841. At Aston-cum-Aughton, the name *Windmill Hill* also survived as a place-name long after the mill had disappeared, mentioned in a Tithe Award of 1834. Indeed, the name *Windmill Close* was given to the field at Swinton where it was known the post-mill stood, mentioned previously. A *Windmill Field* was also recorded in connection with the enclosure of lands at Laughton-en-le-Morthern in 1771, shown on the Enclosure Map of that date, but curiously, not on Jefferys' map of 1772, even though a windmill survived until 1932, when it was painted by Karl Wood, albeit in ruins.[10]

Originally, windmills would have been built on the open fields or common land of the village. The erection of a mill was a privilege granted only to the lord of the manor or church, and with its ownership went certain rights in respect of milling corn known as 'mill soke'. Under this feudal custom, tenants of the manor where required to bring their corn to the manorial mill for grinding. The miller, often a tenant put in by the lord was allowed, for his labour, to retain a predetermined percentage of the flour he produced with the exception of that belonging to his lordship, who could have his corn ground free. It was the duty of the miller to collect the toll, or 'multer' as it was often called, due to the lord, and present it at the manorial court on prescribed dates either in money or in kind.

Failure to abide by and uphold this state of medieval soke law was a serious matter, and in 1573, William Plewman, a miller of York, was fined 13s 4d by the manorial court 'for not attending the Court and for not bringing the Tolle Dishe according to custom'.[11] Similarly, in 1357, John Duffain and Agnes Knight, of Methley, were fined 3d each because 'they do not make suit at the lord's mill, but use a mill to the prejudice of the lord'.

Through his responsibilities, the miller was often the recipient of much mistrust, and Chaucer drew attention to this aspect of the

Figure 3. Enlarged detail of the two Doncaster Gate windmills from a drawing in Christopher Thompson's *Hallamshire Scrapbook* dated 1867. *Rotherham Central Library, Archives & Local Studies Section*

miller's character, observing:

His was a master hand at stealing grain,
He felt it with his thumb and knew
Its quality and took three times his due...[12]

Such observations were not without foundation, and in 1725, William Scutard, the miller of Thorne (Temple Newsam parish), was accused in his absence of falsely setting the stones 'in order to steal the flour of the customary tenants'.[13]

Access to the windmill was paramount and an important consideration in the siting of mills. The roads to a windmill where known as 'mill-ways' and would have had free passage along their entire length, with no obstacles such as stiles or gates, particularly where the route led directly to an isolated mill and did not form part of the network of village highways and byways. This was necessary to enable the manorial tenant to transport his grain to the windmill and back again. Medieval documentary evidence shows that the principal form of transport was the horse, consequently, a mill-way would at least have had the width and substance of say today's bridleway.[14]

In the town of Rotherham itself, two windmills still stood in 1867 on Doncaster Gate with boundaries along St Anne's Hill, and were shown complete on a drawing in Christopher Thompson's *Hallamshire Scrapbook* (Figure 3). These were tower mills and undoubtedly replaced earlier post-mills. A photograph taken around 1872 (Figure 4) shows that by this date they were derelict, one completely roofless and devoid of sails, while the second still retained partial sails which indicate that the earlier drawing is perhaps not as accurate as one might suppose.

Built of stone, the two mills on Doncaster Gate stood five storeys high and had only a slight taper to their walls. One had a curious circular room running around the base of the tower, presumably erected as some form of storage area. In 1822 the two millers listed as working these Rotherham mills were Matthew Crossby and Richard Tasker,[15] who each operated independently even though the windmills were situated near each other (Figure 5).

William Baines' *Directory of Yorkshire* of 1822 records a number of mills still in operation. At Treeton, Robert Taylor was the corn merchant and miller; at Kimberworth, S. Lockwood was the corn miller at Grange Mill, no doubt a site of some antiquity; at

Figure 4. The two Doncaster Gate windmills photographed around 1872. *Rotherham Central Library, Archives & Local Studies Section*

Figure 5. Site plan of the Doncaster Gate windmills (marked A and B) redrawn from the Ordnance Survey Map of 1890. The mill marked A was described as the 'Old Windmill'.

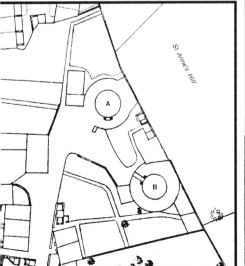

Greasbrough, J. and E. Jackson were the village corn millers; William Brayshaw was given as the corn miller at Wickersley; while at Thorpe Salvin, William Twibble was listed as the miller at Peck Mill and John White was the miller at Moor Mill in the same village.

It is possible that many of these windmills had survived from the previous century, and on Thomas Jefferys' map of 1772, windmills are shown at North Anston, Wentworth, and Brookhouse near Laughton-en-le-Morthen, the latter being still marked on Greenwood's *Map of Yorkshire*, published in 1817.

This last windmill near Laughton-en-le-Morthen, however, may have been Carr Mill, situated one mile north of All Saints' church, which was demolished around 1976. This was said to have measured 25 feet in height and had walls two feet thick. A newspaper photograph taken at the time of its demolition when it stood ruinous, shows that the mill walls had a pronounced taper similar to a surviving windmill at Stutton beside the A64 outside Tadcaster (Figure 6). Indeed, the resemblance in size, shape and material struck me as being so uncanny that the two mills could have been identical twins.

Peck Mill at Thorpe Salvin, mentioned above as still operating in 1822 and shown on Jefferys' map, took its name from the Peck or Pekes family and is said to have been established in the twelfth century, and was held by lease from the lord of the manor by that family until 1546 when they purchased it outright.

Another windmill which survived into the nineteenth century, was the mill at Dalton Brook. This mill was photographed around the end of that century (Figure 7), and while it is shown as derelict with no sails, it is interesting to note that it was not shown on the 1st edition Ordnance Survey map (Figure 8) published some years earlier. The millhouse, however, still stands and was later a public house; today it continues to survive, although recently converted into flats.

The photograph shows a tall narrow tower-mill which had been heightened at some previous date as there is a marked difference in the stonework, and it is covered by a Dutch-style ogee-cap. A curious fact here, is that I can find no millers listed in any nineteenth century trade directories for this windmill.

Finally, the two most instantly recognisable windmills in this area are probably those at Wentworth, one situated on Clayfields Lane in the village itself, now known as the 'Roundhouse', the other, about a half-mile north-west of Wentworth along Mill Lane at

Figure 6. Stutton windmill which stands beside the A64 York - Leeds road, an almost identical twin to the demolished Carr Mill. *The Author*

Barrow in Wentworth township, which are the last surviving examples of at least three windmills known to have stood hereabouts.

The earliest reference to a windmill at Wentworth occurs in 1590, when in that year a series of manorial by-laws was drawn up, one of which read,

> *A Payne*[16] *is layde that ev'ye p'son* [every person] *wythin this Lordshippe doe grynde his corne at the Lorde's wynde myln and horse myln in paine of ev'ye p'son* [paying] *IIIs IIIId* [3s 4d].

To which mill these regulations refer is not clear, but a windmill obviously continued on one site at Wentworth from this time, and was possibly repaired between 1769 and 1770, when the Wentworth Estate Account books mention on 13 November, 1769, 'Christopher Evers in full for the repair of a windmill, etc. upon quitting the same, £26 5s 0d.' A year later an entry of 14 October, 1770, reads, 'John Marshall then and before for work done and materials found in and about repairing Wentworth Windmill in full, £63 0s 6d.'[17]

In 1745, Lord Malton, soon to become the first Marquis of Rockingham, 'built a new wind miln'[18] at Wentworth which was in all probability the mill now known as the 'Roundhouse'. Estate accounts record the 'buying of eighty yards of sail cloth for the windmill'; another entry shows a payment of

Figure 7. The windmill at Dalt[on] Brook photographed around the e[nd] of the nineteenth century. *Rother[ham] Central Library, Archives & Local Studies Sectio[n]*

Figure 8. Site plan of Dalton Brook windmill redrawn from the 1890 Ordnance Survey map, showing the position of the windmill (marked A) which had been demolished by this date. The mill house (marked B) survives to this day.

£2 12s 6d to Jonathan Smith, millwright, while a further entry for the year ending 7 July, 1745, mentions a payment for 158,000 bricks, undoubtedly for the windmill in the village, which is constructed of thin, handmade bricks on a stone base.

That two separate mills stood hereabouts during the same period is almost certainly the case, as mention of 'repairs' to a windmill in 1769 presupposes this, as it would hardly seem credible that a substantially built 'new wind miln' barely 24 years old would be in need of repair by this latter date.

Unfortunately, however, the issue of the number of windmills at Wentworth during this time is complicated and not made entirely clear when the maps for the area are searched. No mills at Wentworth are shown on Joseph Dickenson's *Map of South Yorkshire*, published in 1750, but a single windmill appears on Jefferys' map of 1772, and again, only one mill is marked on William Fairbank's plan of Wentworth dated 1778.

The list of alterations in the Wentworth Estate Rental of 1793, provides further evidence though, which tends to support the idea that two mills existed. A note recalls:

> *John Pearson abated out of his rent in consideration of the windmill not having been wrought part of this year, the same being taken down and rebuilt at Barrow.*

In the same year, the Household Accounts show an entry of a payment to 'Anthony Boulby, bricklayer, for 14 Days wages converting the old windmill into a Cottage called Saxon Tower - £1 15s 0d.' This was the 'Roundhouse', and the name of Saxon Tower suggests that the ornamental crenellations which encircle the roof were the handiwork of Anthony Boulby in 1793. A Joseph Wormack became the first tenant of the cottage called Saxon Tower at Martinmas in 1793, paying a rent of £1 10s 0d annually. A year later, the old wheels, etc. From an 'old mill' were sold by Leonard Wilkinson, an estate foreman.[19]

It is evident that as the windmill of brick, now known as the

Figure 9. The 'Roundhouse', Wentworth village, once a windmill, now converted to a dwelling. *Rotherham Central Library, Archives & Local Studies Section*

'Roundhouse' – formerly the Saxon Tower – survives, then it was another windmill of stone which was taken down and rebuilt elsewhere.

It seems that at times the second Marquis of Rockingham employed his own miller at the Wentworth Mill (Figure 9) and worked the windmill for his own profit; and at other times he rented his mill and the tenant miller laboured on his own account. There was a 'small house' available for the miller's use, but from what period this was provided is unknown. It was taken down in 1788. From payments in the estate accounts for drying oats and grinding malt in 1751, we learn that Richard Hirst was then the miller. In 1769 Chris. Evers rented the mill, house and garden for £18 for one year. The second Marquis of Rockingham took the mill 'in hand' in 1770, and, according to the Memorandum Books that accompany Fairbank's plan, the mill was 'not let' in 1778. The name of another miller comes from the parish register of Wentworth church, which records the death, on 14 October, 1781, of Joanna Welsh, widow of Joseph Welsh, miller to the Marquis of Rockingham. Thomas Booth rented the mill for a period previous to 1784, in which year Benjamin Jackson replaced him. In the latter half of 1791 John Pearson took the place of Benjamin Jackson at the windmilll, and it is possible that John Pearson's father worked the Aldham Mill at Wombwell, for the parish register again supplies the information that William Pearson, son of John Pearson, miller, of Wentworth, and grandson of William Pearson of 'Oldham Mill', died on 13 December, 1794.[20]

Meanwhile, at Barrow, the building of a new windmill from materials provided by the taking down of a mill at Wentworth, must have proceeded with urgency, for it was completed by 1793. The total cost of the work was £382 9s 1$^{1}/_{4}$d, and the following items helped to make up the figure mentioned.

	£	s	d
Thos. Hobson & Co. For mason's work	52	9	5$^{3}/_{4}$
Leonard Wilkinson's expenses for carpenter's work and sundry expenses	135	15	9
Stone from Blacker Quarry	2	15	1$^{1}/_{2}$
James Howard for a flour machine & box	7	9	0
George Chandler for a pair of French mill stones	31	15	0
Messrs. Whittaker & Gill for sail cloths	8	9	7
Messrs. Walker for sundry cast metal goods	48	8	9

Mill Lane, the road or 'mill-way' which led to the new windmill, was
also made at this time, and a substantial house was built for the miller
and his family. The accounts for building and repairs on the
Wentworth Estate contain the following entry for the year 1794:

> *Paid sundries for erecting a new dwelling house, barn and stable, etc.*
> *Contiguous to the new windmill and other expenses relating thereto ...*
> *£313 14s 5d.*

Several enclosed fields surrounding the new mill were transferred
from neighbouring farms for the use of the miller, and John Pearson,
in addition to his first rent of £40 for the lease of the new windmill
for the year ending Michaelmas 1794, paid a further sum of £10 for
a half year's lease, from Martinmas 1793, for the homestead at the mill
and several parcels of land.

John Pearson stayed at Barrow Mill until 1800, when William
Nodder took possession, but he remained only two years, after which
time, a Benjamin Jackson, perhaps the same, or a relative of, the man
who had once been at the old mill at Wentworth, replaced him. By
1825, it is evident from notes and correspondence in the Wentworth
Woodhouse Muniments that Joshua Jackson had charge of the windmill. Possibly he was the son of Benjamin Jackson, although Joshua's
name did not replace that of Benjamin in Earl Fitzwilliam's Rental
until 1833.[21]

Considerable repairs to the windmill took place between 1828 and
1831, but from 1824 steam power had
also been used to grind wheat in the
village, when in that year, Earl
Fitzwilliam paid half the costs with
Joshua Jackson to erect a steam corn
mill near the miller's house. In 1829,
a Matthew Turton built a bone mill,
near the corn mill, for grinding bones
into bone for use in agriculture, and
he also repaired the windmill, having
possibly had the use of it from Joshua,
but this is not clear. Notwithstanding
the amount of work carried out on
Barrow windmill, by June, 1835, the
mill had ceased working, and the
Estate Accounts for the year June
1834 to June 1835 show that Earl

Figure 10. The remains of the windmill
at Barrow, Wentworth, photographed in
November, 1997, which was undergoing
yet another conversion. *The Author*

Fitzwilliam paid his foreman mason, John Sykes, £135 1s 0d 'for converting Joshua Jackson's windmill into 2 cottages' – thus ended several centuries of wind-powered corn milling in Wentworth village. Today, the windmill still stands, and when I visited it in late 1997, it was again undergoing another conversion (Figure 10).

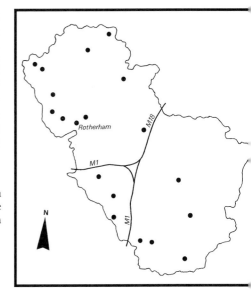

Figure 11. Map of Rotherham Metropolitan Borough showing the distribution of windmills mentioned in the text. Not to scale.

Notes on References

1. Yorkshire Archaeological Society (YAS), *Records of the Knights Templars*, p.131.
2. Ordnance Survey Six Inch Map, 1851.
3. Yorkshire Archaeological Society Record Series (YASRS), *Yorkshire Feet of Fines*, 33 Eliz.I.
4. YASRS, *Yorkshire Feet of Fines*, 13 & 14 Eliz.I.
5. *Yorkshire Archaeological Journal*, Vol.45, 1973.
6. YASRS, *Feet of Fines, Stuart Period*, 12 Jas.I.
7. West Yorkshire Metropolitan County Council (WYMCC), *West Yorkshire: An Archaeological Survey to AD 1500*, 1981.
8. *Anston: Then and Now*, Vol.2, p.36.
9. YASRS, *Feet of Fines, Stuart Period.* 1 Jas.I.
10. Wilson, C. *Checklist of Windmill Paintings by Karl Wood*, 1982. Lincolnshire Museums Occasional Paper No.1.
11. YASRS, *Yorkshire Feet of Fines.*
12. Chaucer, G. *Canterbury Tales* (The Miller's Tale), *c.*1378.
13. Baildon, W. P. (Ed.) YASRS, Vol.29, 1901. *Court Rolls of the Manor of Wakefield, Vol.1.*
14. WYMCC. *West Yorkshire: An Archaeological Survey to AD 1500. 1981.*
15. Baines, William. *Directory of Yorkshire, 1822.*
16. Hey, D. (Ed.) *Oxford Companion to Local & Family History.* 1996. 'Pains. The regulations issued by the jury of a manorial court leet, the breach of which incurred a fixed penalty.' P.338.
17. Wentworth Woodhouse Muniments in Sheffield Archives (WWM/SA), Wentworth Estate Account Books, A.1273.
18. WWM/SA, A.1271 '1745. Built the Temple on the summit of the Hill towards Rotherham, began the new Hospitalls at Barrow, built a New Windmill, finished the Ceilings of the Great Dining Room and that next to it ...'.
19. Clayton, A.K. 'The Wentworth Round-Houses'. *Transactions of the Hunter Archaeological Society,* Vol.VIII Pt.4, 1962, pp.229-233.
20. Clayton, A.K. 'The Wentworth Round-Houses', p.230.
21. Clayton, A.K. 'The Wentworth Round-Houses', p.232.

4. 'REMEMBERED IN STONE': CHURCH MONUMENTS IN THE ROTHERHAM AREA

by Simeon Bennett & Tony Dodsworth

VISITING PARISH CHURCHES IS A POPULAR PASTIME for many people in England and often the parish church reflects the beliefs and mirrors the development of the community it has served over hundreds of years. Paying particular attention to the monuments in a church can add interest to any visit because they, perhaps above all other features in the church, allow us to get closer to individuals who worshipped in that place up to 700 years ago. These human links with the past emphasise the historical continuity of the building and provide the viewer with fascinating details of the costume and armour worn in past ages. Monumental memorials come in a great variety but can be largely classified into slabs, brasses, table-tombs with or without effigies, and 'hanging' wall monuments. The Rotherham area is far from renowned for its church monuments yet careful study reveals that a surprisingly full range of monuments can be found in local churches and that some of them are very fine examples indeed. The aim of this study is to exemplify this range of monuments in and around Rotherham from the thirteenth to the mid-seventeenth century without attempting to be a comprehensive guide to them all. The churches chosen to exhibit the range of monuments in the Rotherham area are St Leonard's, Thrybergh; the Old Church, Wentworth; St Helen's, Treeton; St James', South Anston; St Peter's, Thorpe Salvin; All Saints', Aston; and St John's, Throapham (see Figure 1), but fine examples exist in other churches.

A church monument is the term used for a memorial within a church to a dead person or in some cases to more than one person and less often to a large number of people. Generally such a monument would represent someone of standing in the local community, able to afford the cost of the memorial. The 'common' people would be buried

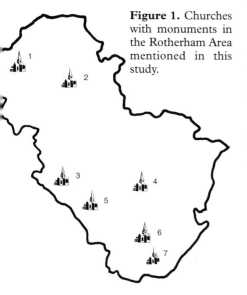

Figure 1. Churches with monuments in the Rotherham Area mentioned in this study.

1. Old Church, Wentworth.
2. St. Leonard's, Thrybergh.
3. St. Helen's, Treeton.
4. St. John's, Throapham.
5. All Saints', Aston.
6. St. James', South Anston.
7. St. Peter's, Thorpe Salvin.

in unmarked graves in the churchyard for hundreds of years until gradually the use of gravestones in the churchyard became more popular. This happened particularly in the nineteenth century when their cost came within the range of ordinary people. The style of monuments used inside the church changed with time and essentially followed fashion. Some types of monuments occur more frequently in some parts of the country than others so few examples of brasses are found in South Yorkshire unlike, for example, Cambridgeshire and Essex. The purpose of the monument was to perpetuate the memory of the person represented. A group of monuments to the same family close together in one church helped to establish their dynastic continuity as well as to reinforce their fundamental link with that place. In some cases they took on the name of the place as their surname, such as at Wentworth, to strengthen their link with that place. In many cases this foremost family in a parish also chose the priest for the parish church to further emphasise their importance to all aspects of life in that place.

Church monuments have suffered in the past with deliberate destruction occurring at times during the Reformation in the sixteenth century and during the Civil War period in the seventeenth century, but compared to many other European countries our domestic history has been peaceful and so quite large numbers survive. Sometimes a medieval effigy survives relatively unchanged (although noses, hands and swords suffer often) but particular attention was paid by the iconoclasts to religious symbols such as angels that are rarely left intact. Much destruction of later monuments occurred with church 'restorations' in Victorian times and more recently through neglect. Some important monuments in the Rotherham area, now inside churches, have obviously in the past spent quite considerable lengths of time outdoors and suffered extensive weathering as a result. The two effigies of medieval clerics now in St Leonard's, Thrybergh, and the effigy of the man and his daughter in St James', South Anston, have all suffered in this way.

Prior to the early part of the thirteenth century burials within churches were few, the privilege usually being reserved for the bodies of the local magnate, founder or benefactors. The earliest monuments that remain tend to be carved slabs which were placed over stone coffins that were let into the floor of the church or interred in the churchyard, sunk to the level of the ground. The most frequent motif on these slabs was the cross, although earlier surviving examples tend to show creatures and foliage carved upon them. Whilst worn and partly broken, what was once clearly an excellently carved cross slab

can be found at St John's Church, Throapham (see Figure 2). The cross is combined with foliage to give quite an elaborate effect. Other slabs survive, carved with motifs of the profession of the deceased; a sword usually indicating a knight, a chalice indicating a priest, a mitre and a crozier representing a bishop. These could be the only symbols on the slab, however in the majority of cases they are combined with a cross. A rare representation is the depiction of a bow as can be found on the crudely carved slab, known locally as the Archer's Grave, at Wentworth Old Church (see Figure 3). The authors know of only one other example of this representation, a slab in Durham Cathedral where the cross and bow are accompanied by a sword.

It is also at the start of the thirteenth century that we begin to see carved representations or effigies on the coffin lids of those interred beneath. For many this is the most appealing part of a monument given the wealth of information and detail they provide regarding the style and development of the clothing or armour worn. The very early effigies that remain tend to be ecclesiastical and are carved in low relief giving the impression of the figure being sunk within a panel on the coffin lid. As more workable material was found and the carvers' skills improved, more undercutting of the figures took place with the effigy becoming free of the slab from which it was carved. The effigies of knights gave the carvers an ideal opportunity to display these skills.

The middle of the thirteenth century heralded the first appearances of the famous cross-legged knight, a style largely unique to England, and one that was to last for approximately the following 100 years. The romantic theory that these cross-legged figures indicate that the person commemorated was a crusader persists in many church guides. This however does not agree with the historical facts, the age of the great crusaders having come to an end before the earliest of these figures appeared. It is generally accepted that the cross-legged attitude was merely a style which coincided with the 'Decorated' period in art and architecture.

The earliest effigial monument in the area can be found in St Helen's Church, Treeton (see Figure 4a). Now positioned upright in a niche beneath the tower is the torso and head of a military figure. This has suffered much neglect and damage over the centuries but it is still of great interest. It was referred to by Charles Hadfield when repairing the church in 1896-7. He described it as 'a stone effigy of a knight in chain mail, placed in a recess by the Western doorway' (where it remains today). The details that remain allow us to reach certain conclusions as to what the figure may have looked like and these are summarised in Figure 4b and Figure 5. Usually with the earlier

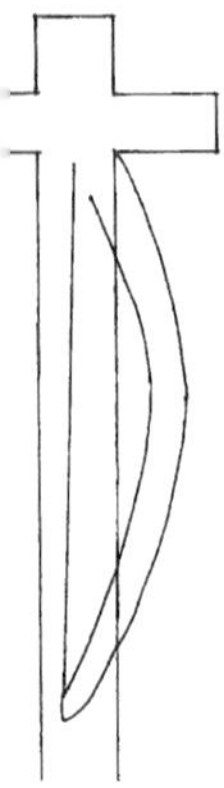

Figure 3. The 'Wentworth Archer' floor slab. *Tony Dodsworth*

50 cm

Figure 2. A cross slab in St John's Church, Throapham. *After Ryder, Saxon Churches in South Yorkshire*

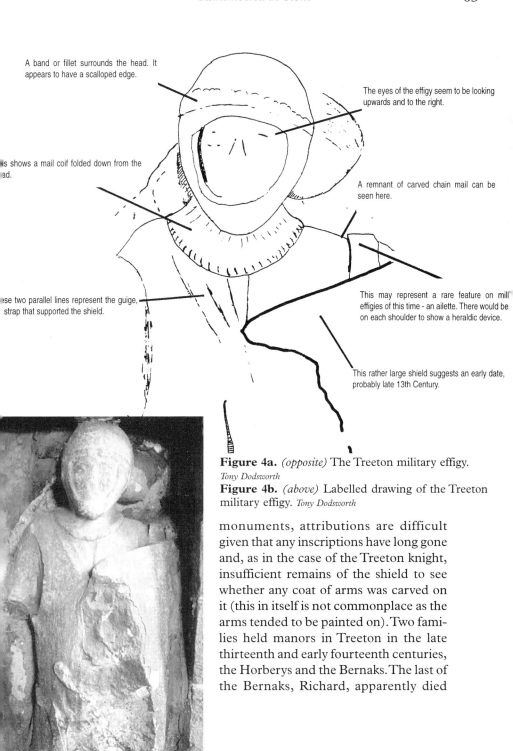

A band or fillet surrounds the head. It appears to have a scalloped edge.

The eyes of the effigy seem to be looking upwards and to the right.

...is shows a mail coif folded down from the ...ad.

A remnant of carved chain mail can be seen here.

...se two parallel lines represent the guige, ...strap that supported the shield.

This may represent a rare feature on mil... effigies of this time - an ailette. There would be on each shoulder to show a heraldic device.

This rather large shield suggests an early date, probably late 13th Century.

Figure 4a. *(opposite)* The Treeton military effigy. *Tony Dodsworth*
Figure 4b. *(above)* Labelled drawing of the Treeton military effigy. *Tony Dodsworth*

monuments, attributions are difficult given that any inscriptions have long gone and, as in the case of the Treeton knight, insufficient remains of the shield to see whether any coat of arms was carved on it (this in itself is not commonplace as the arms tended to be painted on). Two families held manors in Treeton in the late thirteenth and early fourteenth centuries, the Horberys and the Bernaks. The last of the Bernaks, Richard, apparently died

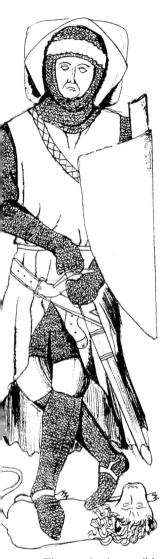

Figure 5. A possible reconstruction of the Treeton military effigy.
Simeon Bennett

between 1317 and 1318 which is rather late considering the style of the effigy.

In general the earlier cross-legged figures give an impression of vigour and action, their hands engaged in the drawing or sheathing of their swords. Around 1340 the military effigies start to adopt a more passive state, lying flat on their backs with their hands held in prayer. It is unfortunate that no military effigies survive in Rotherham from this period but fine examples can be found close by at Barnburgh and Sprotbrough. However, a monument of great interest, due to its unique style, can be found at South Anston (see Figures 6a, 6b and 7). This monument, like the one at Treeton, is fixed upright against a wall and is clearly not in its original position. When Hadfield visited the church in 1910 he said the effigy was under the founder's arch in the north aisle, and some years previously had been brought in from the churchyard. The effect of the weather is obvious with much of the detail worn away. Despite initial impressions the larger figure is not that of a lady as indicated by Pevsner but a male civilian of the mid-fourteenth century. That the figure is male is shown by the ankle length garment and the long hood (on which traces of leaf decoration remain) thrown back over the shoulders. The length of the robe, its long hanging sleeves and the hip belt indicate a date of *c*.1340. The long curling hair is quite normal for a male of this date; no lady unless a maiden would be without a veil, and none would wear anything but a full length garment as is the case with the smaller figure by the side of the male effigy. Both figures rest with their heads on pillows and both are supported by two angels, albeit the female effigy has one at her head and one at her feet. The diminutive nature of the female figure would suggest the person represented died young and, whilst attribution is unknown, it would seem reasonable to assume the monument represents a father and daughter, in which case it is the only such monument of this date in the whole country.

The long, curling hair is crucial in identifying this as a male figure. No lady, unless an unmarried maiden, would be without a veil.

The long hood thrown back over the shoulders indicates this is a male figure.

The smaller figure does seem to be female and the clothes imply a death after leaving infancy.

The long hanging sleeves and the hip-level belt indicate a date of the mid-14th century – more likely the 1340s than the 1350s.

This coffin-shaped monument surely represents a father and daughter. The detail that remains indicates it was a high-status monument.

Ankle-length garment is part of the crucial evidence that this monument shows a male civilian. A female figure of this date would have a full length garment.

Figure 6a. The male civilian and daughter effigy in St James', South Anston. *Tony Dodsworth*

Figure 6b. Detailed artist's impression of the South Anston effigy. *Based on a line drawing from M. H. Bloxham, On Certain Sepulchral Effigies and Monuments in South Yorkshire*

Figure 7. Detail of the effigy in St James', South Anston. *Tony Dodsworth*

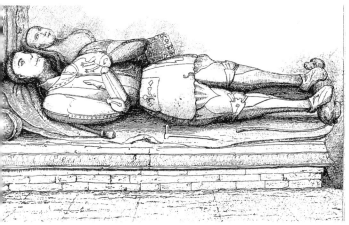

Figure 8a. *(above)* The Gascoigne monument in the Old Church, Wentworth. *W. Cowen from Joseph Hunter's South Yorkshire*

Figure 8c. *(above)* Survivir section of the weepers from tl Gascoigne monument. *To Dodsworth*

Figure 8b. *(left)* Detail of the male figure on the Gascoigne monument. *Tony Dodsworth*

Two rather battered effigies of priests can be seen at St Leonard's Church, Thrybergh. The majority of priests' effigies seem to conform to certain rules – fully recumbent, heads on pillows and hands in prayer. Regardless of geography there is little deviation in the style and design of such monuments. These two have obviously spent many years outside in the open air (they were seen there by Hunter in the 1820s) and have suffered grievously as a result. They probably date from the fourteenth century and may represent two of the three rectors named Reresby from that century.

It was around the mid-fourteenth century that the Midlands tomb workshops came into prominence. The local alabaster quarries provided them with an abundance of material that was easy to carve, thus allowing them to attempt more elaborate and detailed projects that quickly captured the top end of the market. Alabaster was to remain a common material for effigy production for the next 200 years. Alabaster military figures have rarely survived in Rotherham but good examples may be seen elsewhere in South Yorkshire at Darfield and Wadworth. These figures, as mentioned earlier, are depicted straight-legged and rigidly recumbent with their hands usually in prayer. They, and others to be seen in Yorkshire, clearly show how armour developed from part mail and plate earlier in the four-teenth century to almost full suits of plate by 1410. The bascinet (helmet worn beneath the great helm) is nearly always worn on these effigies without the face defences. There is no attempt at portraiture and when military figures of this period are viewed as a whole they are fairly uniform, differences usually being limited to the type of beast supporting the effigy's feet or the crest on the great helm posi-tioned beneath the head.

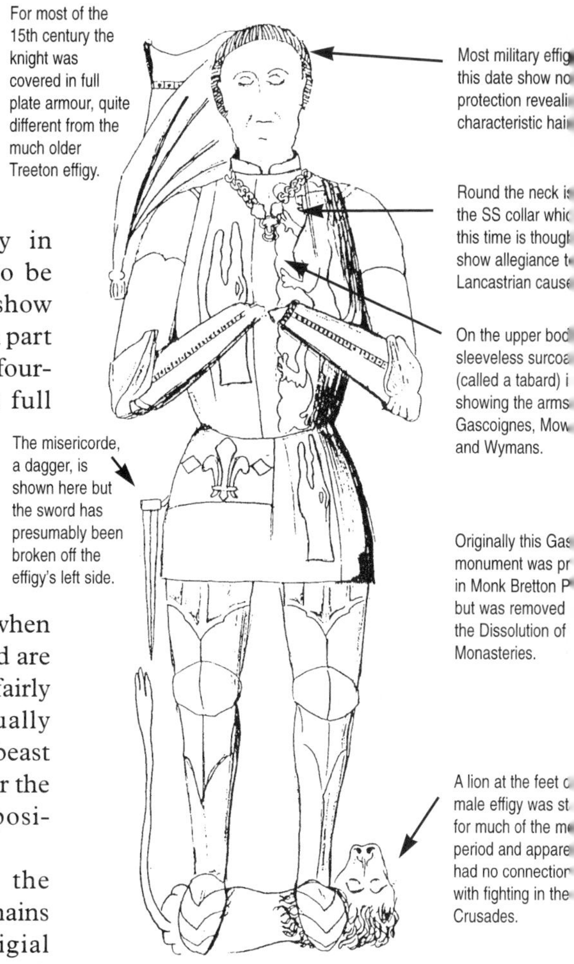

What can be seen in the Rotherham area are the remains of a double alabaster effigial tomb at Wentworth Old Church which is currently in the care of the Redundant Churches Fund. This monument is in a poor state

For most of the 15th century the knight was covered in full plate armour, quite different from the much older Treeton effigy.

Most military effig this date show no protection reveali characteristic hai

Round the neck is the SS collar whic this time is though show allegiance t Lancastrian cause

On the upper bod sleeveless surcoa (called a tabard) i showing the arms Gascoignes, Mow and Wymans.

The misericorde, a dagger, is shown here but the sword has presumably been broken off the effigy's left side.

Originally this Gas monument was pr in Monk Bretton P but was removed the Dissolution of Monasteries.

A lion at the feet o male effigy was st for much of the m period and appare had no connection with fighting in the Crusades.

Figure 9. Male figure on the Gascoigne monument. *Simeon Bennett*

of preservation. Whilst the figure of the knight is fairly complete all that remains of the female's effigy is the battered head and shoulders. A panel from the original tomb chest survives, but this is no longer at the head of the figures as shown in Hunter's illustration of 1831, being now fastened to the south wall next to the door (see Figures 8a, 8b, 8c and 9). The tomb panel consists of two canopied niches with buttresses beneath which are carved the figures of two bare-headed knights with their hands in prayer. They stand on two small pedestals which in their turn rest on two shields. Whilst poorly preserved it can be seen that the two knights or weepers are wearing full plate armour of a style suggesting a date of *c*.1450 and similar to that on the main male effigy. They may represent members of the family of the person represented by the main effigy. The remnant of the female effigy shows the hair loose and confined by a decorated orle (a band round the hair or helmet) rather than the more common veil of a widow. This suggests that the person commemorated possibly predeceased her husband. The labelled drawing of the male effigy in Figure 9 identifies key features of the figure's armour and decoration.

There has been much speculation about this monument by previous writers as to exactly who it commemorates. The arms on the knight's tabard (short open-sided garment) show it to be a member of the Gascoigne family and its style suggests a date from *c*.1460. It is thought that it was transferred from Monk Bretton Priory at the Dissolution of the Monasteries during the reign of Henry VIII. An interesting detail on the male effigy is the livery collar of SS or esses, which it is believed signifies allegiance to the House of Lancaster. Numerous effigies, especially military ones, can be found throughout the country wearing this collar and its first appearance on a monument is believed to be that of Sir John Swinford (died 1371) at Spratton, Northamptonshire. The monument to Sir Edmund Fitzwilliam (died 1431) at Wadworth is also carved with an SS collar around his neck. With the ascendancy of the House of York during the latter half of the fifteenth century some effigies of their followers are depicted wearing collars composed of alternate suns and roses. Fine examples can be found on the effigy of Sir William Ryther (died 1474) at Ryther Church, Yorkshire and Sir Ralph Fitzherbert (died 1483) at Norbury, Derbyshire, the latter being unique in that the collar has the boar pendant of Richard III suspended from it.

Three dimensional effigial monuments were not however affordable by all, and consequently alternative forms of memorial were sought. One such alternative that proved popular was the incised slab. Like the effigies previously mentioned these could be placed on a tomb-chest or let into the floor of the church. Relatively easy to produce, the figure and any other details, such as the canopy or inscription, were simply cut into the surface of the slab and then filled with pitch. The majority of incised slabs produced in England were made of alabaster and large numbers still exist in churches in the Midlands, however examples remain where a different stone was used that was more readily available in a particular area. An example of an alabaster slab can be found in St Peter's Church, Thorpe Salvin (see Figure 10a). It commemorates Katherine, wife of John Sandford, who died *c*.1461. She is depicted beneath a canopy with her head resting on a tasselled cushion and her hands in prayer. Her head-dress is heart shaped and her cloak is fastened by two cords to which appear to be attached a purse. Each foot rests on a dog and at the hem of her gown are carved her numerous children.

Another example can be seen at St Leonard's Church, Thrybergh, carved in sandstone. The carving of the slab is of crude workmanship compared to the Thorpe Salvin example and shows a knight in full plate armour with his hands held in prayer (see Figure 10b). The knight appears to be wearing a sallet style helmet, but apart from that a lot of the armour detail is missing, and the treatment of sword and dagger is particularly poor. Frank Greenhill in his *Incised Effigial Slabs* attributes the monument to Arnold Reresby Esq, died 1485. The cusped style of the armour, sallet and pointed foot defences, (which by 1500 had become more rounded or blunt) would support this date.

St Leonard's Church at Thrybergh is very much the church of the

Figure 10a. Incised slab of Katherine Sandford *c*.1461 in St Peter's, Thorpe Salvin. *From Frank Greenhill, Incised Effigial Slabs*

Figure 10b. Incised slab of Arnold Reresby Esq. *c*.1485 in St Leonard's, Thrybergh. *Simeon Bennett*

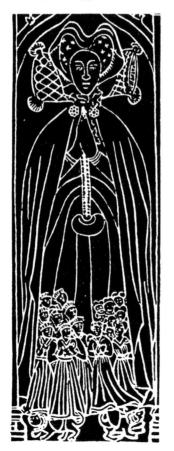

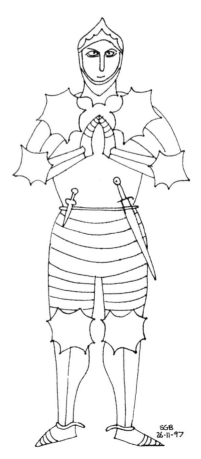

ure 11a. Stained glass showing William esby (1383-1469) in St Leonard's, yybergh. *Tony Dodsworth*

gure 11b. Stained glass of a lady of the eresby family in St Leonard's, aryergh. *Tony Dodsworth*

Reresby family and using the evidence of heralds who visited it in the late sixteenth century it was once almost overwhelmingly used to display links with the Reresby family. As many as 54 heraldic shields were represented in glass in 1584 as well as a series of small kneeling figures representing the Reresby lineage from the reign of King John to the end of the fifteenth century. Most of this family record in glass has now gone, as have a large number of slabs bearing figures of gentlemen and ladies, but two figures still remain. One is believed to represent William Reresby (1383-1469), a former rector of the church and builder of the spire that can still be seen at St Leonard's (see Figure 11a). He is dressed in a scarlet gown and is shown kneeling at what in the past has been described as an altar but appears to us to be much more likely a representation of a shrine, perhaps to a famous bishop or saint. Over his head remains part of a scroll written in Latin 'God be merciful to me a sinner'. Originally this scroll was much longer and was transcribed by Johnston in the late seventeenth century. The other figure is that of a female presumably of the Reresby family and roughly contemporary with William but other than that no more precise attribution can be attempted (see Figure 11b). What can certainly be said is that at one time Thrybergh had one of the best heraldic displays of glass in the whole of Yorkshire and even the fragments left today represent some of the best survivals of medieval glass in South Yorkshire. It represents another very interesting type of church 'monument' in its widest sense.

The sixteenth century saw a number of

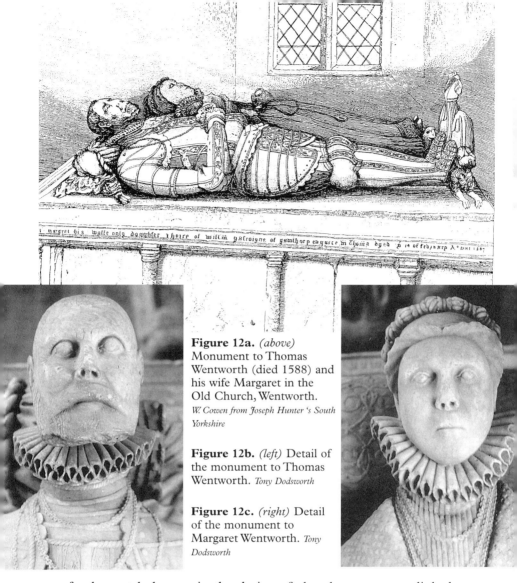

margret his watte onlg daughter. theire of willm gåtroigne. of gamthorp eaquire in Thoma ðged p̃ iå of feb̃js̃ kep Aᵒ DNi 1587

Figure 12a. *(above)* Monument to Thomas Wentworth (died 1588) and his wife Margaret in the Old Church, Wentworth.
W. Cowen from Joseph Hunter 's South Yorkshire

Figure 12b. *(left)* Detail of the monument to Thomas Wentworth. *Tony Dodsworth*

Figure 12c. *(right)* Detail of the monument to Margaret Wentworth. *Tony Dodsworth*

fundamental changes in the design of church monuments linked particularly with the growing influence of the Renaissance in Italy and with the Reformation that altered most people's Christian beliefs and worship in England. The style of the effigies and their settings at the start of the century was essentially Gothic but the new ideas of the Renaissance swept the European continent as the century progressed and were often introduced to England through craftsmen from the Netherlands and Northern France. This influence was first felt in church monuments in the south of the country and particularly in the design of high status tombs such as that for Henry VII in Westminster Abbey. The idea of representing the dead as they were in life was one aspect of the Renaissance and obviously had a profound effect on the design of church monuments, although the change did not take place as swiftly as might be imagined. Essentially the recumbent figure on a tomb chest gave way to figures represented as reclining or kneeling but the pressure of fashion was obviously not strong enough for Sir Thomas Wentworth and his wife Margaret to change their traditional representation on their tomb in the Old Church at Wentworth (see Figures 12a, 12b and 12c), even though it was late in the century, 1588, when he died. Thomas' marriage to Margaret Gascoigne of Gawthorpe was very beneficial for the Wentworth family since she was the heiress of the Gascoigne family which was one of the principal land-owning families in the West Riding of Yorkshire. This link with the Gascoigne family perhaps explains why the Gascoigne monuments from Monk Bretton Priory (mentioned earlier) were brought to Wentworth. In Thomas' will it specifically stated that he wished to be buried close to his ancestors in the church at Wentworth and this continued to be the tradition for most landed families for many more years to come. Men of truly national standing who could have been buried with great ceremony in the major cathedrals of England still usually chose to be interred in small country churches like Wentworth and Thrybergh because they represented the 'hearts' of their families. To see such great historical figures represented in ordinary parish churches is one element of church visiting in England that is so exciting. The detail of clothing and armour shown on Thomas and Margaret's tomb is exquisite even if the relationship of the heads to the bodies of the effigies is slightly less convincing. Both pairs of hands have been broken off, possibly accidentally but more likely deliberately in the second main period of effigy damage during the Civil War in the mid-seventeenth century. The tomb chest they lie on seems surprisingly plain and may well not be the original one. William Cowen's drawing of the monument in Hunter's *South Yorkshire* shows a small headless figure of a woman at the feet of Margaret, the remains of which now stand on the ground beside the chest.

The first period of tomb damage and destruction had been initiated by the Reformation and concentrated particularly in the reign of Edward VI (1547-1553). An attempt was made to destroy all religious imagery on tombs, such as angels at the head of the person represented, and this destruction often included the effigy itself. With the accession to the throne of the Catholic Queen Mary in 1553 these attacks ceased but when Elizabeth followed her in 1558 it seemed the destruction might begin again. Fortunately it was expressly forbidden by the Queen in 1560, so we owe her a great debt of gratitude. From this time until the nineteenth century, no religious imagery was acceptable on funerary monuments, a long-lasting effect of the Reformation. One type of monument that appeared in the late sixteenth century that was entirely new in concept and design was the hanging wall monument. These monuments did not stand on the floor at all but were suspended on the wall by iron supports and mortar. Their popularity was linked to several factors including their relative cheapness and the fact that they need not take up much space in the church. They particularly appealed to families like the Reresbys of Thrybergh whose standing, they obviously believed, required a monument but who were not so 'great' that a large and expensive standing monument would have been appropriate. The architectural setting for the figures often reflected standing monuments of the same date and figures were most often shown kneeling across a prayer desk (called a prie-dieu). Husbands and wives were most often shown with below them figures that represented their children divided into males and females. The labelled drawing of Sir William Wentworth (died 1614) and his wife

Figure 13. Monument to Sir William Wentworth (died 1614) and his wife Anna (died 1611). The drawing by W. Cowen in Hunter's *South Yorkshire* has been labelled to highlight typical features of hanging wall monuments such as this from the late sixteenth and early seventeenth centuries.

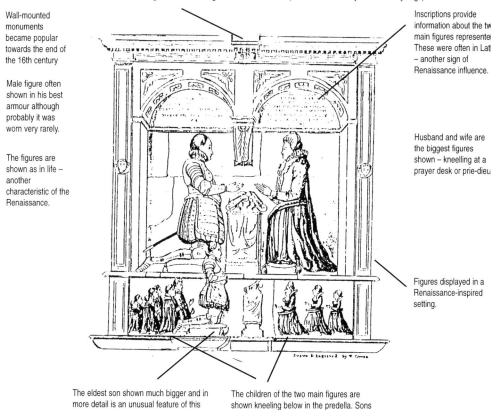

Quite often heraldic devices relating to the two main figures were shown here (as on Lionel Reresby's tomb at Thrybergh).

Wall-mounted monuments became popular towards the end of the 16th century

Inscriptions provide information about the two main figures represented These were often in Latin – another sign of Renaissance influence.

Male figure often shown in his best armour although probably it was worn very rarely.

The figures are shown as in life – another characteristic of the Renaissance.

Husband and wife are the biggest figures shown – kneeling at a prayer desk or prie-dieu

Figures displayed in a Renaissance-inspired setting.

The eldest son shown much bigger and in more detail is an unusual feature of this particular monument.

The children of the two main figures are shown kneeling below in the predella. Sons and daughters are shown separately.

Figure 14. Monument to Henry Sandford (died 1582) and his wife Margaret in St Peter's, Thorpe Salvin. *Tony Dodsworth*

Anna (see Figure 13) illustrates many of the typical features of this type of monument. Some excellent examples locally can be seen in the churches at Wentworth, Thrybergh and Thorpe Salvin.

On the north wall of the chancel at St Peter's Church, Thorpe Salvin, is possibly the oldest example of a hanging wall monument in Yorkshire. This shows Henry Sandford, his wife Margaret and their three daughters (see Figure 14). Typically husband and wife face each other across a prayer desk with the three daughters represented beneath in the part of the monument called the predella. Henry died in 1582 and is represented in armour similar to that of the recumbent Sir William Wentworth. By this time heraldry was an essential element of monumental display and here it is located on the pediment above the figures. The heraldry became increasingly complex as families sought to show through that medium their links by marriage to other armigerous families, the more noble the better! Note also the skull shown above the right hand side of the pediment. The increasing use of symbols of death and mortality on church monuments was one aspect of the changes brought about by the Renaissance, skulls and bones being the symbols most often used. Both were rarely used before the late sixteenth century. Facing the Sandford monument at Thorpe Salvin is a very similar one commemorating one of the daughters of Henry Sandford and her husband Sir Roger Partington, who died around 1604. As the couple were childless no other figures are included on this monument.

A larger and more ornate wall monument can be found on the north wall of the chancel of St Leonard's Church, Thrybergh. This fine monument is for Lionel Reresby, who died about 1587, and his wife Anne (see Figures 15a, 15c and 15d). The form of the monument is similar to the two at Thorpe Salvin but is obviously a more expensive piece. It reminds us that most church monuments, up to this date at

Figure 15a. Monument to Lionel Reresby (died 1587) and his wife Anne in St Leonard's, Thrybergh. *Tony Dodsworth*

Figure 15b. Monument to Francis Copuldy (died 1599) and his wife Elizabeth (née Reresby) the church at Harrington, Lincolnshire. *Roy Morri*

Figure 15c. Detail of the monument to Lionel Reresby – wife and daughters. *Tony Dodsworth*

Figure 15d. Detail of the monument to Lion Reresby – youngest son and swaddled baby. *To Dodsworth*

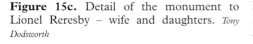

least, were highly coloured and wonderful works of art in their own right. In most cases the colour we see today is the result of restoration but hopefully based on the fragments of colour that remained at the time of the restoration. The monuments in Thrybergh Church were apparently restored in the 1930s and M. Janet Becker (the restorer?) writes in a contemporary leaflet that before renovation the monument had the appearance of slate, but in this case the cleaning brought out the old colours and gilding which only needed to be retouched. The monument to Lionel Reresby and his wife, Anne, was erected by one of their daughters, Elizabeth, who married Francis Copuldyck and lived in Harrington, Lincolnshire. (Note the similarity of the monuments to Lionel Reresby at Thrybergh and Francis Copuldyck at Harrington – see Figures 15a and 15b.) Anne was a daughter of Robert Swift, the rich mercer of Rotherham, who is himself represented with his family on a wall-mounted brass in All Saints' Church, Rotherham (see p.25 in *Aspects of Rotherham*). She brought some much needed wealth to the Reresby family and gave birth to a huge family of seven sons and nine daughters, all represented in the predella. Poignantly one son and one daughter are shown swaddled as babies which presumably means they died very young (see Figure 15d). The male child is shown with a face but not so the female. All bar Sir Lionel are shown in black mourning clothes but are not identical thus suggesting some individual modelling. Sir Lionel appears in white armour, no doubt his best suit! Men continued to be represented in armour on tombs long after the period when it would have been a common occurrence to wear it. In this at least a strong element of tradition is suggested. The decoration around the figures, in the spandrels above and the apron below, is a particularly attractive feature showing golden foliage and red flowers. Lionel and Anne were also remembered in a richly carved oak chimney piece at Denaby Hall and seen by Hunter. He noted the inscription associated with their arms and crest 'Blessed are they, the scripture doth say, that heares the worde of God and keepes yt always'. Note the three shields of arms on the monument's pediment.

Throughout the sixteenth century monuments continued to be made of stone or alabaster but as the seventeenth century progressed more use was made of imported marble (white and black in colour). This was associated with changes brought about by the Renaissance and particularly the increased classicism linked especially to the reign of Charles I. Obelisks were used quite often on monuments as a representation of immortality linking back to ancient Egyptian tradition. These pagan symbols from antiquity were considered acceptable on monuments following the Renaissance when overtly Christian representations of angels, crosses, saints, etc. were not, the pagan symbols though were interpreted in a Christian way.

The wall monument to Sir William Wentworth (died 1614) and his wife, Anna, (died 1611) is shown in Figure 13 with explanatory labels, and in Figures 16a and 16b. This is a good quality example of this type of monument and it has been attributed to Nicholas Johnson, a Flemish sculptor of some renown who lived in Southwark and died in 1618. Many of the best monumental sculptors in England at this time came from the Low Countries. One unusual feature of this monument (see Figure 16b) is that one of the sons, probably the future Earl of Strafford, has been shown much larger than his siblings and with his own prayer desk. This suggests that already at the time of the monument's production his importance had been recognised and so reflected in the monument. The women are all shown wearing the farthingale, which spread the skirt in an exaggerated way. This was first introduced into England in the 1550s and continued fashionable throughout the reign of James I and so well into the seventeenth century.

The monument commemorating John, Lord Darcy and three of his wives in All Saints' Church, Aston, is a reminder not to take all church monuments at face value. Their arrangement now, as shown in Figure 17, cannot be as they were originally and Pevsner

Figure 16a. Monument to Sir William Wentworth (died 1614) and his wife Anne (died 1611). *Tony Dodsworth*

Figure 16b. Detail of the monument to Sir William Wentworth showing his son the Earl of Strafford. *Tony Dodsworth*

states that they are no longer in their original context. The niche in which Lord Darcy kneels is considerably later in style than the effigy itself. There are many well-documented cases of monuments being moved around churches as the centuries progressed and the needs and sentiments of the vicar and his parishioners changed. Occasionally parts of different monuments are put together for convenience or artistic licence, a particular nightmare for the students of church monuments! John, Lord Darcy took over the estate at Aston in 1602 from his grandfather and remained there till he died in 1635. His father, Michael, died in 1588 and was buried at Wentworth. John's four wives, of which the first three are represented on the monument, were Rosamund Freschville of Staveley (died aged 28), Isabel Wray (died aged 60), Mary Bellasis (died aged 19) and finally Elizabeth West (who survived him). His only son, John, died in 1624 at the age of 22 and surprisingly for that time was buried not with his family at Aston but in Westminster Abbey. John, Lord Darcy, certainly had some interesting relatives for his great aunt, Mary, married Henry Babbington of Dethick at Aston in 1560. It was their son Anthony who was the conspirator who gave his name to the Babbington Plot of 1582 that resulted in his execution. (John, Lord Darcy's grandfather, married Agnes, daughter of Thomas Babbington of Dethick and her sister Margaret lived not far away for she married Thomas Reresby of Thrybergh – first son of Lionel Reresby mentioned earlier.) John, Lord Darcy's great great grandfather was implicated in the Pilgrimage of Grace and beheaded for high treason in 1538. Detailed examination of family trees shows how close the links were through marriage between the great families in the area such as the Darcys, the Wentworths, the Foljambes and the Reresbys. These then extended further afield to families such as the Fitzwilliams, the Wyvills, the

Conyers, the Stapletons and many more.

When this chapter was originally planned we intended to include examples of church monuments in the Rotherham area up to the middle of the nineteenth century but the wealth of interest in the local monuments before 1640 meant that an earlier end date had to be selected. 1640 was ultimately chosen because it starts a decade when there was a major dislocation of most aspects of life in England as a result of the English Civil War. The numerous

Figure 17. Monument to John, Lord Darcy (died 1635) and three of his wives Rosamund, Isabel and Mary in All Saints', Aston. *Tony Dodsworth*

monuments of great interest close to Rotherham that post-date 1640 will have to be examined separately.

We hope this present study will have whetted readers' appetites to discover more about church monuments in general and to view examples in local churches in particular. Certainly for us they help to bring alive people who lived many hundreds of years ago and bring us closer to religious communities that worshipped in our churches in the past.

Bibliography

Becker, M. Janet, *The Monuments in Thrybergh Church, Yorks*, 1936. Information Sheet.
Bennett, Henry Leigh, *History of the Church of St Leonard's, Thrybergh*. Pamphlet in Rotherham Local Studies and Archives Section, 942.741 (Small).
Bloxham, M. H., *On Certain Sepulchral Effigies and Monuments in South Yorkshire*, Yorkshire Architectural Society, York, 1850.
Glynne, Sir S., 'Treeton Church Notes', *Yorkshire Archaeological Society*, Vol 15, p.492.
Glynne, Sir S., 'Aston Church Notes', *Yorkshire Archaeological Society*, Vol 15, p.493.
Greenhill, Frank, *Incised Effigial Slabs*, 2 Vols. London, 1976.
Hadfield, Charles, *Pre-Reformation Churches of Hallamshire and District*, 1910.
Hunter, Joseph, *South Yorkshire*, London, 1828-1831.
Kemp, Brian, *Church Monuments*, Shire Publications Ltd., 1985.
Kemp, Brian, *English Church Monuments*, B. T. Batsford, 1980.
Pevsner, Nicholas (revised by Enid Ratcliffe), *The Buildings of England - Yorkshire, The West Riding*, Penguin Books, 1967.
Routh, Pauline and Knowles, Richard, *The Medieval Monuments of Harewood*, Wakefield Historical Publications, 1983.
Ryder, P. F., *Saxon Churches in South Yorkshire*, South Yorkshire County Council, 1980.
Sitwell, Sir George, *Barons of Pulford*, Booklet in Rotherham Local Studies and Archives Section, 942.741/920 RER (Small).
Tummers, H., *Early Secular Effigies in England: the Thirteenth Century*, E. J. Brill, Leiden, 1980.

Further detailed information about church monuments may be obtained from the Church Monuments Society (contact the Secretary - Clive Easter, 62 Abbots Grove, Werrington, Peterborough, PE4 5BT). Members of the Society receive two detailed newsletters each year plus a high quality illustrated journal.

Acknowledgements

We need first to thank Mel and Joan Jones for their usual support and advice when preparing this chapter. The staff of the Local Studies and Archives Section of Rotherham Central Library have once again expertly answered all our enquiries and for this we are really grateful. We have been delighted with the co-operation given to us by the clergy of the churches mentioned in this chapter and wish to thank them - Reverend L. E. Boniface (St Helen's, Treeton), Reverend B. E. Leng (St Leonard's, Thrybergh), Reverend P. J. Coglan (St James', South Anston), Reverend P. Morley (St Peter's, Thorpe Salvin) and Reverend R. W. B. Atkinson (All Saints', Rotherham). We must also thank Roy Young, the key holder of the Old Church at Wentworth and St John's, Throapham, both now in the care of the Redundant Churches Fund. His help and advice made our task much easier. While preparing and writing this chapter we received considerable support from members of the Church Monuments Society and expert help particularly from Brian and Moira Gittos and Roy Morris. This help was invaluable in completing our task. Finally, thanks to Jane for all the hard work of checking and word processing and to Helen for coping stoically with the frequent statement 'we will just visit one last church'.

5. The Expansion of a Great Landed Estate: The Watson-Wentworth South Yorkshire Estate, 1695-1782[1]

by Melvyn Jones

THERE IS A GREAT DEAL OF CURIOSITY about how country estates – not just the house and park but also the surrounding farm-land – came into the hands of their owners. Did they 'steal' them from the common people? Did they win them in battles? Did they obtain them for service to their country? Did they simply buy them? It is often impossible to answer these questions, but there are periods in history when much change in land ownership took place and it is possible to see how some estates were disappearing and others were expanding rapidly. The first half of the eighteenth century is such a period.

The modern interest in landed property in the eighteenth century was initiated more than half a century ago by the Oxford historian, H. J. (Sir John) Habakkuk. Between 1940 and the 1960s Habakkuk published a series of influential papers in which he put forward a number of related ideas concerning changing patterns of landownership.[2] Habakkuk argued that 'the drift of property in the sixty years after 1690 was in favour of the large estate and the great lord'.[3]

During the same period there was, Habakkuk contended, 'an appreciable diminution in the area of land owned by small squires and the landed gentry.'[4] There were five main reasons for these general trends, he argued: the easier availability of long-term mortgages; the burden of the land tax on lesser proprietors; the contribution, for a minority of the great lords, of additional income from government office; the preference shown by a substantial number of rich merchants and other *nouveaux riches* to invest in things other than land; and the widespread adoption by the aristocracy and the greater gentry from the second half of the seventeenth century of the **strict settlement** in contrast with its slower and more limited use by the smaller landowners.

In very simple terms, in a strict settlement a father arranged that on his death his landed estate would be settled on his eldest son – **but only as a life tenant.** The settlement usually took place at the son's coming of age or marriage. The settlement also specified that on the death of the eldest son, his eldest son would inherit. At the latter's coming of age or marriage another strict settlement would be entered into and the estate would survive intact again. Each successive landowner, therefore, became the **temporary owner only** and the estate remained **inalienable** (i.e., it could not be sold). Smaller landowners were slower to adopt the strict settlement than the great proprietors, and their estates were often inherited by daughters or were split among a number of children. Moreover, the inheritance was often in **fee simple** (i.e., the inheritor or inheritors were absolute owners) and the land could be sold, mortgaged or leased as the inheritor(s) wished. These circumstances, ran Habakkuk's argument, put the aristocratic landowners and the greater gentry at a considerable advantage over the minor gentry and the small freeholders when it came to keeping property in their possession and consolidating and expanding their estates.

At first, Habakkuk's conclusions were tacitly accepted or largely supported.[5] More recently, however, his arguments have come under close scrutiny and have been widely challenged.[6] Not all recent commentators have dissented from Habakkuk's views and most critics have supported some aspect or aspects of his thesis.[7] Nor has Habakkuk remained silent during this re-evaluation: he restated a number of his views – with some qualifications – in a series of presidential addresses to the Royal Historical Society[8] and most recently in a major review of the landownership question running to nearly 800 pages.[9]

A number of important components of Habakkuk's original thesis have come under sustained attack. First, the demographic crisis in the first half of the eighteenth century when survival rates of fathers (to their son's coming of age or marriage) and sons (to adulthood) was low, has been shown to be a major influence on landownership trends: in this respect good luck as well as good judgement, bad luck as well as prodigality played a part in the rise of some families and the decline of others. Furthermore, the resilience of and opportunities for the lesser proprietors have been more fully realised, as has the extent to which some great estates were dismantled. More significantly, the strict settlement has been demonstrated to have been elevated to perhaps a somewhat exaggerated role. Finally, and perhaps most important, the extent of regional differences, has come to be more widely appreciated.[10]

In the light of the above, this study considers one South Yorkshire family and one estate. How active were the Watson-Wentworths in the land market in order to expand and consolidate the home estate? To what extent did this rising family enlarge its estate at the expense of middling and small landowners? What proportion of their purchases resulted from indebtedness among middling and lesser proprietors? How many of their acquisitions followed the death of a smaller landowner and the subsequent division of the property among heirs? And, finally, to what extent were the successive inheritors of the estate in question hindered or allowed room for manoevre by family settlement practice, in their attempts to enlarge it and round it off?

The Watson-Wentworth inheritance and subsequent settlement practice

When William Wentworth, third baronet of Wentworth Woodhouse and second Earl of Strafford of the first creation, died in 1695, child-less, his will entirely dashed the hopes of one male relative and created a great landowner of another. The decision by the Earl of Strafford to dispose of his estates as he did was, in Dr Peter Roebuck's view 'the most sensational disposition' among seventeenth and eighteenth century indirect inheritances in Yorkshire.[11] The unsuccessful aspirant to the Strafford estates was Thomas Wentworth, soldier and diplomat, second but first surviving son of Sir William Wentworth of Northgate Head, Wakefield, brother of Thomas Wentworth, first Earl of Strafford. Thomas Wentworth was, therefore, first cousin once removed of the second Earl. His claim was based on the fact that he carried the family name, that the line of descent was male and that he had strong Yorkshire interests.[12] In the event he was not mentioned in the will and succeeded only to the baronetcy and the Earl's secondary title of Lord Raby. Disappointed and angered at not succeeding to the whole or part of the Strafford estates, he did not disguise his enmity towards the inheritor, who was seen as an upstart and an outsider. His self-appointed role as thorn in the flesh of the inheritor may have been at the root of his decision to buy the estate of Sir Gervase Cutler at Stainborough – just a few miles from the seat of his rival – and to erect a new house there which he provocatively called Wentworth Castle.

Thomas Watson (1665-1723), whose inheritance of the Strafford estates had engendered so much envy and ire in his cousin, was the

third son of Edward Watson, Lord Rockingham, and his wife Anne, of Rockingham Castle, Northamptonshire (see Figure 1). His mother was the younger sister of the second Earl of Strafford. He was, therefore, a nephew of the second Earl and although the line of descent was through a

Figure 1. Thomas Watson-Wentworth (1665-1723) inheritor of the Wentworth estate in 1695, and single-minded estate builder. Between 1695 and 1723 he completed 42 separate purchases of land to enlarge and consolidate the South Yorkshire estate.
Courtesy of Commander Michael Saunders-Watson of Rockingham Castle, Northamptonshire where the original painting hangs

female it was more direct than in the case of Thomas Wentworth. Moreover, as a younger son, already 30 years old when his uncle died, and without a professional or military career, Thomas Watson would have no great expectations of landed property elsewhere and therefore his newly acquired properties, particularly his home estate in South Yorkshire, would become his central interest.

Thomas Watson-Wentworth was succeeded by his only son, Thomas the Younger (b.1693), who was created first Marquis of Rockingham in 1746. On his death in 1750 the estates came into the possession of his only surviving son, Charles. The second Marquis died childless in 1782 and the Watson-Wentworth estates were inherited by the Marquis' nephew, William, the fourth Earl Fitzwilliam. Thomas Watson-Wentworth was not active in politics, but his son Thomas was. Thomas the Younger was a keen supporter of the Whig cause and was Lord Lieutenant of the West Riding during the Jacobite rebellion of 1745. The second Marquis, the leader of the Rockingham Whigs, was First Minister in 1765 and again in 1782.[13]

The Strafford estates, inherited by Thomas Watson in 1695, were substantial.[14] In South Yorkshire was the principal house, Wentworth Woodhouse (to be renamed simply Wentworth House), a park and an estate of over 9,000 acres. The Earl's will directed that the inheritor should change his name to Wentworth (hence Watson-Wentworth) and live at Wentworth Woodhouse. There were also substantial Irish properties. One of these in the half barony of Sligo was sold by the second Earl's executors to help pay his debts and legacies amounting to £34,000. The remaining Irish properties were in counties Kildare and Wicklow and covered almost 90,000 acres. The Irish properties, which were not added to between 1695 and 1782, provided a substantial regular income from farm rents and the sale of wood and timber. For example, in the period from 1714 to 1720, gross annual income from Ireland was £7,805, of which almost exactly half came from rents and half from the sale of timber, wood and bark.[15]

Between 1695 and 1782 the Watson-Wentworth estates were resettled on five separate occasions; three times by will (in 1695-99, 1748 and 1782), and twice through marriage settlements (1716 and 1752)[16] All these settlements were strict but contained considerable scope for leasing, exchanging and mortgaging property. The 1716 marriage settlement also contained a general power of appointment (the ability to take the estate out of settlement) and the first Marquis took advantage of this to take a substantial part of the Irish estaes out of settlement during the greater part of his stewardship.[17] Moreover, the scale of purchases was such that between 1695 and 1750 as much as 2,000 acres in South Yorkshire might be out of settlement at any one time.

Estate building in South Yorkshire 1695-1782

Purchases [18]

In the 87 years between Thomas Watson's inheritance of the Strafford estates in 1695 and the death of the second Marquis in 1782 no fewer than 96 separate land purchases added almost 4,500 acres to the South Yorkshire estate at a cost of more than £78,500 (Figure 2). By this means the size of the South Yorkshire property was increased by 48 per cent. The sizes of the transactions varied enormously. At one extreme was a strip in one of Greasbrough's open fields amounting to a little more than one-eighth of an acre and costing £3; at the other was the manor of Whitehall and one third of the manor of Greasbrough, both in Greasbrough township involving an outlay of £11,000.[19] Of the 90 purchases for which the acreages are known, half (46) were of less than ten acres and only ten were for properties in excess of 100 acres. This story of many small purchases is repeated in terms of outlay: 44 per cent of the 94 purchases for which the consideration is known cost less than £150 each.

Thomas Watson-Wentworth was particularly active in the land market in South Yorkshire, making nearly 44 per cent (42 out of 96) of the individual purchases and this was only one of three sub-regional markets in which he was a keen buyer (he also acquired the pocket boroughs of Malton in the East Riding, for his son, and Higham Ferrers in Northamptonshire for himself). There was an abrupt falling off of activity after 1750 so that by the end of that year 84 per cent of the land purchased by the Watson-Wentworths in

Figure 2. Known Watson-Wentworth purchases in South Yorkshire, 1695-1782.

	no.	acreage			consideration		
		a	r	p	£	s	d
Thomas Watson-Wentworth (1695-1723)	42	1,643	0	13	15,902	09	04
Thomas, 1st Marquis of Rockingham (1723-1750)	24	2,116	1	17	36,611	04	10
Charles, 2nd Marquis of Rockingham (1750-1782)	30	726	1	32	26,064	01	10
Totals	96	4,485	3	22	78, 577	16	00

South Yorkshire was already in their possession. Apart from one large purchase of 250 acres in 1777, acquisitions after 1750 were relatively small, fourteen of the remaining 30 being of less than 10 acres and only one being over 50 acres.

Geographically, the way in which the South Yorkshire estate was developed is remarkable for its unevenness. Dr J. Martin, in her study of landownership in Glamorgan, has pointed out the possible relationships between the local land market and local ownership patterns.[20] For example, in a region containing the home estates of a small number of large landowners and few small properties, expansion by purchase could be slow and difficult; if on the other hand the estate of a large landowner was surrounded by the detached holdings of other large owners and by a mixture of minor gentry estates and small yeoman farms the possibility that land would come on to the market at fairly regular intervals was increased appreciably. In the case of the large owners, detached holdings could come on to the market because of a desire to free capital in order to consolidate the home estate: for all owners, great or small, indebtedness or an indirect inheritance might precipitate a sale. In the case of the area surrounding the Watson-Wentworth South Yorkshire estate in the eighteenth century, ownership patterns varied considerably. To the south lay the enormous South Yorkshire estate of the Duke of Norfolk centred on Sheffield. To the west occupying Wortley township and the northern third of Tankersley township was the estate of the Wortley family (the Earls of Wharncliffe). Expansion to the south and west, therefore, was likely to be blocked. In contrast, the areas to the north, north-east and east had more potential for the would-be purchaser. Here, at the end of the seventeenth century, the Watson-Wentworths were already substantial owners and although there were some compact middling estates, the pattern of ownership was very varied and contained a number of detached holdings of large and middling owners as well as fairly compact yeoman farms and many smallholdings often made up of widely scattered strips and closes. It was in this arc, with Wentworth township at its centre, stretching from Hoyland Nether and Wombwell in the north, through Brampton and Wath in the north-east, Swinton and Hooton Roberts in the east and Greasbrough, Kimberworth and Tinsley in the south-east and south that 75 per cent of the Watson-Wentworth purchases were made, with another 20 per cent in the same arc but beyond this inner ring of townships (Figure 3).

Not that the Watson-Wentworths were alone in seeking property in south-west Yorkshire; among purchasers of estates in the first decade

of the eighteenth century were John Savile of Methley, who bought
the Thrybergh estate from the debt-ridden Sir William Reresby in
1705 and, more significantly, Thomas Wentworth, Lord Raby, who
bought the Cutler estate at Stainborough in 1708, another property
brought onto the market through indebtedness.[21] The latter estate lay
only a few miles north-west of Wentworth Woodhouse and its
purchase by Lord Raby, the disappointed pretender to the Earl of
Strafford's estates, was a deliberate act of provocation. The Watson-
Wentworths, though, seemed to have remained unperturbed by this
development and pursued their estate building in the opposite
direction; they appear to have turned their backs on their cousin,
cushioned by their already substatial holdings in Tankersley and
Hoyland Nether which lay between their respective seats at
Wentworth Castle and Wentworth Woodhouse.

Figure 3 shows the level of Watson-Wentworth purchases, in
relation to land already in their possession, in each township or
parish. In Wentworth township, the heart of the estate containing

Figure 3. The level of Watson-Wentworth purchases in South Yorkshire,
1695-1782, by township and parish, in relation to land already in their
possession in 1695.

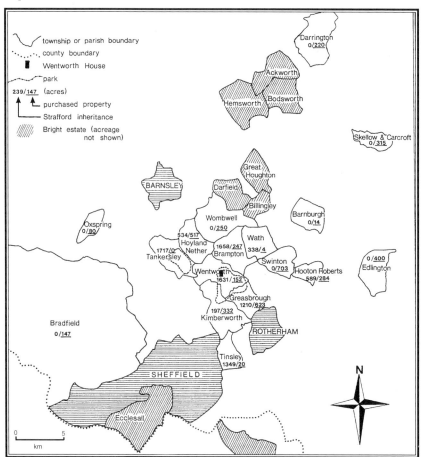

Wentworth House, the park and the demesnes, the Watson-Wentworths had inherited in 1695 an estate of 1651 acres, accounting for nearly three-quarters of the land in the township, and in the next 87 years they purchased another 152 acres in twelve separate transactions. In this township filling in odd gaps was their main concern. Seven of the twelve purchases were under 5 acres and much of the land was spread widely over four open fields.

In Hooton Roberts, five miles to the east of Wentworth lay a detached property, which in 1695 amounted to 589 acres. Although not physically attached to the property surrounding the main residence it may be properly considered with the core of the estate for here stood the dower house of the first Countess of Strafford which she occupied until her death in 1688, the same house to which Thomas Watson-Wentworth and his wife Alice retired when the future Marquis of Rockingham married in 1716. There were three purchases here; two were of only half an acre each but the third, in 1739, added more than 283 acres to the property as a result of a complicated transaction with the Hon. John Finch which involved the exchange of a farmhouse and 90 acres of land in three parishes plus chief rents in another together with purchase money of £1700.[22]

In three townships little or no property was purchased after 1695; in Tankersley in the west (no additions) and Tinsley in the south (20 acres), which both contained large compact holdings of over 1717 and 1319 acres respectively, and Wath (an addition of only about four acres) in the north where there was a much smaller and less compact property. It was in Greasbrough, Kimberworth, Hoyland Nether and Brampton, all sharing boundaries with Wentworth township, that the bulk of the purchases was concentrated.

Strafford property occupied 1210 acres in Greasbrough in 1695, about half of the area of the township. By the time of the second Marquis' death in 1782, the Rockingham estate there covered 2153 acres, almost 88 per cent of the area. Of the additional 944 acres, 261 were acquired as a result of the enclosure of the commons and 60 as part of an exchange with land in Little Houghton, but the remaining 623 acres were bought, from no less than 35 different vendors. Thus more than a third of the South Yorkshire purchases was concentrated in the township. A combination of factors conspired to make this a desirable area for estate expansion: there was a need to consolidate the already substantial holdings, the northern part of the township abutted on Wentworth Park which the first Marquis was keen to redesign and enlarge,[23] there were known coal reserves near navigable water, and control of land in the southern half of the township guaranteed access to the navigable River Don. The fulfilment of these ambitions was aided by the mixed nature of ownership in the township at the beginning of the eighteenth century. Of the 35 land purchases made in the township, 23 were from yeomen, fifteen of which were properties of less than 10 acres. The minor gentry provided four rather more substantial properties of between 20 and 60 acres but the most important purchase was a detached holding of the Wortley family amounting to 431 acres.

In Kimberworth, immediately to the south of Wentworth, small and middling purchases helped to almost treble the size of the holding from 197 to 530 acres. The purchases in this township were restricted entirely to its northern third. Here again consolidation was a major driving force accompanied by a desire, as in Greasbrough, to enlarge the park. In 1714 the 100 acre Scholes Spring was acquired for £960 and by 1726 the first Marquis was able to report that it was 'being cut into Walks for Beauty and intended to be thrown in the Park'.[24]

To the north of Wentworth in the neighbouring townships of Hoyland Nether and Brampton 764 acres were added to the estate, mostly between 1700 and 1750. As elsewhere in South Yorkshire many small purchases from yeomen were combined with the judicious acquisition of the properties of indebted minor gentry and the detached holdings of large owners. Of the last type, Lord Galway's estate in Hoyland, bought in 1750 for £7,500, and one of the last purchases of the first Marquis, proved in the long run, to be one of the most valuable additions to the estate.[25] This property of nearly 337 acres, containing a farm of 126 acres, six smaller farms, five spring woods, thirty-five cottages and two nailors' smithies, lay over the nine feet thick Barnsley coal seam which was already being exploited in a small way in another part of Hoyland township at the time of the purchase. The extension of the Watson-Wentworth estate in Brampton was also made in the knowledge of exploitable coal reserves – a colliery had been working from at least the early 1720s – though the full potential value to the income of the estate could not have been appreciated at the time and there is no evidence to suggest that the acquisition of coal rights was of more than secondary importance in the decision to purchase.[26]

Outside the core townships the largest addition was at Swinton, where there had been no Strafford properties and where purchases served to attach Hooton Roberts to the rest of the core townships. Most of the new land here was acquired in 1712 when the manor of

Swinton with all its lands in Swinton, Wath and Mexborough were bought from Edward Bagshaw of Culworth, Northamptonshire for £4,198.[27] It was in this township, at Kilnhurst, that a wharf was built beside the navigable Don from which coal from the estate's collieries was carried into the lowlands of north Nottinghamshire and north Lincolnshire.

The rest of the purchases in South Yorkshire, with the exception of the late purchase (1777) of 250 acres at Wombwell, which was part of the dismembered Wombwell estate, were widely dispersed from each other and from the core of the estate.[28] Significantly none of them came from yeomen: yeoman purchases were very much associated with small properties acquired to fill in gaps in the core of the estate. They were bought from vendors described as gentlemen or esquires. Two of the purchases were connected with non-payment of debts: 148 acres at Darrington in 1702 where the owner had mortgaged the land to Thomas Watson-Wentworth and had been taken to court for non-payment; and 198 acres at Skellow and Carcroft in 1704 where the owner, William Wombwell, had died owing Thomas Wentworth nearly £5,000.[29] Only one of the detached properties was, as far as is known, bought with a specific purpose in mind: this was the purchase in 1748 and 1749 of 400 acres of woods at Edlington that were acquired to be managed as coppice woods. The remaining five peripheral properties were acquired before 1715 and they may have been bought as bargaining counters in exchanges or part-exchanges or as speculative purchases at a time when it was not clear where the main areas of estate expansion would be, but this must remain a matter for conjecture.

So far the emphasis has been on the chronology and location of purchases. It is now appropriate to look more closely at the sources of these additions to the estate and to enquire into the circumstances surrounding their acquisition. Among the most enduring issues in the landownership debate has been the extent to which the enlargement of great estates was at the expense of the lesser gentry and yeoman farmers and the extent to which indebtedness and the vagaries of succession aided some estate builders and thwarted others.[30]

Purchases, by the three heads of the Watson-Wentworth family between 1695 and 1782, by social class of vendor, are summarised in Figure 4. What is immediately clear from the table is that the number of purchases (omitting the single purchase from a peer) was very nearly equally divided between the smaller occupiers and the gentry. But this simple statistic is misleading: the 48 purchases from the yeoman group amounted to only about 592 acres; a slightly smaller number of purchases from the gentry added more than 3,500 acres to the estate, of which almost two-thirds had been acquired from the esquires, principally from four local families: the Rokebys, the Wortleys, the Wombwells and the Foljambes. Only two of the substantial esquire purchases – the manor of Swinton in 1712 from the Bagshaws whose seat had been at Culworth, Northamptonshire and Edlington Wood from the trustees of the estate of George Liddell Esq. of Hebburn, Co Durham – were from families whose main seat was outside the West Riding.

Bearing in mind the relative crudity of the social classification, the analysis suggests that the enlargement of the Watson-Wentworth estate was not at the expense of one particular group; land was acquired from all groups, but it was the smaller owners and the gentry of the lesser and middling sort who bore the brunt of the Watson-Wentworths' purchasing activity. Its impact on the lesser,

Figure 4. Known Watson-Wentworth purchases in South Yorkshire, 1695-1782, by social class of vendor.

	YEOMEN no	acreage a	r	p	consideration £	s	d
T. Wentworth	16	124	1	22	1,364	00	00
1st Marquis	12	176	3	35	2,984	00	00
2nd Marquis	20	290	1	32	11,425	17	10
Totals	48	591	3	09	15,773	17	10

	GENTLEMEN no	acreage a	r	p	consideration £	s	d
T. Wentworth	18	717	0	36	6,405	06	00
1st Marquis	3	216	1	12	4,550	10	00
2nd Marquis	6	145	3	21	5,415	00	00
Totals	27	1,079	1	29	16,370	16	00

	ESQUIRES no	acreage a	r	p	consideration £	s	d
T. Wentworth	6	759	0	29	7,433	03	04
1st Marquis	8	1,386	0	26	21,576	14	10
2nd Marquis	4	290	0	19	9, 223	04	00
Totals	18	2,435	1	34	38,233	02	02

	PEERS no	acreage a	r	p	consideration £	s	d
T. Wentworth	-	-	-	-	-	-	-
1st Marquis	1	336	3	24	7,500	00	00
2nd Marquis	-	-	-	-	-	-	-
Totals	1	336	3	24	7,500	00	00

middling and greater gentry was widely distributed in the sub-region; on the smaller owners it was concentrated in Greasbrough township where half of the 48 yeoman purchases were located. All the yeoman purchases were in the inner core of townships centred on Wentworth, emphasising their role in the consolidation process. The different roles of acquisitions from the various social groups are also reflected in the average sizes of purchased properties: in the case of purchases from yeomen the average size was just over 12 acres; from gentlemen it was about 40 acres and from the esquires it was 135 acres.

Some reference has already been made to the reasons for land purchase. Most important were the twin desires for consolidation and expansion. In a good number of cases it is clear from the size and location of the property that one or the other was the principal reason for purchase, but in any case the net effect of both individual and groups of neighbouring purchases was both to expand and consolidate the estate.[31] For example, in Hoyland Nether township at the beginning of their stewardship in 1695, Watson-Wentworth properties in the township, amounting to 534 acres, were held in 31 widely scattered blocks and 33 lands and balks or bundles of lands and balks scattered about the remnants of the three open fields. Over the next 74 years five purchases had the effect of almost doubling the size of the property and at the same time substantially reducing the degree of dispersion. When the commons and the remnants of the open fields were enclosed in the 1790s, by which time the property had passed to the fourth Earl Fitzwilliam, practically the whole of the southern two-thirds of the township formed virtually one consolidated Fitzwilliam holding. For the most part income from the newly acquired land came in the form of annual rents from tenants, but in two cases an increase in earnings from what was to be untenanted land was sought. These were the 350 acre Edlington Wood purchased in 1748 and the adjacent Edlington Holts, amounting to 50 acres, in 1749 for use as coppice woods. Coppice woods were also important inclusions in the purchase of Edward Wortley Montagu's Greasbrough property in 1726 and of Lord Galway's Hoyland estate in 1750.

Land was also purchased for aesthetic reasons and for display. At the centre of the South Yorkshire estate, surrounding Wentworth House, lay Wentworth Park, and land for its expansion was purchased on its peripheries in Kimberworth and Greasbrough townships.[32] The largest purchase was the 100 acre Scholes Coppice already referred to above, but the greatest addition to the park came through the enclosure of Greasbrough Common in 1728.

Finally, eleven purchases are known to have been connected to the recovery of debts, mainly the foreclosure of mortgages. The bulk of the land acquired in this way was, however, some distance from the core of the estate and some of it was later resold.

The circumstances surrounding the decision of vendors to sell their properties to the Watson-Wentworths are unclear in a large number of cases. Even where a possible reason can be proffered the evidence is mostly indirect and must be treated with caution. For only 48 of the 96 purchases made between 1695 and 1782 and which still remained part of the South Yorkshire estate at the latter date can a possible reason for their sale be suggested. Of these, nineteen can certainly be attributed largely or wholly to indebtedness: seven were precipitated by the accumulation of large mortgage debts in favour of or assigned to the Watson-Wentworths, one occurred as a result of a debtor dying whilst still owing Thomas Wentworth nearly £5000, and in three of the remaining eleven cases the land was purchased from creditors of indebted owners.[33] Of these nineteen cases seven were yeoman properties, seven were from minor gentry (including a clergyman and a doctor) and five were from substantial gentry landowners. Altogether they resulted in the addition of more than 1700 acres to the estate.

In the case of three purchases from the Rokeby family in 1704, arising from mortgage debts, the role of Thomas Watson-Wentworth was questionable to say the least. The circumstances surrounding the purchases appear to show that his singleminded devotion to extending his estate did not preclude his taking advantage of a weak man's predicament and may even have extended to encouraging the slide into indebtedness.[34]

Of the remaining 77 purchases, unconnected, as far as is known, with indebtedness, information in the deeds reveals that nineteen followed closely on the death of an owner: in four of these instances the land had been inherited by a son, daughter or brother residing in another part of the country, in six cases it had been divided among heirs or, more usually, heiresses. In four instances executors had sold land to clear debts and/or to meet expenses and in another they had been specifically instructed to sell the property and to share the proceeds among the two daughters' younger children.[35] In a further nine cases the vendors were resident outside South Yorkshire but whether these circumstances in any way contributed to the decision to sell is not known.

Finally, two of the purchases, one of 59 acres and the other of 431 acres, both in Greasbrough, were from owners whose substantial estates lay elsewhere in South Yorkshire.[36] The largest of these two purchases was from Edward Wortley Montagu whose large, compact estate lay seven miles to the west at Wortley. There is a strong suggestion that Wortley Montagu bought the property in question with an eye to a quick sale and a substantial profit. It had been bought in 1719 for £7,289 (plus an annuity charged to the estate of £115) by Elkana Horton, brother-in-law of John Gill, in accordance with the latter's will so that portions could be raised for Gill's younger children. Horton disposed of it, for £8,600 (plus a rent charge of £60) to Edward Wortley Montagu in 1722 who in turn sold it to the first Marquis in 1726 for £11,000.[37]

Enclosures

Acquisitions of land following the enclosure of commons in five separate localities added more than 530 acres to the South Yorkshire estate.[38] Two of these, at Bolsterstone and Hallfield, both isolated properties at Bradfield in the Pennines to the west of the main body of the estate, together added less than 25 acres. In contrast the enclosure of Hoober Common in Brampton township near the centre of the estate in 1714 resulted in Thomas Watson-Wentworth being awarded 247 acres. At Greasbrough in 1728 the first Marquis' share of the common was 261 acres. The purpose to which the Greasbrough acquisition was to be put, which abutted on Wentworth Park, was made clear in the award: the land was to be immediately 'inclosed and taken in for a park'.[39]

Exchanges

Between 1698 and 1782, 63 exchanges of land took place in South Yorkshire. Land was overwhelmingly exchanged with yeomen and, with one exception, involved no more than a few acres on each occasion. Fifty-eight were straight exchanges, in the other five money also exchanged hands, ranging from £4 to £100. The biggest exchange involved the transfer in 1750 of land in Little Houghton belonging to the first Marquis to Robert Bingley, gentleman, of Bolton-on-Dearne, in exchange for a messuage and thirteen closes in Greasbrough amounting to 60 acres. The property in Little Houghton was several miles from the outer edge of the core of the estate, the Greasbrough property, on the other hand, was in the expanding core in a township in which a great deal of inherited and purchased Watson-Wentworth land was concentrated.

All except the Bingley exchange took place within the confines of particular townships and all but one of these were located in the core of the estate in the townships of Brampton, Greasbrough, Kimberworth, Swinton, Wath, Wentworth and Wombwell. The concentration of the exchanges in the core and their generally small size reflect their function: they were aids to consolidation. The details of the deeds of exchange make their role quite clear. An exchange in 1739 in Swinton township is a typical example. The first Marquis had two one-acre strips in 'foxlands', a sub-division of the open fields. The exchange involved the interchange of one of the Earl's acres with one belonging to Samuel Savile 'in Order that the said Earls two Acres may lie together'.[40]

Acquisition of land through marriage

Land in South Yorkshire was brought directly into the estate by only one of three brides of the heads of the Watson-Wentworth family. As a result of his marriage in 1752 to Mary Bright, daughter of Thomas Bright of Badsworth, the second Marquis was able to add a substantial gentry property to his family's South Yorkshire estate. The new property comprised six discrete holdings. In the parish of Sheffield, on the borders of Yorkshire and Derbyshire, lay Ecclesall township. Here, together with small acreages to the north in Sheffield township and across the Derbyshire boundary in Norton parish lay a property amounting to about 1,000 acres. Two-fifths of this was valuable coppice woodland; the rest consisted of tenanted farms and a mill on the River Sheaf. About six miles to the east of Ecclesall, in the parish of Eckington in north Derbyshire, lay the Westwell property. This property, in the Rother Valley, was not only the most distant but also the most fragmented of the new possessions.

The rest of the newly acquired Bright properties lay to the north of Wentworth House. In Billingley and the adjacent parts of Darfield called Millhouses was a compact property amounting to about 750 acres. Immediately to the north lay another compact property at Great Houghton of about the same size as that at Billingley. The last two of the six new holdings lay, side by side, another three miles to the north. On the west was a property of more than 1,000 acres lying mostly in Hemsworth but extending northwards into Ackworth. To the east was Badsworth which had been acquired by Mary Bright's great great grandfather, Sir John Bright, more than a century before and which he had made his principal seat. The property covered most of the parish and amounted to 1152 acres.[41]

Sales

Throughout the 87 year period only six sales are known to have taken place in South Yorkshire. They all involved purchased property outside the core of the estate. They comprised either detached or small or distant or highly fragmented properties, or some combination of these, and their sale increased the compactness of the estate.[42]

Conclusion

The socially and politically ambitious Watson-Wentworths constitute an interesting case study of landownership because of their deliberate settling at Wentworth Woodhouse and their high level of activity in the land market. Almost from the day he inherited it, Thomas Watson-Wentworth began to expand his newly acquired South Yorkshire estate through purchase, and this policy was continued by his son Thomas, first Marquis of Rockingham, and his grandson Charles, second Marquis of Rockingham. Major additions were also made as a result of the enclosure of commons and by one judicious marriage. At the same time no opportunity was missed to consolidate the estate through exchanges of land. By 1782, when the second Marquis died childless and it passed to his nephew William, the fourth Earl Fitzwilliam, the South Yorkshire estate covered more than 18,000 acres, almost double its size in 1695.

The development of the Watson-Wentworth estate appears to conform in many respects to Habakkuk's original thesis. Enlargement certainly took place at the expense of lesser landowners, with almost half of the purchases being from yeomen and half from the gentry, two-thirds of the latter being from esquires. Purchases from yeomen were usually small and their major contribution was to aid estate consolidation. Acquisitions from esquires and gentlemen, on the other hand, added 79 per cent of the nearly 4,500 acres acquired by purchase, and the location of the land coming on to the market enabled the Watson-Wentworths to expand and consolidate on a broad front to the north, north-east and east of their pre-existing estate. The extent and speed with which they were able to accomplish their expansionist policy, was aided not only by indebtedness among the gentry and smaller landowners, but also the division, and subsequent sale, of properties among co-inheritors, and by the mix of gentry and yeoman properties, and the detached holdings of other proprietors, large and small, lying in those parts of the surrounding countryside in which they had a prime interest. Besides contributing to the demise of a substantial number of lesser owners, they also brought about, through the marriage of the second Marquis to Mary Bright, the extinction of a major gentry family and estate.

Habakkuk also placed great emphasis on the influence of the strict settlement in the rise of great estates. Although the Watson-Wentworths employed the strict family settlement as the basis for transmitting property from one generation to another it did not, in practice, act as a strait-jacket restricting their degree of freedom; nor did it, as some writers have suggested, hinder agricultural improvement. In the hands of the Watson-Wentworths the strict settlement was a very flexible device. It protected the family's long-term interests by maintaining the inalienable status of the whole of the Strafford inheritance in South Yorkshire and part of it in Ireland throughout the whole of the period in question, while allowing the first two life tenants in particular to set about expanding and consolidating the estate in a single-minded and ruthless way. It was as much their 'psychological strictness', their unswerving belief in their status and destiny, as the legal strictness of their successive settlements that fuelled their single-mindedness towards maintaining and extending their estate.[43]

The deliberate policy of exchanging to consolidate, and therefore to improve, exemplifies their attitude to estate building and improvement within the umbrella of the strict settlement. The marriage settlement between the first Marquis and Lady Mary Finch in 1716 is quite explicit about the role of exchanges:

> ... *It shall be lawful...to Exchange any...parcel of the lands...which lye more Contiguous to or which may be more advantageous and Beneficial for the Inclosing Bettering or otherwise Improving of the other parts of the Mannors, Lands, Estates...*[44]

Their motives were mixed. They combined a desire to consolidate, to beautify, to make an ostentatious display, and, (at least during the time of Thomas Watson-Wentwroth) to out-do their rival at Wentworth Castle, with a genuine interest in improvement. The first Marquis advised his successor that 'If you lay out your money in improving your seat, lands, gardens, etc. you beautifye the country and do the work ordered by God himself'.[45] The second Marquis, in spite of a busy political career, took this advice to heart: he became a noted improver and took a close personal interest in drainage, manuring, grassland management and the introduction of new crops and farming equipment.[46] Writing at length about the Wentworth estate in 1769, Arthur Young was moved to comment that he 'never saw the advantages of a great fortune applied so nobly to the improvement of a country'.[47]

Notes and References

1. I am grateful to Professor J. V. Beckett of the University of Nottingham for reading an earlier version of this paper and offering helpful comments. Acknowledgements are also due to Olive, Countess Fitzwilliam's Wentworth Settlement Trustees and the Director of Sheffield City Libraries for permission to quote from the Wentworth Woodhouse Muniments in Sheffield Archives.
2. H. J. Habakkuk, 'English Landownership 1680-1740', *Economic History Review*, X, (1939-40), 2-17; 'Marriage Settlements in the Eighteenth century', *Transactions of the Royal Historical Society*, 4th series, XXXIII 1950, 15-30; 'England' in *The European Nobility in the Eighteenth Century*, A. Goodwin, ed, (London, 1953), 1-21; 'The England Land Market in the Eighteenth Century' in *Britain and the Netherlands*, Ed. J. S. Bromley and E. H. Kossman, (1960), 154-73.
3. Habakkuk, *Economic History Review*, X, 1.
4. Habakkuk, *Economic History Review*, X, 4.
5. Habakkuk's thesis was generally accepted and supported by G. E. Mingay in 'Landownership and Agrarian Trends in the Eighteenth Century' (unpub. Ph.D. thesis, Nottingham Univ, 1958) and in his subsequent book, *English Landed Society in the Eighteenth Century* (London, 1963).
6. More recent critics of aspects of Habakkuk's original conclusions include C. Clay, 'Marriage, Inheritance and the Rise of Large Estates in England 1660-1815', *Economic History Review*, 2nd series, XXI (1968), 503-18; and 'Property Settlements, Financial Provision for the Family, and Sale of Land by the Greater Landowners 1660-1790', *Journal of British Studies*, XXI (1981), 18-38; B. A. Holderness. 'The English Land Market in the Eighteenth Century: the Case of Lincolnshire', *Economic History Review*, 2nd series, XXVII (1974), 557-75; J. V. Beckett, 'English Landownership in the later Seventeenth and Eighteenth centuries: the Debate and the Problems', *Economic History Review*, 2nd series, III (1977), 567-81; 'The Decline of the Small Landowner in Eighteenth and Nineteenth Century England: Some Regional Considerations', *Agricultural History Review*, III (1982), 97-111; 'The Pattern of Landownership in England and Wales, 1660-1880', *Economic History Review*, 2nd series, XXXVII (1984), 1-22; J. O. Martin, 'The Landed Estate in Glamorgan c1660-1760', (unpub. Ph.D. thesis, Cambridge Univ. 1978); L. Bonfield, 'Marriage Settlements and the "Rise of Great Estates"; the Demographic Aspect', *Economic History Review*, 2nd series, XXXII (1979) 482-92; *Marriage Settlements, 1601-1740: The Adoption of the Strict Settlement*, (Cambridge, 1983)."
7. For example, B. English and J. Saville, 'Family Settlements and the "Rise of Great Estates"', *Economic History Review*, 2nd series, XXXIII (1980), 556-63; *Strict Settlement: A Guide for Historians*, (Hull, 1983).
8. H. J. Habakkuk, 'The Rise and Fall of English Landed Families 1600-1800', *Transactions of the Royal Historical Society*, 5th series, XXIX 1979), 187-287; 'The Rise and Fall of English Landed Families: II', *Transactions of the Royal Historical Society*, 5th series, XXX, (1980), 199-221; The Rise and Fall of English Landed families: III Did the Gentry Rise', *Transactions of the Royal Historical Society*, 5th series, XXXI (1981), 195-217.
9. J. Habakkuk, *Marriage, Debt and the Estates System: English Landownership 1650-1950*, Clarendon Press, Oxford, 1994.
10. It should be noted, however, that at the outset of his more recent three-part contribution to the debate (see note 8), Sir John Habakkuk stated that he intended to discuss the issues 'in general terms, ignoring regional differences...'.
11. P. Roebuck, *Yorkshire Baronets*, (Oxford 1980) p.285.
12. J. J. Cartwright, ed., *The Wentworth Papers 1705-1739* (London, 1883), p.22.
13. For discussion of the Watson-Wentworths' political activity see G. H. Gutteridge, *The Early Career of Lord Rockingham*, University of California Publications in History, 44, (Berkeley and Los Angeles, 1952); C. Collyer, 'The Rockinghams and Yorkshire Politics 1742-1761', *Thoresby Society Publications*, XLI (1956), 352-82; M. Charlesworth, 'Elevation and Succession', and Patrick Eyres, 'A Patriotic Landscape', *The New Arcadian Journal*, 31/32, (1991), 7-75 and 77-125 respectively (the whole of the 1991 volume is devoted to a consideration of the reflection of politics in the land-scapes of Wentworth Castle and Wentworth Woodhouse).
14. S(heffield) A(rchives), W(entworth) W(oodhouse) M(uniments), D1493 (will of William, second Earl of Strafford, 1695); D1496 (sale of part of Irish estate in 1696), D1498 and D1501 (settlement of the Strafford estates in 1696 (South Yorkshire) and 1699 (Ireland)). See also J. P. Cooper, ''The Fortune of Thomas Wentworth, Earl of Strafford, *Economic History Review*, 2nd series, XI, (1958), 15-29.
15. M. Jones, 'Coppice Wood Management in the Eighteenth Century: an example from County Wicklow', *Irish Forestry*, XXXXIII (1986), 15-31.
16. SA, WWM, D1493 (will of William, second Earl of Strafford, 1695); D1527 (will of first Marquis of Rockingham, 1748); D1550B (will of second Marquis of Rockingham, 1782); D1523 and D1831 (pre-nuptial settlement between first Marquis and Lady Mary Finch, 1716); D183 (Pre-nuptial settlement between second Marquis and Mary Bright, 1752).
17. SA, WWM, D1526 (deed of revocation taking the Irish estates out of strict settlement, *c*.1725).
18. The term purchases as used in this paper is reserved for those properties bought between 1695 and 1782 and which still formed part of the South Yorkshire estate in 1782. Properties bought

during this period and subsequently resold are dealt with under sales.

19. SA,WWM, Add(itional Deposit), deed 38, box 19, bundle II and deeds 27, 28 and 29, box 17, bundle IV.

20. Martin, thesis, pp.247-49.

21. Joseph Hunter, *South Yorkshire: The History and Topography of the Deanery of Doncaster,* (London, 1828-31), pp. 40-42 and p.267.

22. SA, WWM Add, deeds 2 and 3, box 20, bundle II.

23. For a description of the first Marquis' house building and park expansion activity see M. Jones, 'Rents, Remarks and Observations: the First Marquis of Rockingham's Rent Roll Book' in *Aspects of Rotherham: Discovering Local History*, Ed. M. Jones, Wharncliffe Publishing , 1995, pp.113-128.

24. SA, WWM Add, deeds 35 and 36, box 33, bundle II; WWM A1273.

25. SA, WWM Add, deeds 18 and 19, box 22, bundle I.

26. The half-yearly rental income from the Low Wood Colliery in Brampton township in 1723 was only £35; a colliery at Tinsley produced a half-yearly rent of only £10 and no rental income was recorded for 1723 for collieries at Greasbrough, Swinton, West Melton, and at Westwood in Tankersley township (SA, WWM, A1273).

27. SA, WWM Add, deed 20, box 34, bundle II.

28. Roebuck, *Yorkshire Baronets*, pp.289-90.

29. SA, WWM Add, deed 30, box 14, bundle III and deed 51, box 32, bundle V.

30. The possibility of a slide into indebtedness among smaller landowners through the combined impact of the land tax and their desire for greater comfort and ostentation, leading to extravagance, was a central plank of Habakkuk's original article (*Economic History Review*, X, 9-10). The possible impact of demographic conditions on estate stability through inheritance by indirect heirs and by daughters has become an important feature of the renewed landownership debate. For example, see Beckett, *Economic History Review*, XXXV, 10, and L. Stone and J. C. Fawtier Stone, *An Open Elite? England 1540-1880* (Oxford, 1984), pp. 100-04 and 108-26.

31. Consolidation at the strip or close level was mostly accomplished through exchange, but it was not unusual for purchases to be made to achieve this end, for example, the purchase in 1710 from George Ellis, Gent., in Brampton township, of 10 lands amounting to two acres, in Narr College Moor (part of the open fields) 'lying between lands of Thomas Wentworth' (SA, WWM Add, deeds 30a and 30b, box 13).

32. By 1744 the park was more than nine miles in circumference, and by 1782 the park enclosed more than 1260 acres, SA, WWM, A1273; WWM, D 1597A.

33. The details of the purchases related to mortgage debts in favour of or assigned to the Watson-Wentworths are contained in SA, WWM add, deed 56, box 18, bundle II; deed 30, box 14, bundle II; deed 20, box 34, bundle II; deeds 71 and 72, box 19, bundle IV; deeds in box 68, bundle II; deeds in box 68, bundle III. The purchase from a debtor (William Wombwell Esq., d.1717) who died still owing Thomas Wentworth nearly £5,000 is recorded in SA, WWM Add, deed 51, box 32, bundle V. Details of the three purchases from creditors of indebted owners are to be found in SA, WWM Add, deed 10, box 13, bundles IV and V; deed 7, box 38, bundle I; and deed 38, box 14, bundle III.

34. SA, WWM Add, deeds in box 32, bundle IV; deeds 5 and 6, box 21, bundle II; deed 55, box 32, bundle V; deed 44, box 32, bundle IV. Rokeby's version of events recorded in the proceedings of the Court of Chancery are quoted at length in Hunter's South Yorkshire, p. 202.

35. SA, WWM Add, deeds 61, 62 and 63, box 18, bundle III.

36. In 1766 a 59 acre farm was bought from William Brook, Gent., of Pickburn. Forty years earlier, in 1726, the manor of Whitehall and one third of the manor of Greasbrough, amounting to 431 acres, was acquired from Edward Wortley Montagu.

37. SA, WWM Add, deeds 27, 28 and 29, box 17, bundle IV.

38. SA, WWM, D1507.

39. SA, WWM, D1507.

40. SA, WWM Add, deed 43, box 35, bundle IV.

41. See Roebuck, *Yorkshire Baronets*, pp. 203-50, for details of the Bright properties; a map of the Bright estates is provided in Appendix 9, p. 378.

42. SA, WWM, D 1523, D1597A, D1639, A1273.

43. On 'psychological strictness', see Stone and Stone, *Open Elite*, pp. 76-78.

44. SA, WWM, D1523.

45. First Marquis of Rockingham, letter to his son, 12 May 1750, quoted in M. Binney, 'Wentworth Woodhouse Revisited - I', *Country Life*, 17 March, 1983, 624-26.

46. W. G. H. Armytage, 'Charles Watson-Wentworth, second Marquess of Rockingham, F. R. S. (1730-1782): Some Aspects of his Scientific Interests', *Notes & Records of The Royal Society of London*, XII (1956), 64-76.

47. Arthur Young, *A six months tour through the north of England*, 2nd edition (1771), I, xvi.

6. THE TROUBLE WITH SERVANTS...DOMESTIC LIFE AT WENTWORTH WOODHOUSE IN THE EIGHTEENTH CENTURY

by Marjorie Bloy

THE EIGHTEENTH CENTURY has been called 'the age of elegance', an age which would have been impossible to create without the assistance of a vast number of servants. The 'servant class' was probably the second largest occupational group in the country after agricultural workers. Most servants were employed by the middle classes; the servants employed by the higher gentry and aristocracy were in a minority and formed a privileged élite among servants. Certainly those who worked as servants in the 'big house' enjoyed a higher standard of living and comfort than their contemporaries who were employed by lesser folk. They were clothed, fed and housed at the expense of their employers and were paid a small wage, albeit irregu-

Figure 1. Typical dress worn by male servants in the eighteenth century: (a) coachman; (b) manservant; (c) farm labourer; (d) hairdresser; (e) craftsman. *Margot Lister, Costume, Barrie & Jenkins*

Figure 2. Typical dress worn by fem. servants in the eighteenth century: (a) fa girl; (b) maid servant; (c) lady's maid; (housekeeper. *Margot Lister, Costume, Barrie & Jenk*

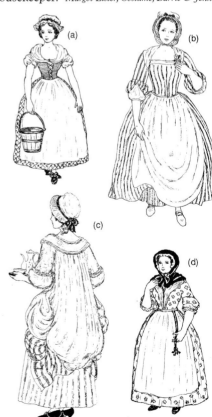

larly on occasion. Their accommodation might be in the attics of the house and their workplace in the basement; their employers might ignore them as persons; they may well have had separate entrances, separate staircases and separate lives from their employers; but they were an essential part of the household without whom the routine tasks of daily life would have been impossible. It was usual for the aristocracy to spend the summer in the country and some preferred to spend much of the winter there too, where their homes were the centre of social and political activity. This domesticity demanded servants, food and wine on a grand scale: the maintenance of a great house was expensive.

A house the size of Wentworth Woodhouse[1] needed an army of servants to keep it running smoothly and to ensure the comfort of its owners (Figures 1 and 2). Likewise the huge estate needed a host of workers to prevent it from going to rack and ruin. In the eighteenth century Wentworth Woodhouse provided employment for the local inhabitants, many of whom lived in Wentworth village because they worked on the estate or at the house. The second Marquis of Rockingham, like his father before him, took care of his employees and was rewarded by faithful service over many years. An almshouse at Barrow for twelve pensioners, established originally in 1694 and rebuilt by the first Marquis, was still maintained by his son (Figures 3 and 4).

Figure 4. Detail of the plaque above the entrance to the Almshouses.

In February, 1753, fifty-four servants were given money from the estate of the late first Marquis. The amounts they received varied from fifteen guineas which was paid to Mrs Hannah Jennet the housekeeper to £2 each paid to John Mann and Henry Wilkinson the

Figure 3. One section of the Almshouses at Barrow as they are today.

gamekeepers. In 1766 there were 39 household servants; in 1767 the number had risen to 88; in 1773 the Marquis employed a total of 97 household staff.[2] However, in 1773 the number of household staff was reduced to 32 during the 'clean sweep' of untrustworthy staff before the numbers were increased again.

All the domestic staff were provided with liveries. The male house staff had 'Scarlott Wastecoats' [*sic*] and breeches, thread and silk stockings, a livery coat, frock coat and greatcoat besides livery hats, frock hats and velvet caps. Each livery had eight yards of velvet lace and sixteen yards of silver lace. Each suit of livery cost £13 13s 6d and was made up of three yards of drabcloth, 42 yards of grey shalloon, 13 yards of yellow cloth, 22 yards of white shalloon, one yard of yellow shalloon, 22 yards of lace, 24 buttons and 32 breast buttons.[3] The Marquis would have paid approximately £225 for servants' clothing in an average year. On top of that was the cost of having the clothes made, often by Benjamin Burgon the house's resident upholsterer.

All the resident staff were fed at the expense of the Marquis. In 1763 the total weight of butchered meat was 27 tons; in 1764 it was almost 30 tons.[4] In January, 1772, 92 servants were provided with food at the Marquis' expense: 67 at Wentworth and 25 in London.[5] Those who were provided for in the steward's room at Wentworth included Dr Bourne the surgeon, Mr Dixon the chaplain and John Thesiger the Marquis' valet, besides the steward himself.[6] Dr Bourne, who had been the Marquis' physician since 1741, appears to have been the resident family doctor at Wentworth Woodhouse although the servants were treated by Dr Simpson[7] and were nursed and/or laid out by Sarah Womack who was more usually employed as a laundry maid after 1772.[8] Prior to that she supplied eggs to the house.[9]

The second Marquis (Figure 5) was conscious of the high costs of running the house. The following figures will give some idea of the expense of simply keeping Wentworth Woodhouse in running order:[10]

	£.	s.	d.
servants' liveries	755	6	5
house expenses	554	0	5
servants' wages	376	16	1
furniture	81	8	0
stables	72	11	11
equipage	59	18	6
gardens	20	13	7

Figure 5. Charles Watson-Wentworth, second Marquis of Rockingham. *Engraving from the original by Sir Joshua Reynolds*

In May, 1770, the Marquis demanded that William Martin the steward should do more to keep costs to a minimum. On 24 May, Martin replied that he was unable to comply since Rockingham was being fleeced by his servants. For example, William Smith the joiner was allowed to buy the wood he needed for a job which had been estimated at £59. The actual price paid for the wood was £117 18s 8d but Smith had been allowed to buy more than he needed. In 1770 William Martin told the Marquis,

> *If your Lordship suffers such things to escape without notice and a reprimand; what I say to them will be of little use and my service to your Lordship of very little significance.*[11]

In August, 1771, Martin resigned and was replaced by Benjamin Hall. Sometime after 9 April, 1772, Martin tried to claim £150 from the Marquis for a quarter's salary and an allowance for a house in Chapeltown.[12] Rockingham replied that his salary was either £150 and a house in Chapletown or £200 and no house. Martin had already been paid £200, and in any case had not worked at Wentworth Woodhouse since December, 1771, although it had taken him until February, 1772, to declare his accounts. Martin apparently was out of work, and was trying to blame his former employer for his plight.[13]

Judging from the lists of servants it seems that the Marquis then began to watch his servants closely because in 1773 there was a big change in the staff.[14] Of the 78 resident staff employed at Wentworth Woodhouse in 1773, only 46 had been there in 1771 and some of them were subsequently replaced, such as the head storeroom maid Sarah Jackson and the housekeeper Mrs Broughton.

The first Marquis of Rockingham's housekeeper was Mrs Hannah Jennet. She still held the post in 1768 at exactly the same annual salary of £30 but after 1766 she was assisted by Elizabeth Broughton.[15] Hannah Jennet's gravestone still stands in the old churchyard at Wentworth (Figure 6): she lived and died on the estate. In 1771 Mrs Broughton was listed as the housekeeper with Mary Evans as her assistant[16] but by July, 1773, Mrs Broughton had been replaced. When she became housekeeper she would have been

Figure 6. Gravestone of Hannah Jennet in the old churchyard, Wentworth.

totally responsible for the stores, linen, servants and the running of the household, albeit under the authority of Lady Rockingham. On 25 February, 1773, Mrs Broughton was married by licence at Wentworth parish church to Edward William Townley, the estate's land surveyor.[17] Two months later the Rockinghams were considering removing Mrs Townley unless she changed her ways.

Benjamin Hall had had a difficult time in trying to establish his authority over the servants at Wentworth after he took over from William Martin. Even the Marquis sympathised with his position and hoped that gradually the servants would get into

a more regular Course of attention to their respective employ-ments, than they have been used to ... & then it will be easier after-wards for you.

Hall had written to the Rockinghams about 'great irregularities' and had enclosed comparative accounts for six months' consumption at Wentworth Woodhouse: they were 'amazed & most agreeably surprised' at the figures, which had fallen substantially in the second quarter. They had agreed to remove the 'grand obstacle' [Mrs Townley] and were pleased with Hall's 'reformations' although Lady Rockingham wanted the changes brought about 'in a right way' because she believed that the 'best Ends are never to be obtain'd by the wrong Means'. She was 'sorry and surpriz'd ... about Betty Dixon [the farm governess] for I really thought she was amongst the very few strictly honest folk'. Hall was told to dismiss Mrs Townley's maids forthwith, but out of kindness to have a word with 'poor Tom' about the conduct of Betty Hankin which made it necessary to sack her, suggesting that she should be placed in a 'lesser family with fewer fellow serv[an]ts & temptations' after which 'she might be more careful of her behaviour & do well'.[18] 'Poor Tom' was Thomas Hankin, then porter at Wentworth Woodhouse but who had been employed by the first Marquis as a footman prior to 1750.[19] Presumably Betty was his daughter.

In May, 1773, Hall had sacked Dolly [Smith] a housemaid whom Lady Rockingham had always thought to be 'a sad Trollop', and clearly plans were progressing to get rid of the housekeeper. Lady Rockingham hoped that 'when the time comes for removing the Main Obstacle to reformation, that all things will come right'. Still, having a general change in staff did cause problems: her ladyship was sure that she did not know

what will become of the laundry, for the last maid I took [Sarah

Womack] - *is very slow & I fear will never do, the Linnen* [*sic*] *at present is not at all managed as it should be.*[20]

Perhaps the versatile Sarah was better at selling eggs or laying out the dead than she was at doing the washing.

Another servant who left Rockingham's service in May, 1773, was Joseph Cattanei, a member of the Steward's Room. He left of his own accord and for understandable personal reasons, moving out of the area altogether. In December the Marquis found himself paying ten guineas to William Poles the Poor Law Guardian to indemnify Cattanei 'from a Bastard Child born in the township of Wentworth'.[21]

By the end of June, 1773, on fully considering the behaviour of Mrs Townley, the Rockinghams were 'of opinion that she can not be continued as Housekeeper at Wentworth'. They were also dissatisfied with the behaviour of Edward William Townley and decided to sack him too 'and most probably as we part with Mrs Townly [*sic*], He would not chuse it'. Rockingham was sorry to have to get rid of him, because he was 'capable of being useful'. However, Townley had been guilty of 'thinking so high of himself' that it had

> *occasioned many of the Improper Things which he may have said & the Improper suggestions which he may have tried to inculcate into others.*[22]

Furthermore, the Marquis instructed Hall to make an inventory of the linen, stores and other household goods left by Mrs Townley: it would appear that she had been diverting various items to purposes other than use at the house and Rockingham did not want the same thing to happen again.

The Rockinghams had already found another housekeeper and a land surveyor to replace the Townleys once Richard Fenton their solicitor had given notice to them. Mrs Croft, a widow with a two year-old son, took over the running of the household and held the post until after the Marquis' death at exactly the same salary as had been paid to Hannah Jennet thirty years before.[23]

A further eight servants were dismissed during the course of 1773. One was the coal carrier Thomas Swift who had begun that job only in January, 1772. The others were two kitchen maids; a housemaid; Sarah Cooper, the baker's maid; Richard Beaumont, the usher in the hall; Thomas Wigfield, the lobby waiter; and one of the stable assistants. All were in a position to divert goods from the house and make a profit for themselves at Rockingham's expense. They were the ones who were caught by the 'new broom', Benjamin Hall. The frauds must have been going on for a long time and it may be that such activities were seen as part of the perquisites of working at somewhere like Wentworth.

In October, 1764, an even worse, and far more public, scandal had affected the Rockinghams: the 26 year-old Lady Henrietta-Alicia (usually known as Harriet), youngest of the Marquis' sisters, had eloped with William Sturgeon, her Irish footman, who had 'attended behind the coach'.[24] The whole family was devastated by the news, [25] and rather than put the letters informing him of the news into his private papers, the Marquis carried them around with him until his wife took them out of his pockets on 29 April, 1765.[26] Sturgeon was unable to keep his wife in the manner to which she was accustomed so Rockingham paid her a quarterly allowance out of his Irish estates. The Earl Fitzwilliam continued to help the Sturgeons after he inherited the estates in 1782. One much repeated story about the Marquis' new brother-in-law - probably apocryphal - came out of this event. Rockingham was a member of White's Club and had gone there shortly after the news of Harriet's marriage had become public knowledge. Dinner was about to be served and a waiter was taking orders. Rockingham, still stunned, was unable to decide so the waiter tried to be helpful. The poor man, who does not appear to have heard what had happened (or maybe he had), invited the Marquis to 'try a dish of sturgeon...'

Problems with footmen recurred in 1773, at the time of the Townley troubles. This time it was Lady Rockingham's footmen who were involved in some untoward activities. Lady Rockingham had begun to insist that Mrs Townley's maids should be dismissed, but her husband had told her that she had

> *no right to order the discharge of these Maids while I* [i.e. Lady Rockingham] *continue Robert* [Needham] *in my service, & there is some truth in that.*[27]

What Robert had done and what happened to him remains a mystery, but by the end of June, 1775, she had dismissed the other footman, William Bruce. Bruce had been 'behaving strangely': he had taken to staying out all night and to frequenting alehouses. Bruce claimed to have married Thompson, another servant, in January, but then he ran off with a juggler. The Marchioness wanted to know if Thompson was 'so great & so unfortunate a fool as to be really married to this poor, idleheaded, good for nothing Creature'.[28] Whether Thompson had married or not, she ceased to appear on the lists of servants at the house.

The Marquis was not very prompt at paying his servants' wages. Sometimes they were paid for two years at a time, in arrears. The domestic servants suffered worst in this respect, since their pay was not high to begin with. Housemaids received £5 a year and kitchen maids £4 10s 0d. This must be compared with, for instance, the molecatcher (five guineas p.a.), stableboys (£5 p.a.) and the pheasant-keeper (£12 p.a.), although the outdoor staff did not receive board and lodging as part of their wages. They were, however, provided with well-built cottages on the estate (Figure 7). The wages bill for 1768 came to £592 4s 6d which included payments for two years in many cases, but was a vast reduction on the wages bill for 1766 which had come to £1062 7s 4d.[29]

Two men employed initially by the first Marquis and retained by his son became successful in their own right. Dominicus Negri, the confectioner to the first Marquis, was employed by the second Marquis not only as a confectioner but also as the keeper of his accounts for a visit to 'Tonbridge Wells' in 1754. Negri ceased to appear on the servants' lists shortly after this but in 1762 Rockingham's London expenses included payments to a confectioner called Negri.[30] The name is too unusual for there to be no connection, and by 1775 there was a D. Negri & Co., Confectioners, in London. The company was used by Rockingham from 1762 until his death in 1782.

William Malpass, a mere Usher of the Hall in 1753, also made good. In June, 1760, Rockingham's accounts show a payment of £2 13s 1d to Malpass for tiles and lime as part of the Marquis' land improvement programme. Malpass took over Edward Butler's Swinton pottery in 1763 and continued to sell household pottery in Britain, Europe and America. Malpass received payments from the Wentworth estates for many and varied services. In 1764 he was

Figure 7. Estate workers' cottages, Lea Brook.

referred to as an inn-holder of Kilnhurst and later the same year he was selling lime to Rockingham and carting it from Kilnhurst to Wentworth. By 1765 Malpass was involved in pottery, ale, carriage and freight, coal carrying and wharfage.[31] From being an usher in the hall, Malpass had gone a long way.

Lord Rockingham took upon himself the responsibility of looking after his staff as and when they were in need. He paid for the nursing of sick servants and if necessary - which it often was, given the medical knowledge and treatments of the day - he paid their funeral costs too. In January, 1766, Robert Goodey fell ill and died. The Marquis' accounts show that he paid 18s. 6d. for nursing and funeral expenses. In 1773 Hannah Smith was paid 6s. for nursing Thomas Palmer, a groom, for twelve days. His shroud cost a further 6s., which says little for the nursing he received. Sarah Womack, the wife of George Womack who was a waiter in the house, supplemented their income by nursing the sick. When Thomas Hobson's apprentice lost thirteen days 'from a misfortune in slipping down and breaking his arm when at Work in the Kitchen' the Marquis paid Hobson 19s.[32] Benjamin Burgon, the resident upholsterer at Wentworth Woodhouse, was 'allowed by his Lordship towards Boarding out & Care Taking of his Wife who is & has been for some Time Disorder'd in her Senses £2 10s 0d',[33] and the cost of Sarah Murphy's wedding (£6 17s 6d) was met by Rockingham.[34] The sums involved obviously were unimportant to a man of Rockingham's wealth but were substantial amounts for servants, workmen and their families.

In 1757 when there was a food shortage the Marquis provided grain but his agent at Ecclesall reported that the people there 'seem to expect something more from you towards buying corn for the Relief of the poor Inhabitants there. If your Lord[shi]p pleases I will make up w[ha]t I have already given them on your Acc[oun]t 10 Guineas'.[35] Again, to the Marquis the amount was small but to the poor it meant the difference between food and hunger: that they expected more is indicative that he was the person to whom they naturally looked to provide charity in times of need.

The Rockinghams became involved personally in the affairs and concerns of their tenants. Two undated letters from Lady Rockingham to her husband show this very clearly. In one letter it seems that 'young Evans' had died and his mother was as yet unaware of it. Lady Rockingham sympathised with the mother and felt that she must

say and do everything kind and comfortable towards her, for let people

have never so many faults when they are oppress'd by affliction,
humanity and Christianity prompts one to give all the comfort one
can.[36]

The Marchioness does not seem to have liked Mrs Evans much. She
did like Captain Newton who lived near Wentworth and who was
dying: he had sent her a dog and a dove. In return she urged
Rockingham to visit Newton before he died and if possible to move
him to somewhere more comfortable. The letter concluded by Lady
Rockingham saying that no doubt the Marquis had already called and
done whatever he could.[37] In 1770 Adam West of Street Farm was
dying: William Martin the estate agent thought it was

exceeding kind of your Lordship to consider West in the manner you
do ... he has a great family [of six small children] *so that any*
kindness your Lordship may chuse [*sic*] *to render him, will be a great*
act of Charity.[38]

It seems that Rockingham did not remove the family from the farm
and in 1773 he was paying an annuity to Edmund West of
Greasbrough Park.[39] Perhaps the most revealing letter with reference
to the Rockinghams' attitude towards their servants - again undated -
is one in which Lady Rockingham gave vent to her feelings at the news
that Lord Grosvenor had lost £26,000 on one bet:

Monstrous indeed! quite wicked in my opinion, so to rob the fatherless
and poor, & even his own family; It is frightful to think what an
acc[oun]*t of our Stewardship we shall have to make at the Great*
Day, for I fear none can say that they strictly fulfil the Divine Will, in
the Gifts he so bounteously bestows. [40]

The maintenance of the house was an ongoing programme and there
were permanent staff to deal with the various jobs. Benjamin Burgon
was an upholsterer, John White a cabinet maker, William Eggart a
gilder. John Salkeld was employed as a painter and John Cooper as a
carpenter. John Salkeld worked hard, but sometimes he must have
been driven to distraction by his employers. One of his jobs was to
paint the house inside and out when the Rockinghams were away from
Wentworth, but Lady Rockingham was likely to change her mind
about the colour schemes. In 1773 the long gallery and Green Room
next to it had been decorated. Once the work was completed she
wished that 'the doors had been painted white, but I fear if they were
done now it would smell' when they returned home, so 'I fear they
must remain as they are except the Painter is quite sure of getting the

smell off in a fortnight or three weeks'.[41] John Smith's sole occupation was to carry coal into each room of the house from the beginning of January until 26 May each year. Any man with that job earned his money: the house consumed nine hundred chaldrons of coal annually.[42] For this, he was paid the princely sum of £7 p.a. Another specialist employed by the Marquis for almost twenty years was Charles Clerici, a scagliola craftsman.[43] Clerici was paid a guinea a week and was responsible for making chimney pieces, pedestals and tables for the mansion. One puzzle concerns the floor in the Great [now Marble] Saloon, which is 60 feet square. Eighteenth century records show that it was almost the singlehanded work of Clerici, but recent work in repairing the floor shows that it was made of pure marble: it can only be assumed that Clerici was a marble craftsman as well. In 1774 Clerici moved to Rockingham's house in Grosvenor Square, London, to work on the interior decoration there.

In May each year the house cleaning began. Men were employed to remove rubbish from the house[44] and William Eyre swept the chimneys for £2. The front of the house was cleaned and painted; the lamp-posts were serviced, cleaned and painted also. All 365 windows were cleaned and the woodwork was painted. Any necessary plastering was done and the gutters were cleaned out. The beds were cleaned and refilled[45] and the carpets were removed and beaten. The general impression is that while Lord and Lady Rockingham were away the whole house was turned upside down.

The park and gardens had their own staff. Listed in the wages bills are such people as gardeners, gamekeepers and under-keepers, a 'rattcatcher' [*sic*], a pheasant-keeper and a mole-catcher.[46] Rockingham also employed a 'ruffrider' [horse-breaker], a post-boy and a dog-feeder.[47] The resident Surveyor of Works was Saintforth Wroe who had charge of 56 men[48] and who was paid £35 p.a. for ensuring that landscaping, repairs and alterations were completed satisfactorily.

The gardens received a great deal of time and attention. The gardener was paid £30 p.a., the same as the housekeeper, and 24 labourers were employed at a total cost of over £20 per month.[49] The peach houses covered about eight acres and were heated by a 'great stove' which had been designed by the Marquis himself. In August, 1772, he was able to ask for pineapples, melons, peaches and other fruit to be sent to him in Wimbledon from the Wentworth greenhouses. Cherries, oranges and grapes were also grown in the hothouses and in September, 1780, the Marquis compiled a list of about 350 'Exotick [*sic*] Plants at Wentworth'.[50] Finding a head gardener who could manage such an extensive range of unusual and difficult plants, besides ensuring that the needs of the housekeeper were met, seems to have been a problem. In 1766 the post was held by James Kennedy; in 1773 it was held by John Turner and in 1782 Benjamin Henderson was the incumbent.[51]

Rockingham also kept an aviary 'containing a prodigious number of foreign birds, particularly pencil and gold pheasants, cockatoos, Mollaca [sic] doves &c., &c.'[52] He had three China geese and two horned owls, peacocks and peahens. He employed an aviary keeper and assistant to look after the birds. Near the aviary was the menagerie which included a bear pit.[53] The Marquis was sent deer and moose from America[54] and other animals such as camels were kept although there was little success with them. The moose was not at Wentworth: it was kept in the garden of the Grosvenor Square house, and no doubt entertained the human inhabitants when it began to bellow at night.

Paul Bowns was employed as the pheasant keeper at an annual salary of £12 although the Marquis took a personal interest in the rearing of the birds. In 1774 he gave orders as to how the pens were to be divided and decided that only golden pheasants were to be bred. Bowns was told to be particularly attentive to the breeding of a large stock of them that year, probably for shooting,[55] possibly as ornamental birds. Whether Bowns took this involvement of the Marquis as interest or interference is debatable.

Other estate workers included a blacksmith, a whole range of stable staff (Rockingham kept a stud at Wentworth), a corn man, butcher, saddler, grooms, gatekeepers, a cowkeeper, a miller and a dairymaid.[56] Wentworth Woodhouse was an economic unit in its own right with a hard core of loyal and reliable staff who lived a life of service to the Marquis and his wife. Many of them received annuities when they retired and all were well looked after by the Rockinghams even though they were no longer in their employment.

Family names recur throughout the records of wages. Joshua Cobb, the head keeper, had started his employment at Wentworth as a hunting groom to the then Lord Malton in 1740.[57] By 1753 he was a groom and by 1766 he was a gamekeeper earning £40 p.a. - £10 more than the house-keeper. He kept that post until at least 1771.[58] Cobb, 'my old Stud Groom and park keeper' died in 1780[59] so the Marquis employed young Joshua in his place, at the same salary, and continued to retain the widowed Mrs Cobb who had worked on the estate for 35 years. Another member of the Cobb family was Stephen, the servant whom Rockingham took with him in

December, 1745, when he absconded from the militia at Pontefract to join the Duke of Cumberland at Carlisle. Thomas and Elizabeth Hankin, Sarah and George Womack, and John and Sarah Cooper are other examples of father-daughter or husband-wife teams working for the Rockinghams.

Wentworth Woodhouse demanded large numbers of employees to keep it operating in what was a labour-intensive age. The craftsmen needed labourers as assistants; all the fetching and carrying had to be done by muscle-power. Even something as simple as washing bottles had to be done by hand: in 1763 Thomas Cusworth spent the whole of October in the brewhouse doing just that.

The trouble with servants, of course, was that they had to be directed and watched, so that untoward activities did not get out of hand. It does seem that the Townley episode was the only one which upset the smooth running of Wentworth Woodhouse: perhaps the Rockinghams were model employers who cared for their staff, perhaps they overlooked misdemeanours - or maybe they were simply lucky.

Notes and References

1. Wentworth Woodhouse Muniments in Sheffield Archives, W.W.M. A1204. Inventory of household goods 1782. Some 130 rooms are listed by name including the winter bedchamber, summer bedchamber, Lord Rockingham's gun closet, Bedlam and pickle closet.
2. W.W.M. R186-46; R186-19; R2A-29; A1100.
3. W.W.M. A1380.
4. W.W.M. A1452. Meat butchered.
5. W.W.M. A1380. List of servants fed at the Marquis' expense.
6. W.W.M. R186-19 and A1380. Servants' wages 1766 and 1772.
7. W.W.M. R186-24. William Martin to Rockingham, 25 November, 1767.
8. W.W.M. A1100 and A5.
9. W.W.M. A234. Account for eggs for the year: £6. 5s. 0d.
10. W.W.M. Unnumbered bundle following R170/R175, September, 1756, to August, 1757.
11. W.W.M. R187-14. William Martin to Rockingham, 24 May, 1770.
12. W.W.M. R191-1. Martin to Rockingham, after 9 April, 1772.
13. W.W.M. R191-2. Rockingham's draft reply to Martin.
14. W.W.M. A1100. List of servants.
15. W.W.M. R186-46 and R186-35b.
16. W.W.M. A1099.
17. Copy of Wentworth Parish Registers, held by Doncaster Archives Department. All housekeepers were addressed as 'Mrs' whether they were married or not.
18. W.W.M. Stewards' Papers 1-1; 2-6.
19. W.W.M. A1380 and R186-46.
20. W.W.M. Stewards' Papers 2-5. Lady Rockingham to Hall, 22 May, 1773.
21. W.W.M. A1100.
22. W.W.M. Stewards' Papers 1-17. Rockingham to Hall, 29 June, 1773.
23. W.W.M. Stewards' Papers 2-8 and A1100.
24. W.W.M. R143-13. Lady Mary Watson-Wentworth(?) to Rockingham, 21 October, 1764. The letter is unsigned, but it does look like her writing.
25. W.W.M. R143-14. John Milbanke (Rockingham's brother-in-law) to Rockingham, 22 October, 1764; R143-15, Duke of Newcastle to Rockingham, 23 October, 1764.
26. The letters, tied together, bear the inscription 'These letters taken out of my Lord's pockets, April 29, 1765'.

27. W.W.M. Stewards' Papers 2-6. Lady Rockingham to Hall, 15 June, 1773.
28. W.W.M. Stewards' Papers 2-14. Lady Rockingham to Hall, 1 July, 1775.
29. W.W.M. R183-35b and A1099.
30. W.W.M. A1298. London expenses 1762.
31. W.W.M. R186-46; A234; R1-403b; R174-4; R192-1.
32. W.W.M. A1100.
33. W.W.M. A1002. 30 April, 1778.
34. W.W.M. A1001. 27 March, 1774.
35. W.W.M. R184. Battie to Rockingham, 2 March, 1757.
36. W.W.M. R168-42. Lady to Lord Rockingham, undated.
37. W.W.M. R168-52. Lady to Lord Rockingham, undated.
38. W.W.M. R187-20. Martin to Rockingham, 23 July, 1770.
39. W.W.M. A1100.
40. W.W.M. R168-9 Lady to Lord Rockingham, undated.
41. W.W.M. Stewards' Papers 2-6. Lady Rockingham to Hall, 15 June, 1773.
42. W.W.M. R140-50. Edmund Burke to Lady Rockingham, 16 January, 1780. A chaldron weighed about 252 cwt., so weekly consumption of coal works out at 22 tons. It was carried through the house in buckets.
43. Scagliola is a kind of artificial marble plasterwork produced from gypsum and glue with a surface of marble dust.
44. W.W.M. A1519.
45. W.W.M. R187-14.
46. W.W.M. A1099. Wages paid in 1766.
47. W.W.M. R186-51.
48. W.W.M. A1380. There were twenty masons, five joiners, thirteen carpenters and eighteen labourers.
49. W.W.M. A1507. Wages paid in 1772.
50. R201b-35. 18 September, 1780.
51. W.W.M. A1099, A1100 and A1101.
52. Arthur Young, *A Six Months Tour Through the North of England,* 6 vols., (London, Strahan and Nicoll, 1771), Vol. 1, 294.
53. This can still be seen. It is now in the gardens of the Wentworth Garden Centre.
54. W.W.M. R187-20. William Martin, June, 1769.
55. W.W.M. A1380. Rockingham's notes, 2 February, 1774.
56. W.W.M. A1099, A1100 and A1101. Wages paid in 1766, 1773 and 1782 respectively.
57. PwF 9145. Rockingham to Duke of Portland, 14 February, 1780. The Portland Papers are held at the University of Nottingham.
58. W.W.M. A1100. List of servants, September, 1771.
59. PwF 9145. Rockingham to Portland, 14 February, 1780.

Acknowledgements

I am indebted to Olive, Countess Fitzwilliam's Wentworth Settlement Trustees and the Director of Leisure Services, Sheffield City Council, for permission to use the Wentworth Woodhouse Muniments; to the Wentworth Estates Offices for permission to use the photographs of the estate buildings; to the occupants of the occupied buildings for allowing the photographs to be taken and to my nephew, Ian Williamson, for his expertise and time in taking them. My thanks also are due to Nottingham University for permission to use the Portland Papers, to Tony Munford at Rotherham Central Library's Archives section and to the staff in the library at Rotherham College of Arts and Technology for locating and providing the contemporary illustrations. I am grateful also to Barrie & Jenkins (publishers) for permission to use the illustrations in Figures 1 and 2 which are taken from Margot Lister's book, *Costume,* pp. 244, 261, 270 and 272.

7. ARCHITECTS OF NO SLENDER MERIT: PLATT OF ROTHERHAM, 1700-1810

by Brian Elliott

ANYONE INTERESTED IN THE CLASSIC architecture of southern Yorkshire will have noticed not infrequent references to buildings associated with the Platt family, especially to those of John Platt II (1728-1810) whose numerous commissions included work on churches and chapels, church monuments, bridges, industrial and public buildings, town houses and great and small country mansions.[1] Geographically Platt's building work and business concerns extended into Cheshire, Derbyshire, Nottinghamshire and Lincolnshire. Today, in the Rotherham area alone, three substantial Platt buildings, as can be seen by reference to Figures 1-3, remain intact: the

Figure 1.1.(*Main illustration*) The Feoffees Charity School, The Crofts, Rotherham, as it appeared in 1965. *Rotherham Archives (2252)*. The building was in danger of complete demolition by the 1970s but thankfully saved and restored in 1980-81 and is now **(Figure 1.2** *(inset)***)** a key feature of The Crofts conservation area. *The Author*

Figure 2. Thundercliffe Grange *c*.1903. Notice the attic storey, added after Platt's work was completed. *Rotherham Archives (1991)*

now restored Feoffees Charity School, Thundercliffe Grange and (the attributed) Ferham House. His versatility in the use and understanding of sculptured and decorative stone can also be seen in several worthy marble monuments within Rotherham's magnificent medieval parish church (Figures 4-5) whilst fine interior features are extant as staircases at Clifton House and Aston Hall.

Figure 3. The stylish front of Ferham House, Masbrough, built for Jonathan Walker in typical 'pattern book' and Platt style; three bays, two and a half storeys, roof pediment, central 'Venetian' window, tripartite doorway and projecting bay windows to left and right, 1780s. Attributed. The listed building is now used as a private nursing home. *The Author*

John Platt II was, as a recent study has shown, from 'a true family of hereditary masons' taking 'great pride in their deep family roots in the profession'.[2] His father, George, described as 'mason', married Elizabeth, daughter of William Rickard of Doncaster, carpenter, at Conisbrough Church, on 7 May, 1727, and settled at Red House, Woodlaithes in Thrybergh parish where John II, the eldest of three sons, was born on 9 March, 1728/29.[3] This John could possibly claim descent from a Richard Platt, master mason, whose name is apparently inscribed alongside the date 1533 on the tower of Mobberley Church, Cheshire.[4] More certainly, as can be seen by reference to the Platt family tree (Figure 6) John Platt II's paternal grandfather, Edmund, who died at Lyme Park, Cheshire in 1715, was also a stone mason. Two of Edmund's sons, John Platt (the elder) and George Platt (John's father) moved into south Yorkshire, probably

Figure 4. The Cutforthay memorial table can be seen by the north door o Rotherham Parish Church. Signed 'J Platt', it was completed in 1799, and therefore one of Platt's last commissions Robert Cutforthay was a Rotherham wine and spirit merchant. *The Author*

leaving their elder brother, Edmund II, to carry on the family business on the Derbyshire-Cheshire border where prospects for all three brothers must have been limited. The older brothers were undoubtedly attracted by more certain commissions via the large and numerous small estates in southern Yorkshire. Thrybergh is not only situated on good quality

Figure 5. Marble monument to Mrs Catherine Buck, 1778, south transept, Rotherham Parish Church, completed at a cost of £80. Catherine was the wife of Samuel, the wealthy Rotherham attorney. Ann (née Fitzgerald), Platt's wife, was the illegitimate daughter of Captain Thomas Buck, son of Thomas Buck of Carnaby, Bridlington and half-brother of Samuel Buck. *The Author*

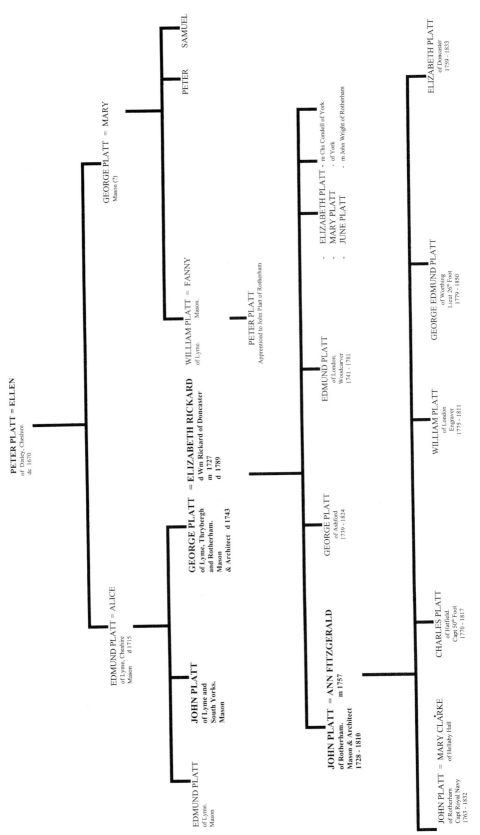

Figure 6. The Platt family tree.

sandstone but also close to the magnesian limestone escarpment, and therefore had considerable quarrying potential. Indeed, George Platt is known to have obtained a small quarry at Thrybergh.[5] The mason's craft continued to be linked to the quarries from which the stone was obtained.

John Platt I ('the elder')

Though information about his work is scanty, the elder John Platt appears to have been the first of the brothers to establish the family business in south Yorkshire. Writing in his journal for 9 and 10 January, 1769, his nephew, John Platt II, who was then adding the dome to St Paul's, Sheffield's new chapel-of-ease (Figure 7), described it as 'built by Mr Tunnicliffe and my Uncle John Platt'.[6] The exceptionally stylish design of St Paul's and the loss of its building accounts has led to conjecture concerning its architect. John Tunnicliffe of Dalton, near Rotherham, who subsequently worked for the first Marquis of Rockingham at Wentworth Woodhouse, has been recently described as a 'likely candidate' but Platt may well have made a contribution to its design.[7] Described as 'the most impressive Georgian building in Sheffield, St Paul's was completed in 1721 but

Figure 7. St Paul's Church. Watercolour by E. Blore, 1819.

because of a dispute over the presentation of the curate remained closed for a further nineteen years.[8] Sadly, one of the best Baroque churches in Yorkshire, it was demolished in 1936. In 1729 the elder Platt was paid £10 10s 6d. for taking down the steeple of Chapel-en-le-Frith church in Derbyshire.[9]

George Platt, 1700-1743

A little more information is available about the work of the younger of the brothers, George Platt, a mason-architect with a growing reputation whose untimely death at the age of 43, apparently from consumption whilst convalescing at Bristol Hot Wells, must have made the continuation of the family business a precarious prospect. His building commissions included executed designs to extend the medieval village church at Chapel-en-le-Frith (1731) where his older brother had recently worked. Seven years later Platt was at Hathersage church, pointing the spire, tower and fabric, said to have been done 'without any scaffold...'[10]

George Platt's most impressive known commission was his contribution to the design and certainly the building of Cusworth Hall (Figure 8) for William Wrightson, MP, between 1740-1742. This was about six years before Paine came on the scene, initially making relatively minor alterations to the fine double-pile house and then adding two pavilions and remodelling the south front.[11] Wrightson had a practical approach to quality control, apparently supervising the building work from a bo'sun's chair attached to scaffolding.[12] Platt

Figure 8. Cusworth Hall, Palladian north front, executed by George Platt in *c*.1741. The curving flight of steps is not unlike an earlier example to be seen at Lyme Hall, Stockport, Cheshire, where the Platts were at work in the 1720s. *The Author*

may also have initiated work at Wadworth Hall, only a few miles to the south of Cusworth, completed by Paine in 1749-50.[13] Godfrey Copley of Sprotbrough Hall was another grateful client, taking the trouble to write to Platt during the latter's final illness. George Platt was buried in Rotherham parish church yard and a monumental inscription, now lost, referred to him as 'Architect and Builder' and 'a Man of great abilities in his profession and the strictest integrity in his dealings'.[14]

John Platt II, 1728-1810

Elizabeth, George Platt's widow, described as 'a woman of excellent understanding and uncommon patience' had the formidable task of bringing up a family of seven children aged between two and sixteen as well as overseeing business until her eldest son, John II, was able to take over.[15] However, despite his youth, John II was already more than familiar with both practical (he was his father's apprentice) and business demands, as can be seen from an extract from one of several letters sent to his 'Honoured Father' in Bristol, dated 28 November, 1742, describing work in progress at Gainsborough and Cusworth:

> *I got my Bill paid at Mr. [Godfrey] Copley's and Mr Tomlinson, with a deal of hums and has. We go on with our diamond paving pretty well, only we want the stone you ordered down the River, but it has been at the waterside almost a week. John Mosely has worked most of the columns for the Doric door... We have nothing material about business only pray send word who must go to Gainsbrough to set the door case and chimney piece if it be ready. All the servants and workmen at Cusworth gives their service to you and is very glad to hear you are a little better.[16]*

Elizabeth, who was to remain a widow for 46 years, may have called upon her craftsman brother, William Rickard, to assist with family/business affairs during John Platt's minority and the support of long serving foreman Thomas Senior.

Masons and Architects

Before examining John Platt's achievements in detail it would be appropriate here to consider the building trade as it existed at the time of his first known commissions. This may help us to understand the term 'mason-architect', often used with respect to the Platts. For most practitioners the art and skill of building was a craft-based occupation that had not significantly changed since medieval times. But there was a nucleus of professionals emerging. In our area and elsewhere James Paine was one of the new independent professionals whose extensive and lucrative practice was both a product of a growing and well-earned reputation and an increasing number of patrons with necessary 'new wealth' – usually from industrial or commercial enterprises, profits of office or smart marriage – so essential to meet the huge costs of large-scale and fashionable building. Craft-based architects could, as we know from the example of John Carr, rise to become professionals of considerable regional merit. There were other worthy men, such as the Platts, who had inherited great building and sculpturing skills along with a first-hand knowledge of stone. They were sought after by both wealthy and middling patrons because of proven skills and relative economy. They were also an essential local component in executing the grand design of the new professionals. Thus, John Platt II worked on buildings associated with both Paine and Carr, and alongside some of the best master craftsmen of Yorkshire. The survival of a small number of Platt drawings also confirms his ability as a draftsman, a skill that Colin Campbell considered essential:[17]

> ...*he must learn Designing, and to draw all five Orders of Architecture, according to their several Proportions.*[18]

'Fashionable country architects', according to Howard Colvin, 'after consulting a client over features' would often assemble a team of craftsmen, and 'sign' their designs to confirm that they had been 'allowed'.[19] Campbell's *Vitruvius Britannicus*, editions of Leoni's *Palladio*, Kent's *Designs of Inigo Jones* and *Rules for Drawing the Several Parts of Architecture* by James Gibbs, were the textbooks of the new building style. There was also a growing bibliography of architectural manuals no doubt 'thumbed to pieces in builders' yards'.[20]

Platt's earliest known commissions date from the late 1740s and anticipated the kind of contrasting work and necessary travel that became salient features of his business. In 1748 we know that he provided an estimate 'for Rebuilding a New Bridge near Stockport' and completed a monument for the Hopkins family in the parish church at Gainsborough.[21]

On 30 December, 1750, 'Mr Platt Mason', was paid £93 11s 0d 'for Mason Work done at ye New House at the Folds', part of a recreational area being created by the Earl of Scarbrough on the Sandbeck estate, only a few years before the commencement of the rebuilding of the Hall.[22] A further sum of £63 10s 0d 'for Mason Work done' appears in the steward's accounts for 24 September, 1751.[23] Platt's abilities must already have been of some consequence since his bills accounted for almost a third of the entire cost of building.[24] The steward's accounts, carefully kept at this time by John Bilham, provide us with a marvellous insight into both the complexities of commissioning and the building process. Building necessitated private arrangements being made for the acquisition and delivery of appropriate materials as well as the recruitment of a variety of largely independent master craftsmen.[25] Apart from the services of Platt, payments were made to suppliers or makers of lead, lime, pitch, bricks, blue slate and 'Westmoreland slate', 'wallstone', 'Roach [Roche] Abbey Stone', ropes (for scaffolding and pulleys), linseed oil (for paint), deals, nails, locks, hinges and ironwork, glass, hair and plaster. Craftsmen employed on site included carpenters, plasterers, metalworkers, bricklayers and masons, slaters and pavers, and plumber-glaziers, again a typical array of independent skill that was required even on such a modest building project. Eleven labourers were also used, accumulating 545 days' work mostly at nine pence per day, mainly for digging and levelling.

Although not involving the Platts, a similar assembly of local craftsmen and materials was required to build a new bakehouse, malthouse, stables, shops and associated structures when the Duke of Leeds began refashioning Barnsley market place from the late 1730s.[26] Interestingly, Platt was called to Barnsley in 1767, redesigning the shambles and rebuilding the old market hall by which time he had an established reputation for 'public' projects,

Figure 9. Penistone Market and former Cloth Hall ('Printing Office'), *c*.1890. *Penistone Almanack, 1953*

having in 1756 designed and built the shambles and butchers' cross at Doncaster, and, more prestigiously and at a cost of £800, completed the fine Market House and Cloth Hall at Penistone in 1763 (Figure 9).[27] Much later, in 1781, he was paid £172 12s 6d by the Feoffees of Rotherham for building a new Market Hall.

Wentworth Castle and Wortley

Platt's first important country house commission came from William Wentworth, the second Earl of Strafford (1722-91) who in 1755 asked him to examine the 'castle in the wilderness' (Figure 10) in the grounds at Stainborough, near Barnsley, which, although only erected in 1728 had fallen into disrepair. After an objection from His Lordship, Platt reduced his estimate of £96 8s 0d to 80 guineas, though he was not afraid to inform his aristocratic patron that 'it will be a Troublesome affair & well Deserves the whole Sum'.[28]

Platt had a practical involvement in executing the new south front of Wentworth Castle, which was probably designed by the Earl himself but supposedly built by Charles Ross of London, even though the latter was only required to attend the site twice a year. One wonders if Platt was what Ross referred to as 'a clever man who understands Drawing and Several Branches of building'.[29] Platt may

Figure 10. The 'miniature castle' at Stainborough. Drawing by E. Darlow, 1932.

Figure 11. The Palladian range at Wentworth Castle, completed for the Earl of Strafford in 1762. *The Author*

have executed the finer masonry work on the thirteen bay and three storey Palladian facade (Figure 11); but we know that he was responsible for carving the six great Corinthian capitals along with the griffin and foliar decoration (Figure 12) contained in the central pediment, completed in 1762, receiving a substantial fee of £642 2s

Figure 12. Wentworth Castle, pediment detail showing carving executed by John Platt. *The Author*

2d for the work.[30] He was also paid £129 17s 4d for the completion of several marble chimney pieces.[31] Platt's journal records that on 2 August, 1765, he had 'Got all finished at Wentworth Castle so as to take off ye men';[32] but he was back at Wentworth Castle for a very special occasion on 5 August, 1766, 'with Lord Strafford, the Duke of Cumberland, and 16 other Lords, Knights and Esqrs. etc' for a dinner celebrating the completion of the front, an invitation surely acknowledging his role in its building.[33] At the dinner the Earl may well have discussed plans for the completion of a Corinthian temple to be built to overlook the south lawn, for Platt was subsequently commissioned to carve the four columns to equate with those on the new range (Figure 13).[34] As can be seen by reference to Platt's building activities summarised in the appendix of this essay, the 1760s were an extremely busy period for the young mason-architect apart from a gap in 1765 due to the start of his considerable business associations with Rotherham Pottery which has been discussed in some detail elsewhere.[35]

Figure 13. Wentworth Castle, The Temple. *The Author*

Figure 14. Wortley Hall, south front. *The Author*

Platt had a long association with Wortley Hall and estate (Figure 14). As early as 1758 Edward Wortley Montagu had consulted him concerning 'finishing the [east?] wing' at Wortley. The original architect of the Hall was the Venetian Giacomo Leoni who had worked with the Platts at Lyme Hall, near Stockport, Cheshire in the 1720s.[36] Wortley Montagu had, according to Joseph Hunter, begun rebuilding the Hall in about 1743 and work continued under the direction of his daughter and heir, Lady Bute, from 1761.

Whilst building work was in progress Lady Bute – when not in London – lived at Wharncliffe Lodge and on the family's Carlton estate at St Helen's where in 1768 Platt recorded the delivery 'of Plans for ye Farmhouse at St. Ellen for Lady Bute'.[37] Sir Sydney Wortley (d.1727) had what has been reliably described as 'a sumptuous mansion' built there, for the convenience of his mistress, probably the reason why the old hall at Wortley fell into decline.[38] It was pulled down in the late eighteenth century but in 1783 the east and south front were still visible when the antiquarian Brooke described it as having seven windows in a row in each facade, was two storeys high and ornamented with Corinthian pilasters, architrave, frieze and cornice, all richly carved. The Wortley arms and crest were carved over the door of the east front and on the pediments of the windows of the south front which also had various busts of goddesses Diana and Astaea said to be still intact.[39] When the present writer visited the site in 1975, St Helen's Farm, though deserted, remained in situ and a small but clearly high status building, possibly once associated with the mansion, was still evident.

Platt's journal contains many references to building work at Wortley Hall. A major project involved work on the west wing offices, starting in April, 1788, and completed by 16 August, Platt recording that he had 'Got on ye roof & dined 40 men' which must have been a splendid sight.[40] Platt was contracted for the work at a fee of £861 11s 0d but continued to be busy preparing estimates and executing work on the interior. On 6 September, 1790, for example, a journal entry shows that he 'sent to Wortley Hall ironwork for ye staircase & lead for ridge of [the] old roof', probably one of his last tasks there.[41]

Thundercliffe Grange and other Local Commissions

Another locally important commission concerned the building of Thundercliffe Grange, near Kimberworth for the Earl of Effingham between 1776-83.[42] Again, Platt's journal enables us to follow the progress of the work, beginning with plans drawn up in February and 'setting out ye house' on 16 December, 1776. Five of Platt's masons/workmen were busy digging the cellars on 9 September, 1778. On 5 April, 1779, Platt agreed to execute the east wing for £905, the building and mason's work apparently sub-contracted to H. Ibbotson. Foundations for the east wing offices began in June, 1782. The Earl hosted the usual celebratory dinner to mark the completion of the main building on 25 October, 1783. Originally of two storeys, 'The Grange' was subsequently extended by the building of an attic storey and remains an impressive sight when viewed from the M1 motorway.

It would be impossible to do justice to Platt's extensive practice within the constraints of this article but suffice to say that prestigious projects in Sheffield during the 1770s such as Page Hall, for the banker Thomas Broadbent, Mount Pleasant, for the Rotherham merchant Francis Hurt Sitwell (for £3,480) and the new Playhouse, further enhanced Platt's reputation as the leading resident architect of the region. It was, therefore, understandable that in 1775 he was in demand in his home town, the obvious choice for the Feoffees of the Common Lands as the architect and builder of a charity school to be located in the old beast market, which he agreed to execute at a price of £235 though insisting that the Feoffees arranged to prepare the site and provide the building stone. Though Platt exceeded the estimate by more than £22 he was, as we have already noted, called upon to build a Market House (though it was never completed) and also to make alterations to the 'Prison on the Bridge' (the old chapel).[43] In 1775 he waived his fee for survey work for the installation of the Snetzler organ in Rotherham Parish Church, apparently enjoying meeting the great man.

For other typical examples of Platt's Rotherham work, clearly influenced by the pattern book but gracefully executed, it would be remiss not to refer to the stables and offices completed for Tooker at Moorgate Hall (1764), Canklow House and Masbrough Hall stable block (1768: Figure 15), as well as Clough House completed in about 1780 for the coal owner John Hirst and, for Jonathan Walker, the extant and very stylish Ferham House, completed in the 1780s.

The Ashford Marble Works

Figure 15. Drawings of Canklow Hall (1767) and Masboro Hall Stables (1768) in typical pattern book style.

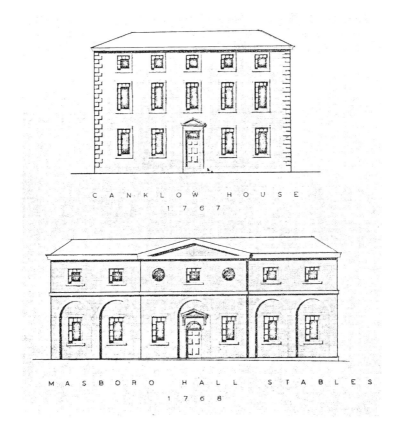

John Platt's work as a sculptor and carver resulted in some twenty commissions for church monuments, usually provided during the winter months, and each costing between £60-80, therefore very useful income before the commencement of spring building works. The work also facilitated the use of marble from Platt's second business concern, his marble polishing works at Ashford, near Bakewell in Derbyshire, where he also rented quarries.[44] The marble was of sufficient quality that it was, in 1789, said to have been 'not only in much request in this Kingdom but is likewise exported to very distant parts of the world';[45] and in 1819 the sawing and polishing works was said to have been 'the first ever established in England'.[46] Platt's enthusiasm was so advanced that he bought out his partners, becoming sole owner but this coincided with his failing health and the works management was entrusted to his less able brother, George, who found the job too difficult, sales suffering to such an extent that in 1811, following Platt's death, the business was repossessed by the landowner, the Duke of Rutland.

Interestingly, Platt also had a very early though short-lived interest in developing the Blue John fluor-spar found at Castleton, apparently inspired by handling pieces in Earl Fitzwilliam's garden at Wentworth.[47]

Final Years

John Platt had four sons but none of them chose to follow their father in his architectural and building practice. In old age, failing health and certainly suffering from the financial setbacks of his business activities, Rotherham's and southern Yorkshire's leading architect experienced a somewhat unhappy final few years. In his will, written in 1804, in which he referred to himself as 'Architect' he left £300 each (from the 'profits' of his estate, after his wife's death) to children, William and George, the former, an engraver, committing suicide in tragic circumstances in 1811.[48] Platt's daughter, Elizabeth was to receive £500 and the residue of his estate was instructed to be shared between all his children: John, Charles, William, George and Elizabeth. Earlier, Platt had sold a quarry that he owned in Rotherham to James Ross, one of his workmen who in fact died in 1805. Platt also sold the house that he had designed and built for himself in the fashionable Westgate area of Rotherham in 1808 to a neighbour for £206, though he continued to live there until his death, at the age of 82, on 14 December, 1810. He and his wife, who had predeceased him by fourteen months were interred in the family vault in Rotherham churchyard and a marble tablet, no longer apparent, was established in the north transept.

It was Joseph Hunter who described Platt as an architect 'of no slender merit' and in many respects he could be regarded, at least regionally and certainly locally, as one of the last of the great builder-architects. Thus by about 1840, as Howard Colvin astutely acknowledged, 'it would have been difficult to discover a worthy representative of a class that was admirable in the history of English Architecture'[49] The age of the contractor had arrived.

Appendix

John Platt II

Age	Year	Commissions & Building Activities *c.*1748-*c.*1800
20	1748	Stockport Bridge, Cheshire, plans & estimates.
	1748	Gainsborough Church, marble tablet for Hopkins family.
21	1749	Gate Burton Hall, Lincolnshire, summer house.
21-25	1749-53	Cusworth Hall, with Paine?
22	1750	Sprotbrough Hall, unspecified works.
22	1750-51	Building work at The Folds, Sandbeck Park, for Earl of Scarbrough.
22-28	1750-56	Ormsby Hall, Lincs. for William Burnell Massingberd.
28	1756	Wentworth Castle, repairs to 'miniature castle'.
28	1756	Doncaster Shambles.
(29	1757	Marriage)
30	1758	Wortley Hall, East wing finished.
32+	1760-65	Wentworth Castle, south front, chimney pieces, garden monuments, etc.
32+	1760-90	Wortley Hall, various building activities.
35	1763	Tankersley Park, building work for Wentworth Woodhouse estate.
	1763	Penistone Shambles (Cloth Hall), for Mr Hallfield of Wadsworth.
	1763	Eckington Church, remodelled south aisle & porch.
36	1764	St George's Church, Doncaster, erection of pews and galleries.
	1764	Bow Bridge, Rotherham.

	1764	Tankersley Park, gothic bridge.
	1764	Moorgate Hall, Rotherham, stables & offices for Mr Tooker.
	1764	Surveyed all County bridges.
	1764	Chimney piece for Lord Lincoln, Clumber Park.
37	1765	Attercliffe Bridge, Sheffield, estimates.
	1765	Masbrough glasshouse for Aaron Walker, John Wright & Dr. Pearson.
	1765	Rotherham Pottery, for Fenney & Wood.
39	1767	Canklow House, for J. Taylor.
	1767	House at Wentworth.
	1767	The Hospital Bridge, Sheffield, estimates for Duke of Norfolk.
40	1768	Masbrough Hall, Rotherham, for Samuel Walker.
	1768	Two houses in High Street, Rotherham, for Earl of Effingham.
	1768	Barnsley Shambles, for Duke of Leeds.
41	1769	Lady's Bridge, Sheffield, under supervision of John Watson.
	1769	Rotherham Bridge widened, under supervision of John Carr.
	1769	St. Paul's Church, Sheffield, completed steeple.
42	1770	Attercliffe Bridge, work carried out under supervision of Jno. Watson.
	1770	Copley monument in marble, Sprotbrough Church.
	1770	Monument for Mr Wolrich, Leeds Parish Church.
43	1771	St Paul's Church, Sheffield, erected vases on balustrade and carved the capitals in the church.
45	1773	Tong Hall, Bradford, erected piers and gates.
	1773	Woodsetts Lock, Chester Canal, built, with Henry Ibbotson.
46	1774	Worsbrough Hall, Barnsley, finished drawing room, for Francis Edmunds.
46+	1774-76	Page Hall, Sheffield, built for Thomas Broadbent.
47	1775	Rotherham Parish Church, erected new organ gallery.
	1775	Hospital Chapel, Sheffield, built, to designs of Thomas Atkinson.
	1775	Canklow Bridge (?) built.
48	1776	A house in Worksop, built for Mr Stovin.
	1776	Hooton Roberts Church, 'repairs'.

	1776	Feoffees' Charity School, Rotherham, built.
	1776-77	Chimney piece & alterations for Sitwell of Renishaw Hall.
	1776-77	Marble staircase for Aston Hall.
48+	1776-83	Thundercliffe Grange, Rotherham, for the Earl of Effingham.
49	1777	A house in Westgate, Rotherham, built for Dr Wilkinson.
49+	1777-78	Mount Pleasant, Sheffield, built for Francis Hurt Sitwell.
	1777-78	Sheffield Playhouse, built (ornamental carving sub-contracted).
50	1778	A house in Sheffield, built for S. Shore, junr.
	1778	Monument to Mrs Catherine Buck, Rotherham Parish Church.
51	1779	Chapel on the Bridge, Rotherham, converted.
52	*c*1780	Ferham House, Rotherham, (attributed) for Jonathan Walker.
	*c*1780	Clough House, Rotherham, (attributed) for Mr Hirst.
56	1784	Marble staircase for Clifton Hall, Rotherham.
57	1785	Monument to Lt. Col. Downes, Rotherham Parish Church.
58	1786	Bossington Bridge (?) built.
59	1787	Marble staircase for Eastwood House.
63	1791	Masbrough Brewery, built for J. Green and Thomas Wright.
65	1793	Monument for Rev. Francis Hall, Tankersley Church.
66	1794	A house in Westgate, Rotherham, for himself.
67	1795	Independent Chapel, Rotherham, alterations for Samuel Walker.
71	1799	Monument to Robert Cutforthay, Rotherham Parish Church.

Drawings and Plans

A small number of Platt drawings can be found in Sheffield Archives (AP508). There are no Platt drawings extant in the RIBA Drawing Collection.

Platt's Journal

Available on microfilm in Rotherham Central Library, Archives and Local Studies Section.

Notes and References

1. Two other short studies have been completed concerning the Platt family: J. D. Potts' *Platt of Rotherham. Mason-Architects 1700-1810*, Sheffield, 1959 (hereafter referred to as 'Potts') and, more recently, C. M. Ross's *John Platt Mason-Architect*, published by Rotherham MBC as a [Clifton Park] Museum Information Sheet No. 11, 1984 (hereafter referred to as 'Ross'). J. H. Cockburn's article, 'A Rotherham Architect and His Family' appeared in the *Rotherham Advertiser*, 8 February, 1936. Howard Colvin's *A Biographical Dictionary of English Architects 1660-1840*, London, 1954 (hereafter referred to as 'Colvin'), continues to be the standard work of general reference. The Yorkshire West Riding volume of Nikolaus Pevsner's *Buildings of England* series, 1967 (2nd) edition, also remains a useful source as does David Hey's Yorkshire volume of *Buildings of Britain 1550-1750*, Ashbourne, 1981.
2. Ross, p.1.
3. Potts, p.1.
4. *Ibid.*
5. Ross, p.3.
6. Potts, p.3.
7. Hey, D. G., *The Fiery Blades of Hallamshire. Sheffield and its Neighbourhood, 1660-1740*, Leicester, 1991, p.281.
8. Potts, p.2.
9. Potts, p.3.
10. Potts, p.4.
11. Hey, D. G., *Buildings of Britain 1550-1750,Yorkshire*, Ashbourne, 1981, p.111.
12. *Ibid.*
13. Leach, P., *James Paine*, London, 1988, p.212.
14. The stone over the Platt family vault was apparently removed during the Corporation 'improvements' of 1950: see Potts, p.4 (fn). The tombstone epitaph is quoted in Ross, p.3.
15. Potts, p.5.
16. Ross, p.4.
17. From Campbell's *The London Tradesman*.
18. Colvin, p.3.
19. Colvin, p.7.
20. Colvin, p.9.
21. Potts, p.6.
22. Beastall, T. W., *A North Country Estate. The Lumleys and Saundersons as landowners, 1600-1900*, London & Chichester, 1975, p.83; and also quoted in Jones M. (ed) 'Sandbeck Hall and Park', in *Aspects of Rotherham 1*, Barnsley, 1995, p.91.
23. John Bilham's Accounts, 1749-51, Lumley Archive, EMA /10 and EMR/3/1. I am grateful to Alice Rodgers for drawing my attention to this source.
24. The total cost being £498 6s 6d.
25. Anyone interested in eighteenth century craftsmen would do no better than consult Geoffrey Beard's works, especially his *Georgian Craftsmen and their Work* (1966) and, more specifically, *Decorative Plasterwork in Great Britain* (1975).
26. Elliott, B., 'Barnsley: The Anatomy of a Yorkshire Market Town and its Neighbourhood, c.1660-c.1760', University of Sheffield M Phil Thesis, 1990, pp.121-22.
27. Hey, D. G., 'Penistone Market and Cloth Hall' in Elliott, B. (ed), *Aspects of Barnsley 5*, Barnsley, 1998.
28. Potts, p.6.
29. Potts p.7.
30. *Ibid.*
31. Potts, p.7; Ross, p.7.
32. Potts, p.12.
33. Potts, pp.7-8.
34. Hey, D. G., *Wentworth Castle. A Short History*, Derby, 1991, p.11.
35. Kiddell, A. J. B., 'John Platt of Rotherham, Potter and Mason Architect', in *Transactions of The*

English Ceramic Circle, Vol.5, Pt.3, London, 1962, pp.172-175 (from a paper read at the Victoria and Albert Museum, 22 April, 1961).
36. Ross, p.7.
37. *Ibid.*
38. Hunter, J., *South Yorkshire*, Vol.2, London, (1831), p.396.
39. *Ibid.*
40. Ross, p.7.
41. *Ibid.*
42. Ross, p.8; also see Goodchild, J., 'Matters of Concern: the Life Story of the Third Earl of Effingham', in Jones, M. (ed) *Aspects of Rotherham 1*, 1995, pp.99-112.
43. Potts, p.16.
44. Ross, pp.11-13.
45. Ross, p.12.
46. Potts, p.9.
47. Ross, p.13.
48. Ross, p.16.
49. Colvin, p.9.

Acknowledgements

For help with sources I would like to express my appreciation to Alice Rodgers and Ron Spensley; and to Tony Munford at Rotherham Local Studies and Archives. Thanks also to Professor David Hey for loaning me a copy of the Potts article. I would like to acknowledge grateful thanks to the Earl of Scarbrough and the Borthwick Institute of Historical Research (University of York) respectively for permission to quote from the Lumley Archive and the John Platt will.

8. Coal Mining on the Wentworth Estate 1740-1840

by Ian Medlicott

The Development of Coal Mining and Mining Technology

THE WENTWORTH ESTATE, located between Barnsley and Rotherham, was one of the two largest landed estates in South Yorkshire during the eighteenth and nineteenth centuries. At its centre stood Wentworth Woodhouse the residence of the Rockingham and Fitzwilliam families.[1] The estate contained rich reserves of coal that included the Barnsley (9 feet), Parkgate (5½ feet), and Silkstone (5 feet) seams (Figure 1). Between the coal seams lay deposits of ironstone, notably the Tankersley, Swallow Wood, and Lidget mines, that were worked extensively in Tankersley parish. The coal and ironstone deposits would have initially been mined where the seams outcropped and there is a record of mining at Cortworth, near Wentworth dated 15 May, 1486.[2]

The market for coal grew substantially as coal replaced charcoal in

Figure 1. Canals, coal seams, and collieries on the Wentworth estate, 1740-1840.

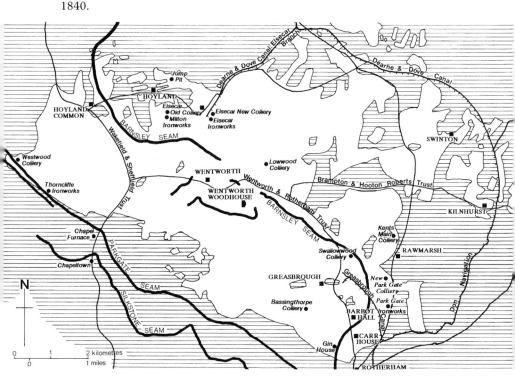

many of the manufacturing processes such as lime-burning and the production of tiles, bricks, glass, and pottery, and in the growing number of forges in the area. A further stimulus came with the adoption of coke in the iron-smelting process, and the introduction of the Newcomen engine, which enabled the deeper coal to be exploited.

During the first half of the eighteenth century coal mining on the Wentworth estate was carried out by capitalist entrepreneurs with the landowner remaining in the background as lessor. On 22 December, 1735, William Spencer of Bramley Grange, agreed to mine the coal in Barbot Hall Farm, Greasbrough Fields, Kimberworth and Ginnhouse Farm. For the coal in Kimberworth and Ginnhouse Farm twelve 'getters' could be employed at £252 per annum, and for the 'Thick Coal', and 'Swallow Wood Coal' in Barbot Hall and Greasbrough Fields, Spencer was to employ no more than six men in 'getting' coal at a rent of £126 per annum. The lease stipulated that a 'fire engine' was to be erected to drain the coal in Kimberworth and Greasbrough to lift the water at least 70 yards from the bottom of the Thick Coal to a sough that had been driven from the River Don, or if the sough was not capable of carrying the water, to lift it to the first capable level. The fire engine or atmospheric pumping engine was probably the first such engine built in South Yorkshire, as it appears that the terms of the lease were carried out, with the engine erected at Carr House.[3] John Bowden of Beighton Fields, Barlborough, Derbyshire, later took over the collieries. The 'Greasbro' field Colliery' was worked until 1749/50 when it was 'laid in', but Bowden continued to lease the Carr House Colliery. William Spencer also leased the Lowwood Colliery from the Earl of Malton on 17 October, 1737:

> ... *at ye yearly rent of 17 pounds and 17 shillings for every man Employed in working ye Colliery afors:^{d} commonly known by y:^{e} name of Lawwood Colliery &c to work six men...*[4]

Spencer sold a half share of the colliery to Richard Bingley of Bolton upon Dearne and Jonathan Smith of Ravenfield, millwright, for £210 on 15 March, 1741. Smith '... having a peculiar Talent in making Machines for mines became Employed by Mr. Spencer for ye purposes...'[5] Several small collieries were also worked on the estate at Elsecar, Westwood, Bolsterstone, Orgreave, 'Cortwood', and Swinton Common, in the 1750s.

The royal assent of the Don Navigation Act in 1726 and its construction as far as Aldwarke in 1733 and Tinsley by 1751, greatly stimulated coal mining in the Rotherham area. Presumably to take advantage of the new markets, William and Thomas Fenton took out a lease of the Bassingthorpe Colliery in 1758. The lease was initially for 21 years to mine the 'Parkgate vein', and other seams, at £324 per annum for the first two years and £648 per annum the remainder. They were allowed to employ sixteen 'Pickmen or Bottom men' plus two men for driving the endway or level, and one man for getting the 'short coals or upper seam' for the fire engine. By 1762 a waggonway had been built for a distance of two miles from the colliery to the Don Navigation near Eastwood lock, and by 1766 iron plates had replaced the wooden rails. An 1820 billhead for the Greasbrough Colliery (formerly Bassingthorpe Colliery) shows a steam-winding engine, a waggon road with horse-drawn waggons leading to the Greasbrough Canal where keel boats waited to be loaded (Figure 2). Between 30 September, 1771, and 29 September, 1780, some

Figure 2. An illustrated billhead of the Greasbrough Colliery in 1820. *WWM, St.P. 13(a) 87, Sheffield Archives*

Greasbro near Rotherham

Delivered to

on

Seven half Waggons of

Wm Fenton,

OLD PARK GATE COALS.

166,393 waggons (approximately 366,065 tons) of coal were sent from the colliery down the Don Navigation. In 1779 the rent was increased to £2,300 per annum, to work no more than 18,500 waggons (40,700 tons), rising to £2,880 per annum on a fixed 8 acres, in 1800.[6]

The conclusion of the Seven Years War in 1763, and the ensuing slump in the coal trade, coincided with the expiry of several leases on the Wentworth estate and the withdrawal of a number of lessees. Hall & Co relinquished the Elsecar Colliery while the lease of the Lowwood Colliery was not renewed following the withdrawal of the executors of Richard Bingley; the two collieries were then worked under direct estate management. In addition, John Bowden gave up the Carr House Colliery at Whitsuntide, 1764, on payment of £600 to release him from the contract.[7]

The major investment associated with coal mining on the estate before 1795, was in the construction of the Greasbrough Canal. The archives indicate that Rockingham visited the Duke of Bridgewater's Colliery at Worsley, near Manchester, and the Bridgewater Canal, noting its dimensions and reductions in the cost of transporting coal. The visit may have influenced his decision to construct the Greasbrough Canal from the Don Navigation to the Bassingthorpe Colliery. The canal would have reduced the cost of transport, provided a regular income, enabled Rockingham to raise the colliery rental, and allowed the more distant coal to be worked.

In 1769 John Varley, an assistant of James Brindley, the engineer of the Bridgewater Canal, made a survey and estimate for two lines for the canal; in 1775 John Smeaton re-surveyed the line of the canal providing an estimate of £5,951 11s 3d; and this was followed in 1778 by a further survey from William Fairbank. In October, 1778, William Jessop, who had been an apprentice to John Smeaton, calculated that the usual charge on inland navigation was $1\frac{1}{2}$d per mile, compared to a waggonway of approximately 3d per ton per mile, including laying, repairs, and keeping the horses. The canal was eventually started with the Estate Accounts recording for the first time on 24 February, 1779, 'Paid Messrs. Jessop & Gott on Account of making a Navigable Canal from Sinderbridge in Greasbrough to Communicate with the River dun – £50.[8] It ran from Cinder Bridge to a junction where a branch went towards Greasbrough village alongside the Ochre Dyke, it then continued parallel to the line of the stream to the Don Navigation, a distance of $1\frac{1}{2}$ miles. Waggon roads ran from the pits to the basins at Cinder Bridge, where limekilns had been constructed, and Ochre Dyke.[9] Fenton rented the canal at £500 per annum, but when he withdrew from mining in 1826/27 the canal became redundant and was later filled in, except for a spur from the Don Navigation to which waggonways ran from the Swallowwood and New Park Gate collieries.

The exploitation of coal in the Elsecar area was transformed by the opening of a branch of the Dearne and Dove Canal into the Elsecar valley in December, 1798. The markets opened up by the canal encouraged Fitzwilliam to sink the Elsecar New Colliery, to the Barnsley seam at a depth of $35^1/_2$ yards, and Darwin & Co to establish the Elsecar Ironworks in 1795, followed in 1801/2 by Walker & Co, of Masbrough, who built the Milton Ironworks with coal supplied from the Elsecar Old Colliery.[10]

The scale of working the Elsecar New Colliery required a more efficient method of drainage and movement of coal from the workface to the point of disposal. A Newcomen-type pumping engine was installed, four-wheeled corves were introduced with underground and surface waggon roads, and steam-driven whimseys to wind the coal to the pit top. Conductors were positioned in the shaft to prevent the corves colliding either with the shaft sides or into each other as they passed. Tipplers poured the coal directly into waggons, the waiting boats, or onto the pit stack, and by 1818 flat ropes were used to wind heavier loads at greater speeds. The increased demand for coal created by the Elsecar Ironworks and the canal brought about an increase in output from 12,710 tons in 1798 to 45,823 tons in 1800.

The collieries were one part of an economic unit, with much of the materials for the mines coming from other estate activities, such as wood for pit props, stone for the buildings and soughs, and bricks to line the shafts. Castings for the engines came from the Elsecar, Milton, and Thorncliffe ironworks, although precision and specialist components were often supplied from the Low Moor Ironworks in Bradford, Butterley Company in Derbyshire, and the Coalbrookdale Works in Shropshire.

By 1790, the continued working of the Lowwood Colliery was in doubt as it approached other landowners' coal reserves and competitors' collieries. Additional acreage was obtained in 1793 on the purchase of the Matthew Roberts estate, with property at Hoober, Wentworth, and Greasbrough, and in 1797 Fitzwilliam sank a new pit at the Lowwood Colliery at Street, near Wentworth, to the Barnsley seam some 100 yards deep. A steam-driven whimsey was erected with castings supplied by Jarratt, Dawson, and Hardy of the Low Moor Ironworks. The whimsey was used both to wind the coal and drain the mine, raising the water from the Barnsley seam some 43 feet to the old Lowwood deep level that ran to Elsecar. At a depth of approximately fifteen yards a seam of soft coal was worked to provide fuel for blacksmiths, coke making, and house fires (Figure 3).[11] Water from the nearby Southwell Colliery, leased from the Southwell Chapter, Nottinghamshire, posed a constant threat to the workings of the Lowwood Colliery. The Southwell lease was acquired in 1810, which enabled a sough to be made from the Lowwood to the Southwell Colliery to drain the workings. It was driven in three shifts of eight hours each, in February, 1812.

In 1819, Fitzwilliam purchased the freehold and leasehold estate of William Wilson Kent with property at Haugh and Rawmarsh, and

Figure 3. A cross-section of Lowwood Colliery, 1797. *MD, 3586K, Allott Papers, Sheffield Archives*

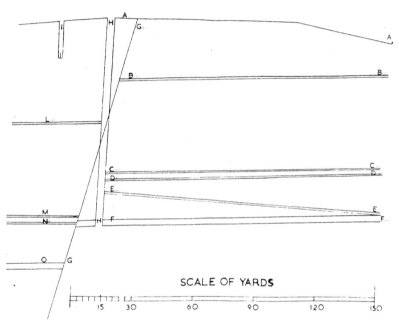

SCALE OF YARDS

15	30	60	90	120	150

REFERENCE

A.. SURFACE OF THE GROUND
B.. ⎰A SOFT COAL THREE FEET THICK SUITABLE FOR BLACKSMITHS, OR TO BURN INTO CINDERS, AND FOR
     ⎱HOUSE FIRES, THIS COAL MAY BE GOT ON THE BASSIT SIDE OF THE NEW PIT, AND WOULD SELL AT 6/PER DC
C.. A SECOND COAL EIGHTEEN INCHES THICK, OF A MEAN QUALLITY AND NOT WORTH GETTING.
D.. A THIRD SOFT COAL TWENTY INCHES THICK, ALSO OF A MEAN QUALLITY AND NOT WORTH GETTING.
E.. ⎰THE DRIFT OR SOUGH BEGINS DRIVEING AT THE OLD LEVEL SOUTH WEST, AND ENDS DRIVEING AT
     ⎱THE NEW PIT NORTH EAST
F. ⎧THE THICK COAL NINE FEET THICK OF WHICH THERE IS SEVEN FEET AND A HALF GOT, THE OTHER
    ⎨EIGHTEEN INCHES IS LEFT FOR A ROOF TO SET THE PUNCHEONS OR PROPS TO KEEP THE ROOF FROM
    ⎪FALLING IN, AND WHEN THE BENKS ARE _ _ _ DRIVEN THIRTY YARDS UPON THE RISE BOARD
    ⎩THE PUNCHEONS ARE TAKEN AWAY AND SET IN OTHER BENKS —————————
G.. THE THROW WHICH THROWS ALL THE COALS TWENTY YARDS DOWN NORTH EAST————
H.. THE PIT NOW SINKING WHICH IS NINE FEET LONGWAY BY SEVEN FEET WIDE —————
I.. A LITTLE PIT SUNK ON PURPOSE FOR WATER FOR THE WHIMSEY —————————

THE THROWS DIRECTION IS SOUTH EAST TOWARDS HOOBER —————————— — ———
     AND NORTH WEST TOWARDS ELSECAR ——————————————————
M.. N.. O.. THE COALS THROWN DOWN NORTH EAST FROM THE PIT——————

Expenses of the Great Engine, new Park Gate Colliery

	£	s	d
The Coalbrook-Dale Company, for Castings - - - - - - - -	830	15	0
The late Jonathan Woodhouse Engineer, for planning &c - -	62	12	6
George H. Barrow, for castings - - - - - - - - - - - - -	227	1	11
Newton Scott & Co - - - d° - - - - - - - - - - - - - - -	87	8	1
Hartop Sorby & Co - - - d° - - - - - - - - - - - - - - -	98	19	3
Josiah Parkes &Son, for applying the Smoke} consuming Apparatus }- - - - - - -	89	0	0
Samuel Sykes for building the Engine House} Chimney &c } - - - -	503	11	0
James Wain, for erecting the Engine - - - - - - - - - - -	258	1	0
	£2157	8	9

Figure 4. The 'Expenses of the Great Engine', at New Park Gate Colliery. *WWM, F70/105, Sheffield Archives*

the Haugh Colliery, leased from the Southwell Chapter. The Haugh and Southwell collieries had previously worked together in competition with the Lowwood Colliery. It was a small mine whose output amounted to only 5,815 tons in 1820, supplying coke to the ironworks in the Rotherham and Sheffield areas and the more distant markets down the Don Navigation. However, during February, 1823, water had risen so much in the 'Haugh Five Feet Coal Pit' that the colliery was stopped, and probably abandoned as no further output figures were recorded.

Fitzwilliam's wealth enabled the purchase of strategically advantageous coal reserves which reinforced his dominance of coal mining in the area,

Figure 5. The New Park Gate Colliery, Westfield Engine House built in 1823. *The Author*

and facilitated the sinking of collieries in Brampton, Greasbrough, and Rawmarsh. The Brampton Colliery (re-named Rainber Park Colliery in 1821) was sunk in 1818. This was a relatively small colliery producing 13,862 tons in 1826. The Swallowwood Colliery was opened in 1823 to a depth of about 60 yards to the Swallow Wood Coal some 5 feet 5 inches thick 'of excellent quality'. A waggon road was laid in Westhill Field in 1825 and following a decision by Viscount Milton, heir to Earl Fitzwilliam, to enter the London market in 1831, a new waggonway was laid to the Greasbrough Canal, a pit sunk, and a whimsey erected. Output rose from 5,232 tons in 1827 to 16,993 tons in 1836. In the 1830s the Kents Main Colliery was opened, with the first output figures recorded in 1837 at 4,208 tons rising to 13,171 tons in 1840.

The single largest investment during the 1740-1840 period involved the sinking of the New Park Gate Colliery, to the Barnsley seam 71 yards in depth. It took three years to open from the initial entry in the accounts in August, 1820, with expenditure rising to £29,478 by 1824, with £33,000 spent on 'freeholders' coal by 1827. The 'Great Engine' cost £2,157 8s 9d to build, with the Coalbrookdale Company providing castings to the value of £830 15s 0d, (Figures 4 and 5). A dry dock was constructed, with a basin to accommodate vessels, and a waggon road 580 yards in length was laid from the pit to the wharf on the Greasbrough Canal. On 17 May, 1823, Joshua Biram, house steward, wrote:

> ... we opened the New Basin yesterday, and begun loading Coals on Board the Fitzwilliam the first Sloop built at the new Yard near the Dry Dock [they also launched a second Sloop there yesterday]. I had a Quantity of roast and boiled Beef and Bread taken to the Wharf and 2 Pipes of Ale, for the different Workmen, and many others partook of it; it being a fine Day there was a great Concourse of People attended; I also had the Rawmarsh Band of Music which enlivened the Scene.[12]

In 1828 output amounted to 45,136 tons with 112 miners employed. Over the period of this study the output of coal rose dramatically from the collieries under direct estate management, from the 603 pit loads (4,115 tons) at the Elsecar Colliery in 1753, to 141,806 tons from six collieries in 1826.

The Market for Coal
The major factor that limited the large-scale exploitation of coal was the distance from a navigable waterway and dependence upon high cost road transport. During the eighteenth century coal from the Elsecar and Lowwood collieries was consumed by local ironworks, forges, farms, limekilns, brickworks, maltsters, and domestic consumers. In spite of the distance from the Don Navigation, coal was carried from the Elsecar Colliery to Kilnhurst, a distance of 5 miles.

Between 2 February, 1754, and 6 January, 1755, some 108 pit loads and 2 pulls (737 tons and 9 cwt) out of total sales of 525 pit loads and 15 pulls (3,585 tons and 15 cwt) or one-fifth, were taken to Rockingham's Kilnhurst wharf. Coal from the Elsecar and Lowwood collieries was transported by boat along the Don Navigation and then overland to the markets on the magnesian limestone to the east, returning with limestone for the limekilns on the estate located at Elsecar, Wentworth, Hoober, and Kilnhurst. The major consumer of Elsecar coal was the Chapel Furnace, Chapeltown, at a distance of $2^3/4$ miles. In 1767 they purchased 595 dozen (1,260 tons) of coal out of total sales of approximately 1,807 dozen and $^1/_2$ pull (3,794 tons and $15^3/_4$ cwt) or 33 per cent. After the adoption of coke in the blast furnaces in 1778 and the surrender of their Westwood Colliery lease in 1791, purchases of coal from the Elsecar Old Colliery increased to 3,067 dozen and 8 corves (6,442 tons and 16 cwt) out of total sales of 7,396 tons by 1798. Most of the coal was sold within a three mile radius of the Elsecar Colliery, but other sales were made to locations in a north-easterly direction, at least as far as South Kirby, and Adwick-le-Street, at a distance of 12 miles. The available evidence suggests that the Elsecar Colliery mainly withdrew from the market to the east of the Don Navigation from places such as Edlington, Wadworth, and Tickhill, the market being taken over by the Lowwood Colliery, after it came under direct estate control in 1763.

The Lowwood Colliery was worked on a larger scale than the Elsecar Colliery, being closer to the Don Navigation, and with the gradient easier over which the coal was carried, as an account for the Elsecar Colliery between 21 April and 19 May, 1753, stated:

> ... we expect no *Extraordinary Sale till most of the Law Wood Coals be gone for they are very Busy Everyday and their Roads both Level and Better repaired than some of our Roads are.*[13]

The lower cost of transport enabled coal from the Lowwood Colliery to be sold further afield, for while local consumers remained an important market, coal was sold to places such as Sykehouse on the lower reaches of River Don (19 miles); Misson, in north Nottinghamshire ($18^1/_2$ miles); and Epworth, in north Lincolnshire (25 miles). Although there was some overlap of markets, where the magnesian limestone outcropped, the Elsecar and Lowwood collieries tended to concentrate on their own geographical areas. The same was true of the Westwood Colliery, whose markets lay mainly to the south, within an area bordered by Oughtibridge, Owlerton, Attercliffe, Ecclesfield, and Chapeltown, but with sales also to Masbrough in Rotherham. Out of total sales of £745 10s 9d in 1796, Swallow paid £302 8s 6d for coal for his Attercliffe works, and Booth paid £46 4s 0d for coal for his Masbrough premises. Some of the estate tenants were obliged to purchase Fitzwilliam coal, the proprietors of the Elsecar Ironworks, for example, had to purchase coal from an estate colliery if there was one within a mile of their works.

Transport costs, especially by road, comprised a major part of the price of coal paid by the consumer. In the 1760s, 1 dozen (42 cwt) of Lowwood coal cost 9s 6d at Kilnhurst, which included 4s 6d for the coal and 5s for leading, while in 1766, 1 dozen Parkgate measure of 94.5 cubic feet cost 5s carriage from Lowwood to Swinton (4 miles) plus 8d 'Wharfage, Stacking and Carters Ab'', but for the next 20 miles to Thorne, along the Don Navigation, it cost only 2s 6d freight plus 2s lock dues.

Sheffield was the most important local market but the cost of carriage limited the amount of Fitzwilliam coal entering the town, even though the price of coal at the Darnall Colliery was double that of the Lowwood Colliery, in 1818. The opening of the Sheffield to Tinsley Canal in 1819, lowered the cost of coal entering Sheffield and on 21 March, 1821, the lessees of the Duke of Norfolk's Sheffield collieries noted:

> *... the open Collieries of Mr Fenton near the River Don, of Mr Edmunds at Worsbro' which communicate with that River from the Dearne and Dove and from which Collieries large quantities of Coal have been recently imported into Sheffield as well as the Colliery opening by Messrs. Booth, Sayle & Company in Estates of Earl Fitzwilliam near Tinsley within three miles of Sheffield in direct opposition to the Duke of Norfolk's Collieries and also a Colliery of vast extent in the opening of which great progress is made by Earl Fitzwilliam near Wentworth and Rawmarsh.*[14]

The dilemma that faced the Fitzwilliam collieries was their over-dependence upon the South Yorkshire iron industry.[15] Attempts were made to widen the geographical market and to seek new uses for the coal and its by-products. A short-lived tar distillery, 1814-18, was established adjacent to the Elsecar New Colliery to produce coke, tar, lamp black, and varnish. In March, 1823, the first shipment of coal and coke was sent from the Swallowwood Colliery to try the Malton market in North Yorkshire, where a Mr Allen commented that he found the coke of 'superior Quality for malting, being more clear of sulphur than what has been in use with us'. By 1823, the extensive waterway system widened the geographical market for coal and enabled Fitzwilliam coal to be carried along the east coast and into Sheffield, Gainsborough, Lincoln, Malton and York. Even so, the cost of transport raised the pit head price of 12s 6d per waggon to £1 9s 3d at York, and £1 11s 6d in Lincoln.

An attempt was made to enter the London market with coal from the Swallowwood Colliery in the 1830s. However, in November, 1832, Benjamin Biram wrote that the prospect of selling Swallowwood coal in London was not good as there had been a 'tremendous supply' over the last fortnight. Viscount Milton believed there would be no new market in London, except for the very best coal, and in an attempt to improve sales he agreed to change the name of the coal, which became known as 'Strafford Main' and the mine the Strafford Main Colliery. By February, 1833, the coal trade:

> ... received severe blow, from great reductions in the price of Coal made at Newcastle, by the Marquis of Londonderry & Lord Durham. I am informed that their Lordships have reduced the Coal at the pit mouth 4/- per Ton.[16]

The result was a complete 'stagnation' of trade and by 16 February, 1833, Benjamin Biram had stopped sending coal to London until freight rates were lower and the price of coal had increased, as they were by then selling at a loss. Fitzwilliam continued to seek out new markets. In February, 1833, a Mr Burstall, from Goole, wrote that the Newcastle proprietors were trying to cut the others from the London market, but he had travelled into Lincolnshire, Cambridgeshire, Norfolk, Suffolk, Essex, and Kent, with many customers prepared to give Fitzwilliam coal a try in the spring. He had already shipped coal to Scotland, Guernsey, and parts of his own coast. In March, 1833, Burstall was sending two boats of Strafford Main coals to Denmark and one boat of Elsecar 'Hards' to Hamburg.[17] In spite of determined attempts to widen the geographical market for Fitzwilliam coal, the collieries remained largely dependent upon the South Yorkshire iron industry, until the coming of the railways.

The Working and Social Conditions of the Miners

Coal mining has always been a physically demanding occupation carried out in a dangerous environment. Unlike some other Yorkshire colliery owners, Fitzwilliam did not employ female miners or boys under nine years of age. At the Elsecar and New Park Gate collieries boys were initially employed as trappers who progressed to horse lads leading the corves; at the age of twelve to fifteen years they worked as jenny boys unhooking the corves on the underground inclined planes, and at sixteen or seventeen they filled the corves at the coal face before advancing to the most senior and highly paid position of 'hewer' or 'collier', who worked the coal. In 1842 the colliers were given one hour for dinner, while the children worked from 6.30 a.m. until 5.00 p.m. with half-an-hour for breakfast and an hour for dinner, making a nine hour working day.

Allowances were given for candles, shovels, and wedges, with flannels provided for wet work. During the eighteenth century the miners received a 'Christmas box' and in February each year a 'feast' was provided. In 1769 the Household Accounts itemised 'The Charge of the Coal Feast' at the Elsecar Colliery, that employed nine miners: malt and hops £1 0 4$\frac{1}{2}$d, beef 14s 3d, veal 3s 1d, bread 1s 2d, butter 1s 4d, tobacco and pipes 11d. Ale and food were provided when a contract was entered into, a pit sunk, a building erected, a colliery opened, or for work carried out beyond what was normally expected. Shortly after Rockingham took control of the Elsecar Colliery, Thomas Smith, overseer, enquired:

Feb 24th 1753
May it please your Hon.^{rble} Lordship
It has Been a Custom for the Colliers & other pit men: to have A weekpull for fire Coals paying Sixteen pence p. Doz.^{n} the price of Getting they Humbly desire yo:^{r} Lordship wo.^{d} Comply with ye above custom.[18]

The custom was continued with the miners receiving coal at cost. Medical treatment was provided for injured miners and by 1806 William Lunn was retained on a salary of £50 per annum.[19] A guinea donation was given to injured miners with a weekly allowance for longer periods off work, calculated according to income and family circumstances. After William Evans was hurt by a fall of stone in January, 1810, Joshua Biram recommended an allowance of 9s a week 'for relief and assistance'. On retirement miners were given a pension that could be continued over several years. Michael Bisby, overseer of the Lowwood Colliery, who was to retire on 1 January, 1794, with a continuation of his wages, received 10s 6d per week until 9 December, 1803. It was the length of time that a miner received benefits that showed Fitzwilliam's actions were not due to economic considerations alone, but to a genuine interest and care for the workforce.

The most common accident was associated with roof falls with relatively few incidents from 'fire damp' or 'choke damp', probably due to good ventilation practices and the shallowness of the coal seams. However, some accidents were due to carelessness, indifference to danger through familiarity, and the blatant disregard of safety rules in order to increase output. On 1 December, 1796, two miners were killed, Samuel Ashforth of Wentworth, who had been at the Lowwood Colliery for only a month, and employed in loading the coal, and Muscroft, a hurrier. They were going into the pit together after the 'pickmen' had gone down:

> *... and according to their Custom the Trunks were tied with a Cord to Keep them on the Pit Hook, when they rest upon the Bottom in order to take the Trunk up without a Person waiting at the Bottom to see that they are upon the Hook, now it is supposed that the Bow of the Trunk had by some means got off the Hook and it hung by the Cord, which was strong enough to take the Trunk to the top, this Man and Boy getting into the Trunk broke the Cord and they fell together to the Bottom Ashforth 25 Years of Age has left a wife & 1 child and Muscroft is 14 Years of age -* [20]

After Richard Jessop was killed by a fall of stone while collecting 'roof coal', his widow received the usual pension of 2s 6d per week. Accidents did occur from 'fire damp'; in April, 1832, for example, John Lee, collier at the Swallowwood Colliery, was killed by an 'Explotion of the Fire Damp'. He survived a few days and left a widow and six children.

Trappers were employed to work the ventilation doors but as there were not sufficient boys to work each door, miners were obliged to open and close them as they passed. The work of a trapper could be lonely as seen in 1842, when Samuel Hirst, aged nine years and four months who worked at the Jump Pit stated: 'I sit by myself. I never have a light. I sit still all day long and never do anything except open and shut the door'.[21] The doors were sometimes propped open in spite of orders to the contrary. In June, 1832, Milton wrote to Joshua Biram, house steward, asking him to rebuke the man responsible for leaving open a trap door as only a few months earlier he had spoken 'strongly' when a similar incident had occurred.

Certain coal seams were more prone to gas and when safety lamps where introduced Milton insisted they be used, but it was not thought necessary for all the miners to use a lamp:

> *As it is not unlikely that the Swallowwood coal will be more liable to explosions than the thick coal it will be right to insist upon the colliers*

using the safety lamps - the colliers should all be furnished with them
& positive orders given that no candles shall be used in the banks at
all. - with respect to the trammers it may not be so necessary tho' better
for them also.[22]

Colliers were often unwilling to use their safety lamps due to their poor light, which affected both their ability to work the coal and their income, as they were paid according to the amount produced. They sometimes unscrewed the safety lamp gauze to obtain a brighter light or discarded them altogether. In a letter written by Milton in June, 1832, he stated that even if a trap door was left open no accident need occur if they would use their safety lamps. They continued to ignore safety rules and in 1852 the propping open of a trap door and the removal of a safety lamp gauze was the cause of an explosion that killed ten miners at the Low Elsecar Colliery. At the subsequent inquest the management was criticised for not ensuring that safety regulations were enforced.[23]

Fire was an additional hazard, which could result in a loss of life, destruction of equipment, and lost production. On 25 January, 1806, the Greasbrough Colliery was set on fire:

... by the Carelessness of one of the Colliers leaving his Candle
burning in the Pit which lately fell in and shut up 7 Men & 2 Boys
– the fire was not discovered till Monday Morning the 27th In^s. they
got some Fire Engines and were trying all the last Week to extinquish
it...[24]

Another fire was reported by Benjamin Biram on 3 June, 1833, when he wrote that on the previous morning the New Park Gate Colliery was on fire. The colliers had descended, but were unable to go far from the shaft due to the smoke and foul air, and all the pits were closed except for the 'drawing pit'. It was suspected that the fire had been started deliberately as it had broken out in a place where people seldom went. There may have been some credence in this suggestion as Fitzwilliam had been making miners redundant.

The coal industry was one of the first to experience the economic advantages of the division of labour. At the Lowwood Colliery, that employed twenty-two miners in 1769, the coal would have been hewn from the coal face by 'colliers', who undercut the seam with a pick to a depth of 2 feet 6 inches to 3 feet 6 inches, with the coal face supported by 'sprags' or short props. Large pieces of coal were split off the coal face with the aid of metal wedges. A 'filler' loaded the corf ready for the 'barrower' to haul it, with the aid of a horse, to the

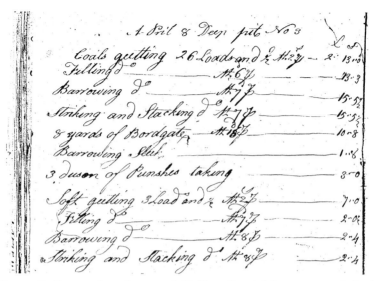

Figure 6. Extract from Lowwood Colliery fortnightly accounts, 8 April, 1769. *WWM, F99a, Sheffield Archives*

shaft bottom. The 'gin driver' wound the coal to the surface where the 'stacker' carried it on a horse-drawn sledge to the pit stack ready for sale. The 'overseer' sold the coal and supervised the colliery (Figure 6).

The colliers in the Barnsley seam worked in a headroom of seven and a half feet with the remaining one and a half feet left to support the roof. The roof coal was collected after it had collapsed following the removal of the props. In 1793, the Elsecar Colliery was drained by a deep level measuring two yards wide and five feet high. The bord and pillar method of mining was used with the banks or work places nine yards wide. To enable a bank to be used as a roadway, two rows of props were placed to support the roof, to give a passage six feet in width. The banks were separated by ribs of coal three feet wide with the ends widened for added support. Running diagonally across the ribs, towards the shaft, 'post holes' were cut for ventilation and to facilitate the movement of corves (Figure 7). When the coal had been worked the men were paid 12d for every dozen props retrieved. The Elsecar New Colliery worked the coal under a similar system in Hoyland and Brampton parishes. A deep level was driven for a mile towards Coley Lane, near Wentworth, with banks 400 yards in length. A plan of the proposed working of the Elsecar New Colliery, by Michael Hague on 21 July, 1794, shows banks ten yards wide, but John Deakin's plan dated 25 October, 1796, called for banks of eight yards in width. The New Park Gate Colliery almost certainly worked the coal by this method, at least until 1835. Other seams may have been mined under a different system, as in the Westwood Colliery, where a form of longwall mining was used, whereby 90 per cent or more of the coal was extracted. A plan of the Westwood Colliery, drawn by Joseph Hague on 9 September, 1794, shows a bank 60 yards in length with packs containing black shale and other materials to support the roof. All the coal was worked except the ribs of coal that were left to support the levels, and even the coal on either side of the boardgate was later removed. Across the bank face two rows of props were fixed and as the coal was worked the back row was removed and placed forward along the coal face. Immediately above the coal was a seam of ironstone that was collected daily after it had fallen down between the packs.[25]

One of the most arduous jobs, that involved a not insignificant degree of danger, was the driving and cleaning of soughs. On 8

Figure 7. A plan of the Elsecar Colliery, drawn by Joshua Biram, 27 September, 1793, showing the bord and pillar method of working the coal. *WWM, MP 56, Sheffield Archives*

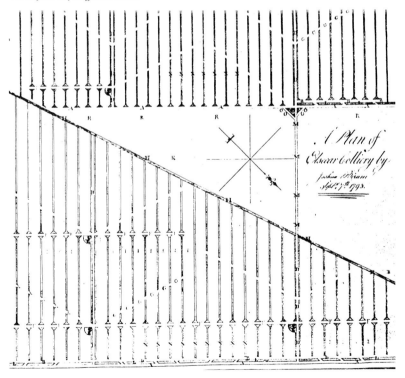

December, 1790, Fitzwilliam wrote: 'I desire you give the men, who were working below, when the water burst in the Lowwood Sough, a guinea...' In October, 1793, when the Lowwood sough was again being cleared, the men were driven out by 'damp'. The sough was only 27 inches high being nearly 'clogged' with mud and 'oker'.

One man and three boys were only able to remove the sediment by stirring it with water and allowing the stream to carry it away. The work was long and tedious, carried out daily 'as long as they are able to bear'. In appreciation of their efforts Fitzwilliam ordered that two guineas be given to them on completion of the work.

Another side to Fitzwilliam's paternalism was the uncompromising attitude towards industrial disputes. On 13 April, 1836, for example, the colliers refused to screen the coal as they were only paid as working 'sleck'. Benjamin Biram suggested that those who had a house should be given notice to quit for they were under an agreement to leave once they ceased to work at the pit. Similar threats of dismissal and eviction were used during the 1840s to discourage the men from joining a trades union.

Fitzwilliam was reluctant to make employees redundant. During periods of low demand the miners were often transferred to other estate activities. Miners at the Elsecar Colliery in the 1760s were employed in clearing ditches, haymaking, and thatching. To avoid throwing men out of work in Elsecar in 1812, Fitzwilliam suggested driving new 'headings' and 'winnings', although none may have been required at the time, making a new road, or any other work until the demand for coal had increased. However, following a slump in the coal trade in 1833, Fitzwilliam wanted a reduction in the 'expences' of the collieries. In reply, Benjamin Biram commented upon the degree of overmanning at the collieries. He believed there was a tendency for the numbers to increase as boys were employed on low wages to attend the horses or to shut the ventilation doors, and as they grew older they were appointed to more important positions, gaining the idea that if they behaved themselves they would be employed for life, which left the collieries 'overstocked' with young men. On 18 March, 1833, Benjamin Biram wrote of the dismissal of ten 'youngsters' at Elsecar and that a similar number could be achieved at the New Park Gate Colliery. On 23 March, 1833, he again wrote about reducing the number of colliers, but would guard against favouritism and dismiss the last employed, unless in individual cases there were good reasons not to.

The expansion of coal mining on the Wentworth estate after 1795 required the employment of more miners. Recruitment, especially of skilled colliers, was not easy in areas of sparse population and therefore accommodation at low rents had usually to be provided to attract the necessary labour. Between 1796 and 1798, some 42 dwellings were built, converted, or repaired for the Elsecar New Colliery, and it was at this time that Old Row and Station Row were built. According to Tremenheere, Mines Commissioner, writing in 1845, the Fitzwilliam dwellings were:

> ... *of a class superior in size and arrangement, and in the conveniences attached, to those belonging to the working classes. Those at Elsecar consist of four rooms and a pantry, a small back court, ash pit, a pig-sty, and a garden; the small space before the front door is walled round, and kept neat with flowers or paving stones; a low gate preventing the children from straying into the road. Proper conveniences are attached to every six or seven houses, and kept perfectly clean. The gardens, of 500 yards of ground each, are cultivated with much care. The rent for cottage and garden is 2s a week.*[26]

The houses referred to by Tremenheere were almost certainly those of Reform Row (Figure 8).

As a paternalist, Fitzwilliam provided many of the benefits of a welfare state, with the provision of injury allowances, retirement and widows' pensions, free medical treatment, schools, and good housing. In addition, the miners were eligible for the St Thomas' Day Donation of beef and 6d and the Collop Monday Charity, and during times of scarcity and high prices, Fitzwilliam gave out blankets and sold rice and herrings at subsidised prices.

Conclusion

The Rockingham and Fitzwilliam families played a vital role in the development of coal mining on the Wentworth estate. It was their wealth and commitment to exploit their coal reserves on a large-scale which played a significant part in the industrialisation of South Yorkshire. In achieving this they did not neglect the welfare of their employees to which they were deeply and genuinely committed.

Figure 8. Elsecar: Reform Row. *The Author*

Notes and References

Abbreviations: WWM - Wentworth Woodhouse Muniments; ACM - Arundel Castle Manuscripts; MD – Miscellaneous Documents; NBC - Newman and Bond Collection; all in Sheffield Archives.

1. Over the period of this study the owners of the Wentworth estate included: Thomas Watson-Wentworth (1693-1750), Earl of Malton 1728, 1st Marquis of Rockingham 1746; Charles Watson-Wentworth (1730-1782), 2nd Marquis of Rockingham; William (Wentworth) Fitzwilliam (1748-1833), 4th Earl Fitzwilliam; and Charles Wentworth-Fitzwilliam (1786-1857), 5th Earl Fitzwilliam.
2. A. S. Ellis, Yorkshire Deeds (part 11), *Yorkshire Archaeological Journal*, Volume 12 (1893), 236-7.
3. WWM, D1727. G. G. Hopkinson, 'The Development of Lead Mining and of the Coal and Iron Industries in North Derbyshire and South Yorkshire 1700-1850', Ph. D. Thesis 1958, University of Sheffield No. 996, pp. 271-2.
4. WWM, F70/3. The term 'man' or 'men' usually refers to 'colliers', 'getters', or 'hewers', who worked the coal.
5. WWM, F70/4-1. Spencer later sold his remaining share in the colliery.
6. NBC, 300.
7. WWM, A241.
8. WWM, A267. William Jessop was a founder partner in the Butterley Ironworks, Derbyshire. John Gott was the resident engineer on the Aire and Calder Canal.
9. John Goodchild, *The Coal Kings of Yorkshire*, (Wakefield, 1978), pp. 30-31, Plate 2.
10. For a more detailed study of coal mining in Elsecar see: I. R. Medlicott, 'Elsecar: The Making of an Industrial Community, 1750-1830', in B. Elliott (ed.) *Aspects of Barnsley 5*, (Wharncliffe Publishing, Barnsley, 1998). After the Elsecar New Colliery opened in 1795, the Elsecar Colliery became known as the Elsecar Old Colliery.
11. MD, 3586K, Allott Papers; A. K. Clayton, Coal-Mines-Local History, Part 1, Chapter 7, pp. 36-41, unpublished typescript 1985, Sheffield Archives.
12. WWM, F107/251. The Westfield Pumping Engine was still at work in 1918. Joshua Biram, house steward, had responsibility for the collieries.
13. WWM, F95/11.
14. ACM, 246. WWM, F107/134.
15. In 1810 the Elsecar New Colliery sold 13,503 dozen (28,356 tons and 6 cwt) or 58 per cent of their coal sales to the Elsecar Ironworks, with the Elsecar Old Colliery supplying 6,615 dozen and 11 pulls (13,893 tons and 8_ cwt) or 77 per cent of sales to the Milton Ironworks.
16. WWM, G40 (i). Benjamin Biram was taking over more of his father's duties, to whose position as house steward he later succeeded.
17. WWM, G40 (i).
18. WWM, F95/8.
19. WWM, A74.
20. WWM, St. P. 6 (6).
21. *Reports from Commissioners. Children's Employment (Mines)*, 1842, p. 71. The Jump Pit opened in 1816, to a depth of 60 yards, was looked upon as an extension of the Elsecar New Colliery. For a general survey of the employment of children in mines in the Barnsley area see M. and J. Jones. 'Child labour in mines in the Barnsley area: Evidence from the Children's Employment Commission', in B. Elliott (ed.) *Aspects of Barnsley 4* (Wharncliffe Publishing, Barnsley, (1996) pp. 81-93.
22. WWM, St. P. 4 (vi).
23. G. Mee, *Aristocratic Enterprise* (Blackie, Glasgow, 1975), pp. 124-128.
24. WWM, St. P. 5 (i).
25. WWM, F100/14, MP55,56, F70/82. John Deakin was employed, 'inspecting and directing the working and management of the Collieries', Michael Hague was 'overlooker', of the Elsecar Old Colliery, and Joseph Hague was 'overlooker', of the Westwood Colliery.
26. Mee, *Aristocratic Enterprise*, p.141.

Acknowledgements

I am grateful to Olive, Countess Fitzwilliam's Wentworth Settlement Trustees and the Director of Sheffield City Libraries for permission to quote from and reproduce documents in the Wentworth Woodhouse Muniments held at Sheffield Archives.

9. COLLIERY TRAMROADS OF NORTH-WEST ROTHERHAM

by Graham Hague

Introduction

THROUGH THE EIGHTEENTH CENTURY the River Don was steadily made navigable upstream from the Humber towards Sheffield. This was achieved by building locks and cuts to bypass weirs and shallows. Aldwarke was reached in 1733, Rotherham in 1740 and Tinsley in 1751, from where the road to Sheffield was improved. The success of this scheme encouraged industrial growth in South Yorkshire which in turn increased the demand for coal which had been mined on a small scale since the sixteenth century.

By the 1760s Rotherham coal was travelling down the Humber to Hull, up the Derwent to the Malton area and up the Trent and Foss Dike to Newark and Lincoln. This trade was based on relatively early river improvement and predated the canal era. The opening of the Sheffield Canal in 1819 finally gave direct access to Sheffield.

The value of the canal for transport continued well into the twentieth century, principally to the power stations at Blackburn Meadows, Mexborough and Doncaster, which took much of their coal by water until closure in the 1970s and 1980s. The last water-borne coal was from Cadeby Colliery to Doncaster in 1981. Coal staithes within Rotherham were situated at Kilnhurst, Roundwood, Aldwarke Main, Holmes and Jordan, each fed by railways of varying lengths.

The low hills rising to the north and west of the River Don at Rotherham were rich in coal at a shallow depth and where they were cut through by side streams outcrops of the Barnsley, Parkgate and Silkstone seams occurred. Exploitation of this mineral wealth was generally encouraged by the major landowners such as the Rockinghams, their successors the Fitzwilliams, and the Howards of Effingham. Usually coal working was let to coal masters like the Fentons at Greasbrough. It was down these side valleys in the eighteenth century that several simple wooden-railed tramroads were constructed to take coal to the River Don. Through the nineteenth and early twentieth centuries these tramroads developed into rather more substantial mineral railways. It is the tramroads and mineral railways that served the Warren Vale area, the Parkgate valley and the Greasbrough areas that are the subject of the following pages (see Figure 1). The Kimberworth area followed a similar pattern but this will have to be the subject of a future article.

Figure 1. Map of the Don Navigation and the associated colliery tramroads north and west of Rotherham.

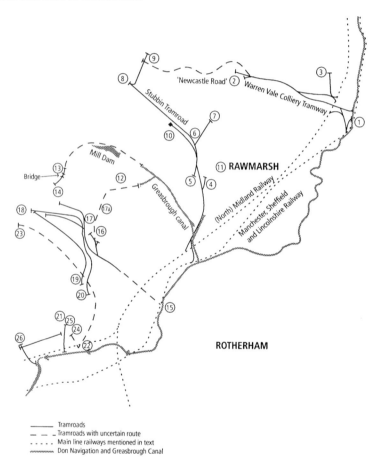

1. Kilnhurst Colliery and Staithes	17. Site of 'Long Bridge'
2. Warren Vale Colliery	17a. Site of Old Engine and Lower Engine
3. Glebe Farm Colliery	18. Greasbrough/Old Parkgate Colliery
4. Westfield Colliery	19. Bradgate Horse Croft Staith
5. Swallow Wood Colliery (Parkgate)	20. Bradgate, Bradgate Road Staith
6. Parkgate/New Deep Colliery	21. Kimberworth
7. Kent's Main Colliery	22. Walker's Ironworks
8. Higher Stubbin Colliery	23. Plantations, Ironstone bell pits
9. Low Stubbin Colliery	24. Swallow Wood Pit (Holmes)
10. New Stubbin Colliery	25. Garrow Tree Hill Colliery
11. Rawmarsh	26. Jordan Colliery
12. Greasbrough	
13. Squirrel Castle Engine House	
14. Whitegate Colliery	
15. Rotherham	
16. Bassingthorpe Spring Wood	

The Warren Vale Colliery Tramway

Warren Vale has a history of coal mining going back nearly four centuries with a record of a miner being injured at Abdy in 1616.[1]

The first reference to rail transport occurs in the Rawmarsh Inclosure Act of 1774[2] where a piece of ground was staked out over Rawmarsh Common for the purpose of making a tramroad for conveying coal. The Inclosure Award and map of 1780/81 indicates a 'Newcastle Road' running eastwards for two and a third miles from near Low Stubbin towards the River Don Navigation at Kilnhurst – linear plot no. 53, awarded to Lord John Murray, 40 feet in width totalling 11 acres 3 roods and 9 perches. The route commenced at Stubbin Lane (SK 421978) close to fields nos. 544 and 546 leased by Murray to William Inman as a coal pit and sough. Lord John Murray (1711-1787) was the eldest son of John Murray, first Duke of Atholl, who held extensive estates in Perthshire. In 1758 he had married Mary Dalton of Banner Cross Hall, Sheffield, where they subsequently lived. It is not clear how long the 'Newcastle Road'

Figure 2. Warren Vale *c*.1910 with the surviving buildings of Victoria Colliery on the left. The colliery tramway used to cross the road but had been removed by the time the Mexborough and Swinton Tramway was opened in 1907. A tram can be seen approaching from Rawmarsh. The new Warren Vale Road was opened in 1932 although the old lane still survives below it. *Rotherham Library photo No. 11150*

remained in operation but it is not shown on Teesdale's map of 1828.

The next tramroad operators in Warren Vale were the important Wakefield coal masters John and Joseph Charlesworth who took a mining lease from Earl Fitzwilliam in 1835. The Charlesworths had noted that the Greasbrough mining operations of the Fenton family were being run down and concluded that mining at Warren Vale could replace that source of supply. The sinking of the shaft commenced in 1837 and coal was won in the Kent's Thick seam in 1839. The Rawmarsh Colliery Victoria Pit was appropriately named after the new queen although the mine was also called Warren Vale Colliery by 1852. Victoria Pit was just east of the Rotherham to Swinton turnpike road at SK 442976 (see Figure 2). The 1840 One Inch Ordnance Survey map shows the tramroad running for one and a third miles beside the Collier Brook to canal staithes at Kilnhurst (SK 463970) on an alignment similar to that of the Newcastle Road.

The 1850 Six Inch Ordnance Survey map shows the colliery layout with two engines situated one either side of the turnpike road, three converging tramways and an inclined plane – the colliery being situated on a plateau of land above the brook (Figure 3). The Charlesworths ceased mining at Warren Vale Colliery in 1897, concentrating on their much larger colliery at Kilnhurst. This had been sunk to the Barnsley seam as the Thrybergh Hall Colliery in

Figure 3. Warren Vale or Rawmarsh Colliery in 1850 beside the Rotherham to Swinton Turnpike Road with a miscellany of colliery buildings. Three converging sidings unite with the main tramway heading east towards Kilnhurst staith. *Ordnance Survey 1st Edition Six Inch Map*

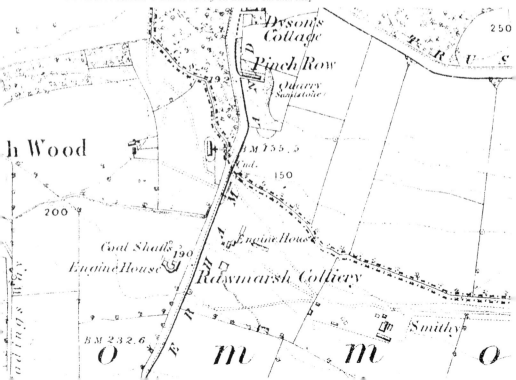

1858 by Robert Passenger and Co., passing to Charlesworths by 1871. This colliery had its own links to both the Midland and Manchester, Sheffield and Lincolnshire Railways and canal staithes adjacent to the colliery. The Warren Vale site remained as a pumping pit. The 1890 25 Inch Ordnance Survey map shows Victoria Pit already disused, with the main colliery, by then a drift mine, situated just west of the turnpike road – with the tramway crossing it on the level. Soon after 1850 a siding was connected to the Midland Railway (opened 1840). This became disused after 1897 as did the canal staithes with only the link to Kilnhurst Colliery remaining.

Further mining operations, just north of Victoria Colliery, were carried out by the Warren Vale (High Hazels) Coal Co. between 1935 and 1942 after which the Warren Vale Colliery Tramway went out of use except for the lower section which through the 1950s and 1960s still linked Kilnhurst brickworks to the colliery. Kilnhurst Colliery continued in operation until 1987 after which the pumping station at Warren Vale was closed. The tramway was of standard gauge. It was originally horse-drawn but later used steam locomotives and was always shown as the Warren Vale Colliery Tramway on Ordnance Survey maps between 1890 and 1947.

Nearer to Kilnhurst, Charlesworths worked the Glebe Farm Colliery – also known as Swinton Parkgate Colliery – from *c.*1845, with a short tramroad to the Midland Railway, as shown on the 1850 Six Inch Ordnance Survey map. The colliery appears to have had a short life.

Charlesworths also worked collieries in the vale at Swinton Common (SK 444988) and Warren House (SK 430981) but neither was rail served. Swinton Common Colliery was originally a collection of small early nineteenth century pits, mostly supplying the nearby Rockingham Pottery, but that closed in 1842. The colliery was resunk in 1874 to supply the needs of Swinton. Earthworks near Glebe Farm on the 1890 25 Inch Ordnance Survey map suggest the beginnings of a rail link up to Swinton Common but nothing was completed and the site is now obliterated by houses. Charlesworths' mining operations in the Warren Vale area were sold in 1924 to Messrs. Stewarts and Lloyds, who continued to work them until nationalisation in 1947.

The Warren Vale Tramroad Route Today

Perhaps the best place to start is the graveyard at St. Thomas's Church (built 1859 – the year after Kilnhurst Colliery was sunk), which offers good views up Warren Vale. Here a winding wheel from the colliery has been re-erected with a stone inscription 'Kilnhurst Colliery 1858 – 1989 They shall not be forgotten'.

Much of the tramway route can be walked today through a pleasantly forgotten South Yorkshire landscape. Past marshland – the effect of mining subsidence – which has created its own ecology and bird life, beside the quiet brook, then higher up the Vale, views of rolling farmland, a vital wedge of countryside between Rawmarsh and Swinton. At the Kilnhurst Colliery site only the pithead baths remain and there is no trace of either canal staith. Where the tramway passes under the Midland Railway at Beechwood Lane it retains its own bridge with stone piers and iron beams, built in 1840, and widened in 1901. Some former colliery brickworks buildings survive here as does Beechwood House, long occupied by the colliery manager.

Half a mile west of the railway bridge the former link to the Midland line joins the main tramway. A low embankment runs to the Collier Brook crossing, though no bridge survives and neither is there any trace eastwards. At the junction are several spoil mounds with sliding runs still visible. At their eastern end beside the tramway is an oval brick shaft (built from Kilnhurst bricks). From the spoil mounds there is a typical South Yorkshire view down the vale and across the Don valley. From time to time trains cross on the Midland line and sounds of shunting can be heard at British Steel's Aldwarke works.

The tramway climbs steadily beside the brook for another half mile, occasionally with low embankments or cuttings. It then begins to climb away from the brook up Warren Vale Incline but is soon lost in a large rubbish tip which has obliterated all traces of Victoria Colliery. The tramway route passed under the embankment of the Warren Vale Road (A633), constructed in 1932, then crossed the almost forgotten old road and passed the Warren Vale Colliery site before terminating in a still extant cutting. The dam wall of the colliery reservoir survives to the south-west.

The 1774 'Newcastle Road' continued westwards for about one mile. There is today a small ledge on the south bank of the Collier Brook through and just east of Birch Wood which could have been the tramroad route, though I believe the sewer from the Manor Farm Estate also passes this way. It should not be confused with the Roman Rig embankment on the north bank. The Manor Farm Estate has obliterated any further traces at Low Stubbin. Green Piece Cottages of 1850 were an interesting 'L' shaped group of stone-built miners' cottages at Harding Avenue, but only the datestone has been preserved. To the north the mine manager's house and a few late nineteenth century cottages survive at Warren House Colliery.

The Parkgate Area

The earliest tramroad at Parkgate was laid down in 1747. The route is uncertain but Jefferys' map of 1772 shows a 'Fire Engine' i.e. Newcomen atmospheric engine, just south of Upper Haugh. It presumably followed a course similar to the Stubbin Tramroad and terminated at the Don Navigation near Eastwood old lock (SK 433940) from where coal would be transported on a level pound to Rotherham. The colliery was operated by John Bowden of Beightonfields near Renishaw. Bowden also worked mines in the Renishaw area and at Kimberworth and Greasbrough at this time. The small stream that flows down the Parkgate valley is called 'Old Sough', sough being the term to describe a tunnel driven into a hill-side to drain a mine, presumably that sunk by John Bowden.

The Earls Fitzwilliam succeeding the second Marquis of Rockingham were the major landowners in the Parkgate valley and in the nineteenth and earlier part of the twentieth century worked most of the pits themselves rather than leasing them as elsewhere. In the early nineteenth century Joshua Biram was their mineral steward but in 1831 he was succeeded by his son Benjamin. Benjamin Biram died in 1859, aged 53, and both father and son are buried in Wentworth churchyard.

The Greasbrough Canal

The canal was built by the second Marquis of Rockingham and opened in 1781 to improve the transport of coal from the Greasbrough collieries (*qv.*). A five-eighths of a mile branch was built in 1823 when Westfield Colliery was sunk and the Parkgate Ironworks founded. The branch was built to the point where a lock would have been required (SK 434949). Here were built limekilns and coke ovens. The Sheffield and Rotherham Railway was opened between those towns on 31 October, 1838. When it was extended to the Greasbrough Canal in 1839 a small basin was provided close to the North Midland Railway crossing. It can have seen little use since coal traffic soon ceased from the Greasbrough area whilst the Stubbin Tramroad was soon linked direct to the Sheffield and Rotherham Railway. The basin is shown on the 1850 Six Inch Ordnance Survey map but had disappeared by the time the Manchester, Sheffield and

Lincolnshire Railway built its Parkgate Ironworks branch in 1873. Although the Greasbrough arm was closed and filled in *c*.1840 the Parkgate arm remained in use until the early twentieth century. Little traffic was handled after World War I and *c*.1920 the upper 300 yards were filled in when additional railway sidings were required. The boatyard still did some trade, repairing Humber keels in its dry dock, up to 1928, but the site is now obliterated. John Newbould, licensee of the nearby *Fitzwilliam Arms*, was proprietor in 1839.

The Stubbin Incline

From the Greasbrough Canal the Stubbin Incline was steadily extended up the Parkgate valley. The Westfield Colliery branch opened in 1823 (SK 434956) with an extension to Swallow Wood Colliery by 1831. The Swallow Wood seam also contained ironstone which was sent down the tramroad to the Parkgate Ironworks. Benjamin Biram was at the time experimenting with a three ton wagon made of iron instead of wood for use there.[3] By 1837 the tramroad had reached Parkgate Colliery, later known as New Deep (SK 432962) and up an inclined plane to Higher Stubbin (SK 419974). Benjamin Biram records in his diary in May of that year that he had ordered rails from the Milton Ironworks at Elsecar for use on the Stubbin Incline. At the same time another rather steeper incline rose from Parkgate Colliery to Kent's Main Colliery (SK 436967), passing under a small viaduct at Haugh Road. It seems to have had a short life being shown disused on the Six Inch 1850 Ordnance Survey map. The colliery was however resunk 350 yards to the north-west where it operated into the twentieth century, supplying coal to Rawmarsh by road. It was run by the Knaptons followed by the Hagues.

At the southern end there was a link to the Sheffield and Rotherham Railway by 1840 and it was soon doing good business in transporting coal to Sheffield at the expense of the canal. Drake's *Road Book* published that year, states that

> *Uniting with the Sheffield and Rotherham Railroad. …Earl Fitzwilliam has formed a branch railway to his collieries, which is traversable by locomotive engines and colliery wagons.*

Indeed the Earl had his own coal agent, Jeremiah Sellars, at Sheffield Wicker Station from 1840 to 1860. It is likely that strengthening of the track would have been required at this time to cater for the change from horse to locomotive haulage.

The tramroad was extended by 750 yards in *c*.1870 from High

Stubbin to a new pit at Low Stubbin which worked the Barnsley seam.[4] The main line was now two and five-eighths miles long. It rose from the canal at 80 feet above sea level in one mile to 155 feet at New Deep, then took a straight line across the hillside for one and one-eighth miles to a summit of 375 feet at Higher Stubbin before dropping 255 feet to Low Stubbin. Low Stubbin Colliery was quite close to the upper terminus of the 'Newcastle Road' mentioned in the Rawmarsh Inclosure Act (see Warren Vale).

The biggest change in the valley occurred with the opening of the New Stubbin Colliery in 1915 to work the Parkgate seam. This was a much larger enterprise than its predecessors which steadily ceased production. Swallow Wood Colliery closed before 1900 but its approach siding remained until 1978 to act as an escape route in case of a runaway on the main line. Westfield Colliery also ceased mining coal last century but remained as a pumping station until recently. It retained a siding until the conversion of the pumps to electricity in 1926. Higher and Low Stubbin Collieries closed in June, 1920, and shortly after, the upper section – above the Bank Pit Brickworks – closed. This section with a gradient of 1 in 27 was always worked as a rope hauled incline, though a steam locomotive was used for shunting at Low Stubbin. With loaded traffic being downhill a self-acting incline would have been appropriate except that this needs a midway passing loop, but one has never been shown on the relevant Ordnance Survey maps. New Deep at the incline foot is the only place where a passing place is shown. New Deep Colliery closed in April, 1924, whilst the brickworks remained in operation until the 1940s and still retained a siding.

The new Stubbin Colliery branch apparently was initially worked as a rope incline in 1915 but by steam locomotives from 1924 and by a pair of Hudswell Clarke 0-6-0 diesels between 1958 and the colliery closure in July, 1978 – after which all rail traffic in the Parkgate valley ceased. Coal production at New Stubbin in the late 1960s averaged 480,000 tons annually of which 10 per cent went to the landsale depots, 30 per cent went to the British Rail sidings for power stations, etc. and 60 per cent went to the coke ovens of the South Yorkshire Chemical Company at Mangham Road.[5] The South Yorkshire Chemical Company operated between 1919 and 1975 and the loss of its major customer hastened the closure of the colliery. Coal to the coke ovens was transported in some ancient 12 ton wagons right up to closure – quite a vintage sight in Parkgate on the generally overgrown track. Coal to the British Rail sidings used 16, 21, and latterly 33 ton wagons and they were taken down the incline behind an N.C.B. locomotive in ten or twelve wagon trains. The line always remained the property of the National Coal Board, a relatively rare arrangement in South Yorkshire.

The Route of the Greasbrough Canal and Low Stubbin Incline Today

a) The Greasbrough Canal

The lower 800 yards of the canal, now called the Fitzwilliam Canal, is still in water. It was recently restored by Rotherham MBC and the towpath can be followed north of Rotherham Road. There is a good general view from the nearby railway bridge.

Where the Don Navigation towpath crosses the Greasbrough Canal, part of the former swing bridge turntable and quadrant wall survive. The Manchester, Sheffield and Lincolnshire Railway crossing is now a fixed girder bridge. The swing bridge here was controlled from an adjacent signal box and rail traffic was held up every time a barge entered or left the canal. Three hundred yards to the north three stone arches built by the North Midland Railway in 1840 still cross the canal. Just beyond is a picnic site. This was originally the site of the basin serving the Sheffield and Rotherham Railway and later became a coalyard served by the Low Stubbin Tramroad. Access from Rotherham Road was along the stone sett track which passes under the westernmost arch. The Manchester, Sheffield and Lincolnshire branch of 1873 – which also served the later coalyard opened in 1935 – also passed under this arch, then rose up the now grassed ramp between the canal and the stone retaining wall that carried the tramroad towards the Midland Railway. The 1903 25 Inch Ordnance Survey map shows this layout most clearly. The upper 300 yards of the canal are now filled in and inaccessible.

b) The Low Stubbin Incline

Much of the route has been converted to a footpath and can be followed up the valley from Greasbrough Road. At the approach to Westfield Pumping Station the earlier route and the more gently curving realignment to New Stubbin can still be identified. Horses now graze in the space between. At Westfield many of the early nineteenth century buildings remain and all are built of the creamy sandstone so typical of buildings on the Fitzwilliam Estate. The atmospheric pumping station (Figure 4) is dated 1823 and the boilerhouse and workshop are attached. It worked thus until 1926 when electric pumps were installed and it continued to pump until 1990 when mining ceased west of the river Don. The atmospheric engine was dismantled in 1934.[6] Also surviving here are Westfield House, long occupied by the mine manager, the stables and smithy and a row of miners' cottages, whilst the offices stood until recently.

Virtually no trace of the Swallow Wood branch remains although a stone adit was still visible in 1986. At the site of Parkgate New Deep Colliery a circular brick shaft eight feet in diameter survives together with spoil mounds and the lower slope of the Kent's Main incline. Low Stubbin incline and the New Stubbin branch diverged here. New Stubbin Colliery was demolished in 1990 and today two concrete pillars mark the site of the shafts. It was probably the most typical of the Fitzwilliam collieries and had hardly altered since its opening. Buildings were mostly in panelled brickwork with round-arched windows and hipped slated roofs with the twin steel headgear rising above. Just to the south of the colliery cricket ground is a stone arched adit dated 1869, once an access to the Swallow Wood Mine but now mostly submerged by earth. The Old Sough nearby has orange staining from the ironstone.

Figure 4. The Westfield Colliery engine house dating from 1823 still survives on Westfield Lane, Rawmarsh with its boiler house attached. The datestone is on the lower arch. The beam engine bob used to protrude through the upper opening but was replaced by an electric pump in 192? when the present wheel and concrete frame were added. *The Author*

Low Stubbin incline between Greasbrough Lane and the Roman Rig, including the brickworks site, has disappeared under colliery spoil – which has now been regraded to provide school playing fields. Examples of bricks stamped 'EFW' can still be found around the area. The upper incline can be followed to Higher Stubbin where the colliery site is now a market garden. Part of the route to Low Stubbin Colliery survives though the cutting at Higher Stubbin has been infilled.

There is a splendid view at Higher Stubbin both down the valley towards Rawmarsh Church and Rotherham and across Wentworth Park including Hoober Stand which at an elevation of 517 feet is the highest point in Rotherham.

The Greasbrough Area

The Fenton Collieries
Coal mining was active in the Greasbrough area for 200 years, and from the pits several tramroads established links to Rotherham and the Don Navigation.

The most important coal masters were the Fentons who for a century were the largest colliery owners in Yorkshire – though much of their activity was in the Leeds and Wakefield areas. In 1757 Thomas and William Fenton took their first lease of 21 years from

Figure 5. Part of 'A plan of Bassingthorpe Colliery' drawn by William Fairbank in 1774. This shows the main line of the Fenton wagonway running to the south and east with several branches serving shallow pits in Bassingthorpe Spring Wood. *Rotherham Central Library*

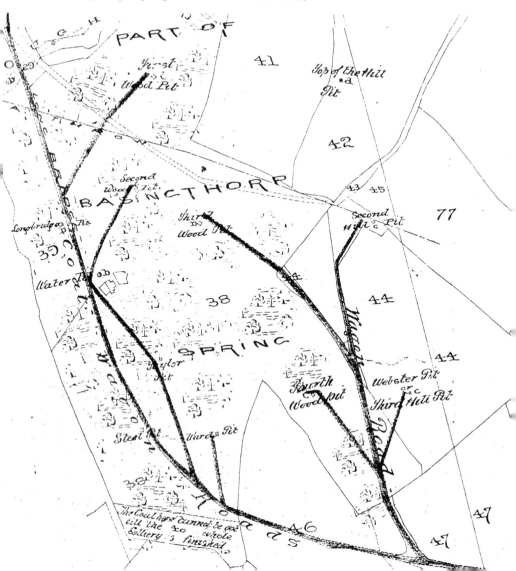

the second Marquis of Rockingham.

The Fenton pits in the Bassingthorpe Spring area were linked to the Don Navigation by 1763, by a wooden-railed wagon road about 13 miles long, running south-eastwards to near Rotherham canal wharf. By 1766 iron plates had been attached to the rails to reduce friction and wear. In March of that year two employees of the Fentons were caught stealing a length of these plates.[7]

The first reliable map of Bassingthorpe Colliery was that drawn by William Fairbank, the Sheffield surveyor, in 1774 (Figure 5). This shows two parallel wagon roads running from near Town Lane north and south of Common Lane (now Wingfield Road) and joining at the northern entrance to Bassingthorpe Spring Wood. The route headed south, then east through the wood to join another road from within the wood. The route continued south-eastwards approximately following the still-surviving footpath in the ravine running past Clough House, then across the wharf nearly where the [Beatson Clark] Glass Works are, to the canal side.[8]

From the upper wagon roads many branches ran to individual pits worked by groups of miners, for example, Firth Pit and Evans Pit. At the time when the above map was drawn it appears that ten pits were in operation producing 20,000 wagon loads per annum, half of the total coal sold along the Don Navigation. A new engine, Lower Engine, was built between 1774 and 1777 enabling lower seams to be worked. There were also inclines constructed below ground, for example in 1815 at Great Whimsey Pit. Whilst the bulk of coal at Greasbrough was being mined by the Fentons, leases had also been taken by John Bowden and John Hurst.

As mining operations extended northwards to the Whitegate area, the Bassingthorpe wagon road became overcrowded and increasingly expensive to operate, so the Marquis of Rockingham decided to construct a canal from the River Don at Eastwood up to Greasbrough and to build feeder tramroads to the several collieries. A survey was commissioned from John Varley in 1769 and, with variations, was eventually constructed by William Jessop in 1781. A plan of the canal as built was drawn up by William Fairbank in 1783. It was 1½ miles long with four locks and terminated at Cinder Bridge, with a short branch to Ochre Dyke Bridge. Water was supplied from the stream running through Wentworth Park, probably by enlarging Mill Dam which is nearest the canal head and is far too large to supply only a corn mill. There is no trace today of the 600-yard-long feeder Varley planned to link the dam with the canal head. The enlarged Mill Dam and the Greasbrough Canal are both shown

Figure 6. Surviving bridge on the Whitegate tramroad at Town Lane, Greasbrough built *c*.1781. It is constructed of stone with brick arches and central pier. *The Author*

on Teesdale's map of 1828.

The canal always belonged to the Marquis or the Fitzwilliams. Cinder Bridge became a small canal colony with cottages, the *Ship Inn* and limekilns, all now demolished. (Another *Ship Inn* survives near Ochre Dike Bridge).

From Cinder Bridge a tramroad extended through Wentworth Park, running alongside Mill Dam then through Morley Plantation and up an incline near Squirrel Castle engine house to Whitegate Colliery. A twin-arched bridge (Figure 6) survives at Town Lane (SK 406956) with openings 6 feet 6 inches wide and 8 feet 6 inches high and also a 100 yard length of route at the incline top. The engine house in Squirrel Castle Plantation was demolished some years ago but its foundations survive, and there are spoil heaps nearby. It was a three-storey structure with hipped roof and was latterly a house. The colliery site was lost *c*.1980 when the Wingfield estate was built.

The tramroad from Ochre Dike bridge ran along 'Wagon Road' then uphill to join the existing wagon roads in the Bassingthorpe area, passing close to Lower Engine, Old Engine and the sough that drained the mines, now all lost in housing. The darker patches of grass near Fenton Road probably indicate locations of former mine shafts.

These wagon roads are typical of mid-eighteenth century mining transport, where frequent branches were built above ground to shallow pits. They were also influenced by the land rising at a similar inclination to the Parkgate seam below. Greasbrough Colliery, sunk a century later, had one shaft with railways radiating underground along the seam.

The wooden wagons used were typical of those long used on Tyneside. They were approximately 7 feet by 4 feet and 11 inches at the top, 4 feet and 2 inches deep with concave sides and having a capacity of two tons. They ran on a track of approximately 4-foot gauge and were commonly drawn in short trains by oxen.

The Fentons' Greasbrough mining operations ceased in the late 1830s and the canal and wagon roads were closed. By now the workable seams were nearly exhausted; William Fenton had died in 1837 and his nephew and heir Kirkby Fenton had neither the interest nor the business skills to keep the 'Empire' going. Within a decade much of the canal was filled in, and Earl Fitzwilliam built Low Coach Road on the section below Glossop Lodge as part of a more easily graded carriage route between Wentworth Woodhouse and Rotherham. The Fentons' Rotherham residence was Car House and several generations lived there, the last being William.[9] The house was rebuilt in 1815 and demolished in 1964.

The route of the Bassingthorpe wagonway today

From the site of Clough House there is still a view eastwards towards the glassworks, canal and All Saints' Church, but in between, the route is obscured by new factories. There is an old quarry here, perhaps at the site of John Hurst's colliery which was advertised for sale in 1804. This colliery would also have used the wagon road.

The route westwards, rising steadily beside a small stream, can be seen, though opencasting to the north has disturbed adjacent land and obliterated most of the easterly wagon road branch. However, where it enters Bassingthorpe Spring Wood, heading for 'Third Wood Pit' (see Figure 5), a low embankment survives with a shale mound and shaft hollow at the pit site. On the main line the branch to 'Second Wood Pit' has a shallow cutting leading to a similar mound and shaft hollow. (A winter visit with low sun angle is best for recognition.) Note that near 'First Wood Pit' are several cuttings with concrete slabs which survive from later workings. The main line crossed the stream flowing out of Hudson's Rough on 'Long Bridge', a timber trestle bridge on a similar alignment to the surviving earth embankment of the Greasbrough Colliery Company's railway. Also crossing the stream here is the Roman Rig, but traces of that are now slight. The Hudson's Rough stream drained into a small reservoir which supplied 'Old Engine', which is shown on Jefferys' map as 'fire engine'. The two westerly arms are now obliterated by school playing fields or housing.

Old Parkgate or Greasbrough Colliery (SK 400950)

It was not long after the Fentons left the Greasbrough area that others were mining coal again, reflecting the improvement in mine pumping and the growing demand for coal in Rotherham.

Benjamin and Jonathan Sellars & Co. were sinking their Old Parkgate Colliery in 1850 on Town Lane near Scholes Coppice. In September, 1853, a lease was assigned to them for 21 years with an agreement to carry down a railway to a coal staith at Horse Croft on Low Lane, and also to construct a carriageway towards Masbrough - the future Bradgate Road – on the land of George Wilton Chambers. Also 'to deliver to George Wilton Chambers there such Parkgate coals as he shall require at a price of 5s 7d per ton soft coal and 6s 8d per ton hard coal'.[10] (Note that the present Wortley Road was not constructed until 1865, under the Rotherham and Four Lane Ends Trust (Wortley) Act of 1862.) Sellars' colliery appears in directories between 1852 and 1871 with an entry for Bradgate staith between 1860 and 1871. The lease map shows the course of the proposed railway running south of Hudson's Rough. It must have been of light construction and after closure was soon returned to agriculture.

The colliery was reworked from 1879 by the Greasbrough Coal Company and *c.*1886 another railway was constructed down to a staith at the junction of Wortley Road and Bradgate Road. This line passed to the north of Hudson's Rough and it remained in use until 1909 when the colliery closed and the Greasbrough Coal Co. became a merchant rather than a mining company.

The colliery became the Remount Farm and the site is now the *Hook Line and Sinker* public house. From the public house there are good views over where all the former lines used to run. The railway was one and three quarters of a mile long, running east then south

Figure 7. Embankment on the Greasbrough Coal Company's railway built *c.*1886, between Bassingthorpe Spring Wood and Hudson's Rough. The timber tressle bridge on the Fenton Wagonway (see Figure 5) was near to this spot. *The Author*

towards Bradgate and was operated by two standard gauge Manning Wardle 0-4-0 saddle tanks. The upper section followed an alignment quite similar to the northern arm of the Bassingthorpe wagonway and is now lost in playing fields. The embankment where it passed through Bassingthorpe Spring Wood is still visible and has become a pleasant wooded footpath (Figure 7). The southern section has become the alignment of Fenton Road.

Bradgate Colliery (SK 411935)

The last bite of the Greasbrough cherry was by Newton Chambers and Co. of Chapeltown who worked a colliery at Bradgate Road in the Robinson's brickyard quarry and in Hudson's Rough, in connection with their Grange Colliery. It worked from 1921 to 1963 and had a wagon staith close to the drift mine entrance.

Notes and References

1. Wath Parish Register.
2. Rawmarsh Inclosure Award – Rotherham Central Library, Parker-Rhodes Collection, ref 63/B – 96.
3. *The Elsecar and Milton Ironworks* by A. K. Clayton, p.41.
4. Recorded in Joseph Ibberson's *Book of Sections*, published in 1873.
5. 'The Atmospheric Engine at Parkgate' by G. T. Newbould, a New Stubbin colliery official, *Transactions of the Newcomen Society*, Vol.15, 1934-35.
6. Information sheet prepared by the N.C.B. Area Surveyor in 1970 – also lists certain closure dates.
7. West Riding, Pontefract Quarter Sessions Roll, April, 1766.
8. John Guest (1865) *Relics and Records of Men and Manufactures at Rotherham*, p.55.
9. White's Directory 1833 – Parish of Greasbrough.
10. Articles of Agreement between B. & J. Sellars & Co. and George Wilton Chambers, September 1853 – Rotherham Central Library, Item 170/B.

The following publications give much useful background information.
Charles Hadfield (1972) *The Canals of Yorkshire and North East England*, David and Charles.
John Goodchild (1978) *The Coal Kings of Yorkshire*, Wakefield Historical Publications, covers the Charlesworths' operations at Warren Vale and the Fentons at Greasbrough.
Sections of Strata of the Coal Measures of Yorkshire, compiled by W. H. Wilcockson, 1950.
G. G. Hopkinson (1957) 'Development of the South Yorkshire Coalfield 1500-1775', *Transactions of the Hunter Archaeological Society*, Volume 7.
White's and Kelly's Street Directories of the Sheffield and Rotherham area published between 1833 and 1974.

Maps
Jefferys' Map of Yorkshire, 1767, revised 1772.
Teesdale's Map of Yorkshire, 1828.
The following Ordnance Survey Maps:
1 inch to 1 mile, 1840.
6 inches to 1 mile, sheets 283 and 289 published in 1850 and 1947.
25 inches to 1 mile Editions of 1890, 1903, 1923 and 1934 (individual sheets vary by a year or so).

Acknowledgements

I would particularly like to thank the staff of Rotherham Central Library Archives and Local Studies Section and Sheffield Local Studies Library for their usual courtesy and help in producing the many relevant documents. Also to my fellow archaeology friends for their suggestions, particularly to John Goodchild regarding the Greasbrough area.

---

10. COAL FOR COMMERCE: SUSTAINING A MANUFACTURING ECONOMY

---

by Trevor Lodge

Rotherham...may fairly be considered as the centre of the great South Yorkshire coalfield, large and important collieries being worked in all directions around. It is also in many other respects a busy hive of industry, and possesses undoubted advantages as an industrial centre.

The Rotherham and District Annual, 1917

The Question of Supply

It was impossible for the Victorians and Edwardians to imagine a civilised world without coal. As the prime source of energy, coal fuelled the furnaces of industry, ran the country's railways and was the power behind Britain's dominant Royal Navy and merchant fleet.[1]

On the domestic front, coal burned in the open grate provided warmth, hot water and a means of cooking food. And, in the days before electricity was generally available, light for streets, homes and factories was provided by coal gas, the first true convenience fuel available 'on tap'.

The over-riding concern to secure fuel for their immediate and future needs was reflected in the almost morbid preoccupation the Victorians had with what came to be known as the Coal Question. Capitalists and politicians alike shared a real concern that the UK's coal reserves would not last, and both were at a loss to see how it would be possible to sustain the country's burgeoning industrialisation without coal.

The Local Scene

Nowhere was the 'thirst' for coal more evident than in Rotherham. Without a plentiful supply of suitable coal and its derivatives (especially coke and gas) the whole of the town's basic industries – iron, steel, brass and glass – would have ground to a standstill.

The economic ramifications of Rotherham's coal, however, went far beyond the town and its immediate surroundings. The present article considers the inter-relation of coal, iron and steel, and reveals a situation all too often neglected by economic historians, namely the dependence of Sheffield steel on coal – especially Rotherham coal.

The manufacture of iron and steel consumes large amounts of energy, and in consequence the Victorian steel barons were very alive to the Coal Question. A natural enough outcome was that many of the big iron and steel companies took steps to secure long-term coal supplies by acquiring their own collieries. This trend became of increasing significance to Rotherham, such that by 1920 six of the nine large collieries within a four mile radius of the town centre were under the control of just two such companies, John Brown and Co. Ltd. and the United Steel Companies Ltd.

Between them, these two steel companies were then employing over 70 per cent of the 19,000 miners working in the collieries within this area. Furthermore, if we include the 2,000 miners at Thurcroft Colliery, marginally outside our arbitrary boundary but very much part of United Steel's Rotherham group of collieries, the figure rises to 75 per cent.

Clearly, the manufacturing activities of Brown's and United Steel had a major influence on Rotherham's coal industry. Before we look in more detail at the local mining activities of these two large companies, it will be useful to consider also how coal was previously made available to local industry.

The Role of the Landowners

Prior to the Parliamentary Company Acts of 1855-56 and 1862, which allowed for the formation of large joint-stock companies in mining and manufacturing, the local coal markets were essentially controlled and/or directly supplied by major landowners, keen to capitalise on coal lying under their estates. Notable amongst these in South Yorkshire were the Duke of Norfolk, Lord Wharncliffe and Earl Fitzwilliam. Within this framework, the region's iron smelters and founders of the eighteenth and nineteenth centuries, especially those operating the relatively large ironworks at Rotherham, Chapeltown and Elsecar, were either supplied with coal direct by Earl Fitzwilliam, or mined it under leasing arrangements from Fitzwilliam or other local landowners.[2]

In Sheffield, both the steel trades and domestic consumers were supplied from the Duke of Norfolk's nearby collieries in Sheffield Park. Indeed, thanks to this advantage of location, Norfolk enjoyed a virtual monopoly of supply to Sheffield from the early 1700s until about 1820, after which time Earl Fitzwilliam began to market his coals more aggressively in the town. Fitzwilliam's efforts in this matter had a direct bearing on the creation of the region's nineteenth century transport base, and also served as a strong influence to attract important metallurgical industries to Rotherham (rather than Sheffield), so need to be considered more fully.

Broadly, Fitzwilliam adopted a three-pronged approach for marketing his coals more effectively, and to break Norfolk's monopoly in Sheffield. Firstly, he developed/enlarged his own coal mines around Greasbrough and Rawmarsh, in conjunction with promoting improvements to the River Don Navigation, which allowed him to transport these coals more effectively. When the canal link from Tinsley to Sheffield was opened in 1819 he was finally in a position to challenge Norfolk's monopoly.

Secondly, and acting in parallel with these initiatives, Fitzwilliam took steps to attract suitable metal-working industries to his Rawmarsh coalfield, where they could enjoy the benefits of cheap coal mined in the immediate vicinity. He therefore made land available in 1823 under favourable leasing conditions which encouraged two such businesses to become established at Park Gate on sites neighbouring his Low Stubbin Colliery. One was for the production of wrought or malleable iron, initially under partners Sanderson and Watson, and was soon known as Park Gate Forge. The other, under William Oxley, was devoted to what was previously regarded as a Sheffield specialism – the conversion of Swedish bar iron to steel. Fitzwilliam's choice of lessees was most astute. By selecting two businesses which operated in rather different markets (so were not commercial rivals) he further fostered conditions which were more conducive to their long-term success. The foresightedness of his plan can be gauged from the fact that the successor companies to both his original lessees are still in business today, trading respectively as the Rotherham complex of British Steel Engineering Steels and the Parkgate Steelworks of Aurora Forgings Ltd. By his actions Fitzwilliam established Park Gate as an 'industrial estate' fully a century and a quarter before such enlightened developments were adopted more generally for fostering the manufacturing economy of an area.

For the final part of his marketing strategy, Fitzwilliam leased the coal under certain parts of his estates to capitalists or joint stock companies keen to sink and develop collieries, taking in these instances only the royalty payments for coal extracted as his profit. This indirect approach was in contrast to the situation at Elsecar and

Greasbrough/Rawmarsh, where he worked the coal himself, using a steward to oversee the mines.[3] The leasing of a large tract of coal beneath his Tinsley Park estate was particularly notable, and its relevance is considered in greater depth later.

Gauging the Demand

With the coming of the railways, Earl Fitzwilliam took further steps to improve transport links between his Rawmarsh (Stubbin) collieries and Sheffield by actively promoting the Sheffield and Rotherham Railway in the mid-1830s. Opened in 1838 as a passenger carrying line, the line became Fitzwilliam's personal coal 'conduit' to Sheffield in August of the following year when a branch off the main line at Holmes to the Stubbin pits was opened. All but one of the coal wagons working on the Sheffield and Rotherham Railway belonged to Fitzwilliam![4]

Of particular interest is the evidence presented to the House of Lords Committee established to examine the need for a railway between Sheffield and Rotherham. Even at this early stage, Sheffield's steel industry was quite sizeable. W. Vickers, of steel makers Naylor, Hutchinson Vickers & Company told the committee on 6 July, 1835, that there were then 56 converting (i.e. cementation) furnaces in the town, together with 62 crucible furnace shops containing a total of 554 crucible melting holes. Speaking of the need for a plentiful supply of cheap fuel, Vickers said that coal was consumed in the various works:

> *By the Steam Engine Boilers for the Purpose of raising Steam; and by converting Iron into Steel; when in the Bar into Cast Steel; and by all the Processes of the Reduction of large Masses of Steel into small Masses, and of the various Manufactures of Cutlery and Hardware of every Description.*

Based on information supplied to him by Samuel Wingfield (Naylor Hutchinson's clerk), Vickers computed that Sheffield's total coal consumption, industrial and domestic, was 505,000 tons per annum. Of the 331,000 tons used in the works, steel conversion/casting consumed 93,000 tons, the '1,000 different' manufactories a further 200,000 tons and 'Engine Coal' amounted to 38,000 tons. (There were at this time 76 stationary steam engines in the town, with an aggregate estimated rating of 1,353 horsepower). Vickers had calculated that one third of the price of bar steel was made up from coal consumed in its manufacture.

On the following day (7 July, 1835) Samuel Jackson of edge tool makers Spear and Jackson enlightened the committee as to the source of the fuel. Nearly half of the coal used in Sheffield came from the pits of Hounsfield & Company, tenants to the Duke of Norfolk. The balance was provided by Booth and Company at Tinsley and a Mr Chambers (Jordan Colliery). The point was also made that there had been a general reduction in prices when Earl Fitzwilliam's coal was first available by the canal, and Vickers was of the opinion that the proposed railway, by reducing transport costs, would make Fitzwilliam's coal even more available.

Ten years after the opening of the Sheffield and Rotherham Railway, coal consumption had increased markedly. Dr R. A. Mott, writing in the National Coal Board's house magazine *Coal* in July, 1947, listed Sheffield's coal consumption for 1848, though regrettably does not indicate his source. The figures were: 312,000 tons for house heating; 188,000 tons (as coke) for crucible steel manufacture; 46,000 tons (as 'soft coke') by 'manufacturers' (edge tools, etc); 11,000 tons (mostly as coke) by iron and brass founders; 80,000 tons for steam engines; 32,000 tons for steel converting (cementation) furnaces; and 28,000 tons (mostly as coke) by the railways. The total came to 800,000 tons – almost a 60 per cent increase over the 1835 figure.

By creating such a surge in the demand for coal, the railways altered the whole scale of development of the collieries.

Company Coal

Following the example of South Yorkshire's ironmasters – cited earlier – Benjamin Huntsman & Co. set the trend for local steel makers by acquiring a lease from Earl Fitzwilliam to work coal under Tinsley Park.[5] Fitzwilliam had developed a colliery at Tinsley in 1819 to coincide with the opening of the Tinsley-Sheffield section of the South Yorkshire Navigation and Huntsman's lease – on 1,200 acres of 'mineral property', almost all of the coal under the Parish of Tinsley – was obtained sometime between 1841 and 1849. One version of the story is that Huntsman acquired the lease by buying out one Mr Booth (or his executors). Booth had been connected with Tinsley Park Colliery in the 1830s, using it as a source of coke for his iron-smelting blast furnace operations at the Park Iron Works in nearby Attercliffe.

For a short period in the 1860s, Huntsman also had a lease on the Nunnery Colliery from the Duke of Norfolk so briefly had control over most of the Sheffield coal market. Subsequently Tinsley Park

Colliery passed to a joint stock company, the Tinsley Park Colliery Co. Ltd., registered on 23 April , 1898, with H. F. Huntsman as chairman. A strong link with the Huntsman family of steel makers was apparent for many years. A Tinsley speciality was beehive coke, much in demand by Sheffield's traditional crucible steelmakers, Huntsman & Co. included. The colliery also supplied coal for more general heating applications in steel melting and processing.

Not only did the entry of John Brown & Co. Ltd. into coal follow a somewhat different pattern to Huntsman's, but the company as a whole was destined for much greater things, and ultimately rose to become a recognised world leader in its field. The company grew from modest beginnings in 1837 when its founder, John Brown, borrowed £500 from the Sheffield Banking Company to establish a business on his own account. Trading from the Atlas Works in Sheffield's East End, Brown soon realised that the fast growing railway network offered incredible business opportunities. Indeed, he made his first fortune from the conical spring railway buffer, which he invented and patented in 1848. With partners William Bragge and John Devonshire Ellis he expanded into other lucrative markets, particularly the supply of wrought iron armour plate for the Royal Navy's 'ironclads' from the 1850s, and railway rails made from revolutionary Bessemer steel from the 1860s.[6]

As events unfolded, the Atlas Works would become one of the first of a new generation of works established on the Don Valley flats in Sheffield's East End, which numbered employees in hundreds rather

Figure 1. Engraving of the Atlas Works about 1890, with the chimneys of coal-fired furnaces and boilers much in evidence.

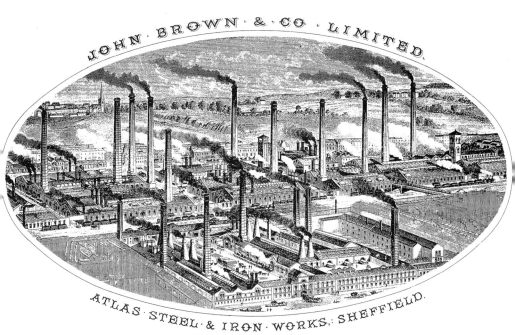

than handfuls (Figure 1). The potential for further expansion was so great that in 1864 outside capital was obtained by floating the business on the Stock Exchange as a limited company.

John Brown & Co. Ltd. was registered with a capital of £1 million, an unheard of sum for the time. The company acquired Aldwarke Main and Car House Collieries in Rotherham in 1873, and by 1891 was engaged in sinking a completely new colliery at Canklow – Rotherham Main (Figure 2). By 1900 the combined output of these collieries was 6,000 tons per day – 4,000 tons from the Aldwarke Main complex alone – and they provided employment for 4,000 miners. Not content with this, in 1909 Brown's acquired the share capital for Dalton Main Collieries Ltd. which operated Roundwood Colliery and had recently developed a large pit at Silverwood.[7] By this stage Brown's had a lease on some 7,000 acres of coal bearing lands in Rotherham.

In 1914, the Jubilee Year of the limited company, the chairman was able to tell shareholders that the company was one of the largest producers of coal in South Yorkshire, with an output (including that of its subsidiaries) of 2½ million tons per annum.

Nor were matters on the steel side static during the intervening years either. In 1903 Brown's obtained a controlling interest in steelmakers, Thos. Firth & Sons Ltd. of the neighbouring Norfolk Works. The output of the Atlas Works at this time was some 50,000 tons of steel (mostly from openhearth furnaces) with Norfolk Works contributing 6,000 tons of crucible steel and 30,000 tons of openhearth steel.[8] Steps were also taken to secure outlets for steel products (forgings, etc.) by a process of vertical integration.[9] The most notable of these was the purchase of the Clydebank

Figure 2. Edwardian view of Rotherham Main Colliery.

Figure 3. An example of a standard gauge railway wagon used to transport coal. This particular example appeared in an advert for John Brown & Co. Ltd. Many wagons of this type were later built by Craven's Carriage and Wagon Works in Sheffield, a John Brown & Co. subsidiary from the 1920s.

Engineering and Shipbuilding Co. Ltd. in 1899. Today, John Brown of Sheffield is no longer a household word but John Brown of Clydebank, once just a subsidiary, is still known the world over as the builder of the famous Cunard Queens. Even further expansion into other engineering concerns was to follow – for example, the acquisition of Craven's Railway Carriage & Wagon Co. Ltd. in 1919 – but is outside the scope of the present study (Figure 3).

The other company of principal concern to us at this stage is the United Steel Companies Ltd. This conglomerate was not created until 1918, but the relevant parts of the jigsaw were taking shape well before this.[10] In reality United Steel owes its origins to the Bessemer steel rail trade which took the Sheffield region by storm in the 1860s. One of the companies involved, Samuel Fox & Co. Ltd., can be traced back to a humble wire-drawing business established by Fox in 1841/42 at Stocksbridge, north-west of Sheffield. Fox was one of the world's first steelmakers to adopt Bessemer's pneumatic method of bulk steelmaking, following hard on the heels of John Brown and Charles Cammell (another Sheffield steelmaker).

The unbridled success of the Bessemer steel rail trade established by Brown, Cammell and Fox was largely responsible for several others setting up in the same line of business, including partners Hampton and Radcliffe at the Ickles, Rotherham. Their business experienced several ownership changes in the 1870s (mainly due to financial upheavals) but by 1883 was trading as Steel, Peech & Tozer Ltd. (SPT).

Both Fox's and SPT continued to grow successfully by responding to market demands, and were heavily involved in the manufacture of railway materials by the early 1900s – especially tyres, axles, wheels and springs. The two companies had already forged a working alliance by 1915, partially at the instigation of the Ministry of Munitions, which was keen to maximise the country's wartime steel output.

Full amalgamation came in the closing months of the First World War, when SPT's chairman, Henry Steel, appreciated that his business would be more effectively cushioned against the economic ups and downs of a very uncertain future if it could become powerful enough to acquire its own raw material sources and obtain captive outlets for its products.

The amalgamation was achieved in two stages. In 1917 SPT joined with Fox's and the pair proceeded to acquire the Frodingham Iron & Steel Co. Ltd. at Scunthorpe and the Workington Iron & Steel Co. Ltd. in Cumberland. One year later this newly formed group, now formally constituted as the United Steel Companies Ltd. acquired Rothervale Collieries Ltd. With Rothervale they were not buying an unknown entity, for both SPT and Fox's were longstanding Rothervale customers and were fully cognisant with the quality of its coals.

Figure 4. Treeton Colliery looking down the aptly-named Pit Lane with colliers coming off shift.

Rothervale Collieries Ltd. had been incorporated in 1875 to acquire the properties of the Fence Colliery Co. Ltd., which comprised Fence Colliery (opened *c.*1842) and Orgreave Colliery (1851). The new company quickly put in hand the sinking of Treeton Colliery (Figure 4). At the time of their acquisition by United Steel, the Rothervale properties were made more attractive on account of the modern coking and by-products plant being erected at Thurcroft Colliery (sunk 1909-13).[11] Developments at Thurcroft were somewhat hampered underground due to the presence of geological problems, with a major fault of 150 yards displacement encountered in the two shafts.

United Steel's Rothervale Collieries branch was certainly not regarded as marginal to the business of making steel. Walter Benton Jones of the original Rothervale Collieries Ltd. joined the infant United Steel board of directors and such was his calibre that by 1928 he had risen to become chairman of United Steel – a position he held for over 30 years.

Though it never gained the glamour that Brown's enjoyed, United Steel was also destined to become a giant in its own right, and by 1940 would be responsible for producing 20 per cent (one-fifth) of the steel output of the entire British Commonwealth. Its potential had been apparent to the American iron and steel consultants, Brassert's, who were engaged by United Steel in the 1920s with a view to outlining a blueprint for future developments.[12]

According to Brassert's report, dated 1929, United Steel was by then one of the two largest iron and steel producers in Great Britain. Operating on four major manufacturing sites, it possessed 20 blast furnaces, three Bessemer converters, 46 openhearth steelmaking furnaces, 14 rolling mills and numerous downstream activities. Crude steel output (i.e., before rolling/finishing) amounted to 1.5 million tons per annum. Its Rothervale coal reserves comprised 260 million tons (74 million still to be proved) under 10,000 acres of leased mining royalties. Weekly outputs from the Rothervale collieries amounted to 12,000 tons at Treeton (falling to 8,000 tons in the summer) and 17,000-19,000 tons at Orgreave. Production at Thurcroft was still rising as development proceeded, and the 12,000 tons weekly output was expected to rise to 20,000 tons. In addition, the coking plants at Orgreave and Thurcroft were weekly contributing 4,000 tons and 2,000 tons of coke respectively to the business.

Rotherham's only integrated steel producer, the Park Gate Iron & Steel Co. Ltd., rather surprisingly did not move to secure a direct interest in the mining of coal.[13] Known colloquially as 'Park Gate Forge' the works had passed through a number of owners in the nineteenth century but at each stage was still reliant on Earl Fitzwilliam's nearby Stubbin Colliery for its fuel requirements. Additionally, in the 1920s Earl Fitzwilliam promoted the South Yorkshire Chemical Works, a large by-product coking plant on Taylor's Lane at Park Gate which supplied Park Gate Iron & Steel's blast furnace needs. This arrangement pertained until 1975 when the No. 2 blast furnace at Park Gate was blown out for the very last time (Figure 5).

Iron and steel barons other than those we have considered in some detail continued to show an interest in South Yorkshire coal, often with unexpected outcomes. Kilnhurst Colliery was acquired in the late 1920s by Stewarts and Lloyds Ltd., a steel tube manufacturing conglomerate with plants in Scotland and the West Midlands. It must have reported favourably on the venture since two other Scottish companies, Wilson & Clyde Coal Co. Ltd. and the Coltness Iron Co. Ltd. then took steps to acquire jointly the neighbouring mining property at Warren Vale. Significantly, Stewarts & Lloyds had plans for a monster greenfield industrial development in the East Midlands, but did not give the go-ahead for the Corby Iron, Steel and Tube Works until it was satisfied that Kilnhurst coal was of sufficient quality and availability to sustain the venture.

Consolidation

As business ventures, steelmaking and mining were poles apart. The

Figure 5. Iron-smelting blast furnaces at the Park Gate Iron & Steel Co. Ltd., erected about 1905. These consumed considerable quantities of coke supplied from the South Yorkshire Chemical Works.

steel industry may be considered speculative insofar as markets may prove volatile and demand for the product fluctuate, but the actual process of manufacture was fairly predictable.

Adopting proven techniques gave a very good chance of reproducing past performances and maintaining product quality. In this sense the industry carried a low element of risk.

Mining, on the other hand, was always much more speculative. There were many unpredictable variables which contributed to the uncertainty, mostly related to geology. Factors such as the nature of the rock strata, especially the presence of faults, the nature of the coal seams themselves and the condition of the roof and floor in the mine could all conspire to make the coal expensive or difficult to work. Furthermore, underground galleries could be additionally troubled with water and explosive/poisonous gases. As we have already noted, both Brown's and United Steel experienced these vagaries when developing their Rotherham pits.

The high risk to investment capital in coal mining was a major factor which encouraged joint ventures since these effectively spread the risk. If a company or individual partially invested in several colliery properties, the law of averages meant that there was a good chance that some of these would prove sound and counter losses from the occasional poor investment. A straightforward example of not putting all one's eggs (capital) in one basket (mine). Virtually the whole of the Doncaster coalfield was developed on this basis, with two giant Derbyshire-based iron-smelting businesses dominating the scene – the Sheepbridge Coal and Iron Co. Ltd. and the Staveley Coal and Iron Co. Ltd.

By the end of the Edwardian era, for example, Brown's had joined forces with Sheepbridge to sink and develop Rossington Colliery south of Doncaster. Somewhat closer to Rotherham, Sheepbridge was associated with the collieries at Tinsley Park, Dinnington and Maltby. Similarly, Brown's was associated with the collieries at Maltby and Cortonwood (Wombwell) through Charles B. B. McLaren, a company director of all three concerns.

I have chosen the term networking to describe the widespread phenomenon of common directorships which fostered links between companies even when they were not necessarily officially connected in joint ventures. It was not uncommon for a steel company owner or director to acquire a significant financial stake in a colliery undertaking and in return accept a seat on the colliery company's board of directors.[14] These directors common to both were then in an influential position to encourage co-operation and trading between the two concerns. It was only natural that they would encourage their steel company to buy coal from their colliery, in return for the colliery purchasing mining consumables (e.g. forgings and castings) from the steel company (Figure 6). For example, through its Chairman, Charles Markham, Park Gate Iron & Steel was associated with Bullcroft Main and Hickleton Main collieries at Doncaster. A similar pattern of consolidation was repeated throughout UK heavy industry, and by the 1930s networking had evolved to such an extent that a socialist academic group, the Labour Research Department, published in 1935 a modest pamphlet by W. Fox entitled *Coal Combines in Yorkshire* so that Labour MPs and trade union activists could better appreciate the true situation.

Legislation had actually been passed in the mid-1920s to encourage greater co-operation within the mining industry generally. The Mining Industry Act of 1926 resulted in far-reaching consequences in the re-organisation of UK coal mining and, amongst other objectives, encouraged the amalgamation of smaller companies in the interests of greater efficiency. Another result was the creation of marketing co-operatives. *The Iron and Coal Trades Review*, on 9 November, 1928, reported details of several such co-operative schemes, including the Rotherham and District Collieries

Figure 6. Silverwood Colliery illustrates well the phenomenon of networking. Sunk and developed by Dalton Main Collieries Ltd., it was largely equipped by engineers Markham & Co. Ltd. of Chesterfield. Much of the steel was provided by the Park Gate Iron & Steel Co. Ltd., another company controlled by the Markham family. Finally, for good measure, Markham & Co. Ltd. was later absorbed by the John Brown group!

Association, which was the selling agency for Brown's Rotherham collieries, Dalton Main Collieries Ltd., United Steel's Rothervale collieries (and the associated colliery at Samuel Fox & Co. Ltd., Stocksbridge) and Tinsley Park Colliery Co. Ltd.

Public Ownership

Nationalisation of the collieries was supposed to rid the industry of capitalistic affiliations, or networking, which the labour movement viewed with some suspicion. State control of the industry was first seriously considered in the aftermath of the First World War by a Royal Commission, but the issue was shelved as unworkable despite a worsening situation which, unchecked, ultimately led to the General Strike of 1926. Then, during the Second World War, the mines were run in the nation's interests through the Ministry of Fuel and Power, bringing full nationalisation a step closer. The deed was finally consummated by the post-war Labour Government in 1947 as part of a wider programme which sought state ownership for the mines, railways, public utilities (gas, electricity) and the steel industry.

Nationalisation of the pits proved to be something of an anticlimax for the miners, who had expected so much – too much, as events turned out. The reality was that little changed (at least initially) and their new bosses, the government-appointed National Coal Board, seemed no better than the coal barons they replaced.

Not only the miners felt betrayed. Former colliery owners were often embittered at what they regarded as derisory levels of compensation offered by the government for their mining properties. This was particularly the case with the more progressive mining companies which had invested heavily in new equipment immediately before the war years, only to see insufficient account of this expenditure being taken in the subsequent compensation value. The deeper long-term forebodings of iron and steel companies to the loss of their collieries were aptly paraphrased in the history of one local large coal, iron, chemical and engineering conglomerate. In *A History of Newton Chambers and its People*, Harold Elliott refers to a passage from Shakespeare's *The Merchant of Venice* to describe the real fear felt within the company at the prospect of losing its colliery properties, especially the knock-on effect this would have on the future well-being of the remaining business. 'You take my house', said Shylock, 'when you do take the prop that doth sustain my house'. The fact that it was uttered by a money lender rather detracts from its nobler sentiments, but Elliott was reminding his readers in a most elegant manner of the very close bonds which perforce existed between the coal, iron and steel industries.

The larger coal and steel combines which lost their collieries on nationalisation were dealt a further blow when their iron and steel manufacturing assets were seized by the state in 1951 as the final enactment of Labour's nationalisation programme. This particular exercise, however, was essentially still-born, since a Conservative government was returned to power before full state control of iron and steel came into force, and the relevant Act was speedily countermanded.

Under the New Regime

The collieries around Rotherham at the time of nationalisation were still of sufficient size and number to justify grouping them into a separate administrative unit within the NCB's North-Eastern Division – the No. 3 Area (Rotherham). By a quirk of geography, the former United Steel's Rothervale collieries (Orgreave, Thurcroft, and Treeton) passed to the N. E. Division's Area No. 1 (Worksop).

Under the state, Brown's pits had varying fortunes. The early closure of Rotherham Main in 1954 came as no real surprise, bearing in mind its poor geological circumstance. Aldwarke Main lasted a few more years, closing in 1961 as its reserves became depleted. Silverwood, as the most recent sinking, obviously had the greatest reserves and continued in production until 1994.

On balance, the former United Steel Rothervale Collieries fared better than many. All were still in production by 1980, and only gradual depletion of reserves brought about closure – Orgreave in 1981, Treeton in 1990, and Thurcroft in 1991.

New Stubbin Colliery proved to be a good investment for Earl Fitzwilliam and his successors, remaining in production until 1978. The surface buildings then stood substantially intact for several years pending a decision regarding the site's suitability as a mining museum, but sadly this came to nothing.

Coal Still Supreme?

By the early 1950s, the steel barons faced a sort of Hobson's Choice, being compelled to draw most of their energy requirements (coal, gas, electricity or any combination thereof) from state controlled enterprises.

A growing availability of cheap fuel oil allowed them some flexibility, and many gave a new lease of life to their ageing openhearth steel melting furnaces by adopting oil-firing instead of using coal-derived producer gas. This option was exercised by all the big local steelmakers, including Steel Peech, Park Gate and Fox's. Oil was also now employed increasingly for reheating steel prior to rolling or forging, and coal-fired reheating furnaces were phased out.

Revolutionary new steelmaking technology, introduced generally in the 1960s, finally rendered energy-intensive openhearth steelmaking obsolete. Basic oxygen steelmaking (BOS) was adopted at many integrated works for general steel grades, and electric melting for engineering and alloy steels of the types traditionally manufactured in South Yorkshire. By the mid-1960s most of the region's alloy and stainless grades were being produced in electric arc furnaces, including some giant 100 ton units of previously unconceived rates of production.[15] Consequently, coal regained much of its importance in supplying energy to the South Yorkshire steel industry, albeit indirectly, since the lion's share (over 80 per cent) of English electricity at this time was generated in coal-fired power stations.

Since then, coal's power base has gradually been eroded as alternative means of generating electricity have gained prominence, i.e., nuclear power and oil-fired power stations. The whole process has gathered momentum of late with the commissioning of a number of compact generating stations fired by natural gas which have directly replaced ageing coal-fired stations. This so-called 'dash for gas' poses a real threat to the viability of South Yorkshire's deep mines, and coal now shares an uneasy alliance with natural gas as one of the two fossil fuels used to generate most of the UK's electricity.

Meantime, our iron and steel industry generally has evolved in such a way that there is now no advantage to be gained from closer co-operation with UK coal producers. Direct consumption of coal by the UK steel industry is confined to its conversion to coke for use in ore-smelting blast furnaces, and the technology of modern blast furnaces is such that coke made from UK coal is no longer suitable as part of the furnace burden, or charge.[16]

Today's Legacy

All the Rotherham collieries mentioned in the narrative are no more: none survived long enough to be privatised following the break up of British Coal (the successor to the National Coal Board). The once great John Brown empire is fragmented, and save the yard at

Clydebank, what remains is a shadow of the former enterprise. The Atlas Works is largely cleared away, though some parts have been redeveloped and are now incorporated in Sheffield Forgemasters Ltd., itself a product of 1980s reorganisation and currently going through yet further ownership changes. Of the United Steel Companies' steel enterprises in South Yorkshire, Stocksbridge continues to thrive, now under British Steel ownership, but the former Steel, Peech & Tozer complex at Rotherham has, like John Brown's, suffered fragmentation and partial closure. 'Parkgate Forge', once heavily dependent on fuel from its landlord, Earl Fitzwilliam, continued to grow and was radically modernised during relocation in the 1960s. The original business has evolved into British Steel's Aldwarke, Roundwood and Thrybergh complex, which has an annual liquid steel capacity in excess of one million tonnes and is now one of the key sites in Europe for the manufacture of engineering steels.

Physical reminders of Rotherham's coal mining legacy – some in unexpected circumstances – are few and fast disappearing. The absolute gem has to be the early nineteenth century stone built engine house tucked away on Westfield Road at Rawmarsh which served the long-gone Low Stubbin Colliery. More typical of the boom period pits (1870-1910) are the substantial brick buildings of the former Brown's Car House Colliery on Greasbrough Road. This pit was an old sinking which closed for production before the First World War, and only the fact that it was used after that time as a service pit for nearby Aldwarke Main Colliery rather fortuitously guaranteed their survival.

Former colliery company houses are still much in evidence and probably merit a special study. Of particular note in the present context is Ellis Street at Canklow, which perpetuates the name of the first chairman of John Brown & Co. Ltd., and the rather fine terraced properties on nearby West Bawtry Road which Brown's had erected

Figure 7. Former John Brown colliery officials' houses on West Bawtry Road, Rotherham.

for its deputies and undermanagers at Rotherham Main Colliery (Figure 7). Parts of Thurcroft could be classed as a model mining village, although perhaps not quite up to the standards of Woodlands, north of Doncaster, which received national acclaim when it was specially built for miners at Brodsworth Colliery.

The Future

To the uninformed, the region's heavy industry which survives is free of the shackles which once bound it to coal. However the link remains, even if it is not readily apparent. All steel melting, rolling and shaping in South Yorkshire uses electricity as the major energy source, and coal remains very much part of the equation since it is still responsible for generating some 60 per cent of the region's power.[17]

Of coal's future role in power generation, and therefore to manufacturing industry, we cannot comment with certainty. Of its past contribution to both there is no doubt. Ever since coke displaced charcoal for iron smelting from the mid-1700s onwards, coal and derived fuels have been one of the sheet anchors of South Yorkshire's metallurgical industries. It has been a long and distinguished partnership, and is only now entering its Indian Summer.

According to figures from the Department of Trade and Industry, in 1996 UK coal-fired power stations consumed 48 million tonnes to produce 40 per cent of the country's electricity needs. This figure has been estimated to halve by the year 2000, and early in 1998 the All-Party Parliamentary Coalfield Communities Group gave the stark prediction that coal's share of the market 'will disappear altogether between 2005 and 2010 unless the decline is arrested.'

Making that decision – ' UK Coal or no? – against the alternative of a foolhardy growing dependence on politically-fickle fuels, imported from an increasingly energy-hungry world, will form the basis of our Coal Question for the new millennium. We have very likely already arrived at the wrong answer.

Notes and References

1. It is generally accepted that the end of the Edwardian era marked the high point of the British coal industry's contribution to the country's economy. British annual coal production first exceeded 200 million tons in 1897, and between 1901 and 1910 output averaged 220 million to 260 million tons annually. The all-time record was achieved in 1913, when 287 million tons were mined. South Yorkshire was somewhat out of step in this overall situation. Its absolute output and its share of UK output continued to rise after 1913 because of the contribution from large pits being opened out in the Doncaster area, a process largely completed by 1930.
2. An excellent general introduction to the development of the South Yorkshire coalfield, including the part played by the landowners, can be found in the first three chapters of *Studies in the Yorkshire*

Coal Industry, edited by J. Benson and R. G. Neville (Manchester University Press, 1976).

3. *Aristocratic Enterprise* (Blackie, Glasgow and London, 1975), Graham Mee's account of the coal mining activities of the 4th and 5th Earls Fitzwilliam, though it ostensibly covers the period up to 1857, does not really address the 5th Earl's direct and indirect coal marketing strategies, even though they were all largely in place by the 1840s.

4. F. Whishaw, *The Railways of Great Britain & Ireland*, 1842, J. Weale, London; reprinted in 1969 by David and Charles, Newton Abbot. Whishaw further records that Earl Fitzwilliam was 'the only coal-owner at present using this line'.

5. The inclusion of Tinsley Park Colliery in a narrative preoccupied with 'Rotherham Coal' is fully justified since Tinsley was actually part of the Parish of Rotherham until 1911, when it passed to Sheffield. The Benjamin Huntsman concerned was none other than the son of clockmaker Benjamin Huntsman, who invented and perfected the technique of crucible steel melting.

6. Sir Allan Grant, *Steel and Ships*, 1950, Michael Joseph Ltd., London.

7. This desire to secure further coal reserves was probably due to unfolding events at Rotherham Main, which was proving to be a poor investment. Much water had been met with during the sinking, and as underground development proceeded it soon became clear that the pit was in a bad location. It was sited on the edge of a large trough in the geological strata formed by two major and many minor faults, and was not able to sustain a viable output. Indeed, though it employed some 2,000 miners up to the First World War, it was virtually closed down through the 1930s and 1940s, requiring only some 300 employees to keep it on a care and maintenance basis. Unlike Rotherham Main, Silverwood was a particularly good investment, producing 1.25 million tons annually by the late 1930s.

8. I have estimated that these combined quantities of steel would have required upwards of 400,000 tons of coal per annum for melting, rolling and processing.

9. Integration is a term used by economic historians to describe business amalgamations. Vertical integration can be either backward integration – the acquisition of a raw material supplier – or forward integration, which here would apply to acquiring a steel consuming business. The other type of integration is horizontal integration, when two 'like' companies amalgamate and then effect savings by rationalising wasteful duplication.

10. See P. W. S. Andrews and E. Brunner, *Capital Development in Steel*, 1951, Blackwell, Oxford, for a fuller account of the United Steel Companies Ltd.

11. By-product coking plants were also established elsewhere in the coalfield meantime, those at Rotherham Main, Silverwood and Tinsley Park being of relevance here.

12. Report on the Properties and Operations of the United Steel Companies Ltd. by H. A. Brassert & Co., published in 1929 for private circulation.

13. An integrated steelworks (not to be confused with economic integration – see note 9) was one which took in iron ore and coal/coke as raw materials, and on one site proceeded to smelt the ore to make iron, then convert this into steel, and finally roll this to billets, bars, sections, plate, etc. Most of Sheffield's steel plants were non-integrated works, buying in pig iron for steelmaking from producers elsewhere.

14. These examples have been verified by *The Mining Manual* and *Mining Year Book*, for 1926, published jointly by Walter R. Skinner and *The Financial Times*, London.

15. The Park Gate Iron and Steel Co. Ltd. adopted the rather novel Kaldo process, sourced with so-called hot metal (i.e. liquid iron) from the company's blast furnace plant but this was atypical of the region as a whole, and barely lasted ten years (1964-1974).

16. This gradual decrease in demand by iron smelters and foundry industries was reflected in the closure of local by-product coking plants. The Tinsley by-product plant was actually closed down permanently in 1942 as a precautionary measure against air raids, since glare from the ovens would have served as a beacon for the Luftwaffe. Rotherham Main and Silverwood ovens lasted until the early 1960s, and the South Yorkshire Chemical Works closed in the mid-1970s. Closure of the Orgreave coking plant about 1992 marked the end of coke production in the Rotherham area.

17. In the last 25 years, for example, some 40 million tons of quality engineering, alloy and stainless steels have been computed as that share of the total output of South Yorkshire steel which has been melted with electricity supplied from coal fired power stations.

Acknowledgements

My thanks are due to fellow industrial historians Roy Etherington, Gordon Green and Ken Plant for their willing assistance, extended over many years. All the illustrations are from my own collection.

11. THE STOVE GRATE, RANGE, AND DECORATIVE CAST IRON INDUSTRY OF ROTHERHAM

by Chris Morley

Rotherham is pleasantly situated in a valley near the confluence of the Rivers Rother and Don: it is by no means a handsome town, but contains a spacious and rather elegant parish church...The town is in a very thriving condition: its inhabitants carry on a considerable trade in coals, and other articles by the river Don: and have the benefit of a very excellent weekly market on Monday. On the other side of the bridge is the village of Masborough, where the extensive and far-famed iron-works belonging to Messrs.Walker are carried on; these were begun in 1746 by that worthy, enlightened, and enterprising character, Mr. Samuel Walker, in conjunction with his brothers Aaron and Jonathan, and almost every kind of cast-iron articles are now manufactured at them, besides cannon of the largest calibre; the bridges of Sunderland and Yarm were also cast at the foundries of Masborough.

SO IS ROTHERHAM DESCRIBED in the 1829 edition of *Patterson's Road Book.*[1] However, this description is slightly out of date because the Walkers had transferred their patterns and machinery for the manufacture of cannons from Masbrough to the Gospel Oak Iron Works in Staffordshire in 1822[2] and by 1829, the Walkers' Ironworks had been sold as a number of varied factories.[3] Nonetheless, the above passage shows that the Walker enterprise had been, of great importance to the town, and their legacy was to continue long after they had moved from South Yorkshire.

The Walkers of Masbrough and the 'luxury' stove grate industry

A blast furnace had been erected on the Holmes Goit at Masbrough in 1740 and, because there are no records of this furnace working in conjunction with a finery, it has been assumed that it produced only recastable pig iron.[4] In 1745-6 the Walkers moved to Masbrough, building 'a casting house with two air furnaces [reverberatory furnaces for re-melting pig and scrap cast iron] and a smithy adjoining'. It was an extension into the production of heavier castings than could be handled at their original site. Unfortunately, we have no knowledge of the types of castings made at the two foundries in these early years other than that some small bushes, and possibly shoe-buckles were among the initial five tons produced at Grenoside. By 1748 they were making cast iron cooking pots,[5] and in 1756-1757 the company purchased the lease of the blast furnace for their own use. Sad-irons and ship ballast were added to their output in 1764, prod-ucts that were to grow in quantity over the ensuing years, and by 1774 guns were also being produced.[6]

The Walkers became well connected with major manufacturers, not only in ironworking but also in textiles and engineering. In 1750 Samuel Walker had entered into a steel making partnership with John Roebuck of Sheffield whose sons had been among the founding partners in the Carron Ironworks[7] and in 1763, they were purchasing pig iron from Carron on preferential terms.[8]

The entry of the Walkers into stove grate production cannot be dated, but if it followed the pattern of Carron or Coalbrookdale then it must have occurred in the 1770s. A book, *The Stove Grate Maker's Guide*[9], published in 1771 contained illustrations of numerous designs for cast iron stove grates, many of them enriched by cast-on decorative detail, and, no doubt, a copy had been made available to the Walkers' management. This, and the migration of workers between Darby's Coalbrookdale Ironworks, the Carron Company's works and Walkers' own foundry brought ideas and surely designs to Rotherham.[10] Charles Green, a noted nineteenth century designer and critic who hailed from Sheffield, wrote:

As to the Walkers stoves, to the art student they are indeed a very valuable study, forming as they do a chain in art history, of which the works of Wedgwood, in pottery, and Bewick, in wood engraving, are notable examples; these artists in their works strove to make their art-work pleasing by the introduction of pretty and cheerful every day subjects. Thus among the Walker Stoves are some eminently fitted for the nursery, on which rabbits, doves, etc., are beautifully modelled; the drawing room stoves possibly show a group of musical instruments, dancing figures, etc., and other stoves, symbolical designs suitable to their several rooms; but never under any circumstances do we find subjects introduced which leave an unpleasant impression on the mind.

It is to be regretted that the name of the artist is not known, but it is a question worthy of attention whether some of the artists engaged upon Wedgwood ware did not also work on the Walker stoves, seeing that the work is done in the same style and with equal talent. There is one notable circumstance which may help a decision. Flaxman was largely engaged in Wedgwood work; and in Rotherham Church, and some other places in the neighbourhood, are specimens of his sculpture. Was that connection with the Walkers, and did it influence their designs?[11]

Unfortunately, Green did not record the locations of those stove grates he had identified as being of Walkers' make. There are many examples of Walker cannons scattered around, but no identifiable domestic castings.[12]

Nineteenth century expansion of the mass-production stove grate industry in Rotherham

There can be little doubt that it was the result of the Walkers' training of pattern makers and moulders that gave the Rotherham area an ironfounding tradition. Rotherham was also blessed by having excellent waterborne communications with the rest of Britain, allowing the easy transport of its products to the emerging markets generated by the increasing use of cast iron in both industry, and in domestic applications. The communication with other parts of Britain was further improved following the appearance of the railway to Rotherham, and it is from this date in October, 1838, that we can date the growth of Rotherham's stove grate industry.

The stove grate industry was a child of the Industrial Revolution and its sustenance was the urbanisation, on a massive scale, of our towns and villages and the cancerous growth of street upon street of terraced houses built to accommodate the every increasing industrial workforce. The owners and landlords of workers' dwellings, to safeguard and protect their properties, installed 'all iron fireplaces', appliances that had previously been considered to be luxury items, developed for the homes of the affluent who had demanded fireplaces that were reasonably efficient, smoke-free, and safe, and it was from these expensive appliances that the cheap products suitable for profitable, mass production were developed. The monotonous rows of mean town housing needed heat and cooking facilities, which, because of the ever present risk of fire and consequent damage to the property – the risk of injury to the occupants was not a consideration – had to be safely contained within a fire-proof area, a fireplace. So the stove grate maker developed, from the stove and fireplace products of the art castings departments of the large iron works, the stove grate for general use. However, in the early days the large iron works, such as those of the Walkers, of Coalbrookdale, and of Carron, were unable to satisfy the demand even following the standardisation of sizes, and impressive outlays on pattern equipment and production methods. Local builders, therefore, sought local producers, and throughout the first half of the nineteenth century small foundries were established in all localities to meet the demand for heating and cooking appliances and domestic ironware. The life span of many of these small foundries was short for they were incapable of competing for wider markets because of incompetence, under-capitalisation, or because they produced poor products (they were often pirated from patterns obtained by purchasing a product from another foundry); and many of them were, in today's terminology, 'cowboys'.

However, in those places that had an established ironfounding industry and tradition, such as the Rotherham and Sheffield areas, mid-Shropshire, the West Midlands, and Falkirk, places where there was also a means of transport by waterway or by rail, the stove grate and light decorative casting industry became established as a staple trade.

The 'New Foundry'

It is now necessary to retrace our steps back into the eighteenth century. Some twenty years after the Walkers had established their foundry at Masbrough, **Messrs Clay & Co.** were ironfounding at the **Rotherham Foundry** supplying cast iron products to the Wentworth estate during the period 1765-1770.[13] However, previously, in 1763, they had been purchasing pig iron from the Carron Company[14], most likely via the Carron agent in Sheffield, Benjamin Roebuck.[15] They were still operating from the Rotherham Foundry in 1780. Between 1780 and 1799, Clay & Co. had also opened the New Foundry at Masbrough and earlier, in 1772, they had taken a lease on the Chapel Furnace and its associated forge and slitting mill at a rental of £106.[16] In an indenture, dated 15 January, 1799, Messrs. Clay & Co. agreed to sell the New Foundry premises, and the business, to Ebenezer Elliott, the father of the 'Corn Law Rhymer', who had been a clerk at the Walkers' Ironworks and had joined Clay & Co. as their chief clerk. The transaction cost Elliott £375, payable by annual instalments of £31 5s 0d (£31.25). Besides the New Foundry, Elliott also had an ironmongery on Rotherham's High Street, described as 'a dark, dirty, dingy place'[17], although this business may have been established after he had taken over the foundry. Unfortunately, business declined after Elliott had become the operator, even following the investment of his son's wife's dowry into the firms. Ebenezer Elliott junior, after inheriting the New Foundry upon the death of his father, was forced into bankruptcy and closed the foundry in 1818. William Glossop, a linen draper from Rotherham, in partnership with a man called Roberts, then attempted to run the New Foundry as a profitable concern but they were forced to close down and vacate the premises in 1822.

There is no evidence to show that the New Foundry made stove grates. We can only presume that it did so based upon the fact that when Yates took over the buildings, stove grate patterns were stored in them.

'Sandford & Yates' and its successors

James Yates (b. 22 April, 1798) was the son of the manager of the Walker Foundry who, following his apprenticeship as a pattern maker, transferred to the Gospel Oak Ironworks at Tipton in Staffordshire, a works that had recently been acquired by the Walkers, where he was employed in a managerial capacity. Upon the closure of the Masbrough Works by the Walkers in 1823, Yates returned to Rotherham and, in partnership with Charles Samuel Roberts Sandford, purchased all the 'General Goods' patterns from the Walkers' foundry and commenced operating as ironfounders in the New Foundry premises. **Sandford & Yates** appear to have been successful from the beginning. By 1825 they were employing 30 staff making all manner of cast iron goods including kitcheners, stoves, fittings for stables and cattle byres, cast shovels and spades, cooking vessels, and frying pans.[18] They then took over another ex-Walker operation engaged in wrought ironwork and forging, that of Burdekin & Fairbairn and, to accommodate the expanded business, Sandford & Yates built a large new forge at the New Foundry site and re-named the whole premises the **Phoenix Works**. The Rotherham Foundry was, in 1833, another early acquisition. It had been operated by S. Kirk, (who had possibly taken it over from Clay & Co.) and later, in 1829, by a partnership between Messrs. Kirk and Kidgell. William Kidgell had commenced making stoves and fenders on Allen Street, Sheffield, in about 1825; in 1829 he joined Kirk, a manufacturer of cast shovels and spades at the Rotherham Foundry, on the Rotherham bank of the River Don and sometimes called the Buttercross Foundry

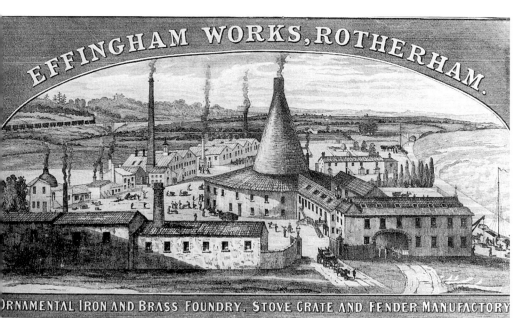

Figure 1. Effingham Works prior to 1855, possibly as early as 1844, showing the collection of buildings leased by Yates from Martha Beatson in 1838. The earthenware factory is shown by the domed structure protruding from the roof at centre left. The tall chimney belongs to the steam engine with the flax mill behind. The railway can be seen at top left, and the Don Navigation at the extreme right. The centrally situated conical structure belongs to Beatson's glassworks as do the buildings in front and to the right of it. The open space in the foreground is part of the Tenter Meadows where the later Effingham Works was to be built. *Rotherham Central Library*

from its proximity to that site. It was a small foundry squeezed between the Market Place and the river, approached by the lane that also served the killing shambles.[19] It probably used some buildings that were, originally, part of the eighteenth century Rotherham Pottery. **Kirk, Kidgell & Co**. were listed as makers of cast shovels and spades, and stove grates, in 1828.

By 1838 both Sandford and Yates felt that the combined businesses of foundry and forge were incompatible in that both sides were competing for capital investment and management time. They agreed to part, Sandford taking over the forge and Phoenix Foundry, and Yates the Rotherham Foundry side of the concern. In May, 1838, Yates signed a lease with Martha Beatson and others for an 18 years term on property that had formerly been an earthenware factory and included several cottages, sheds, a stable, an old fax mill, a flint grinding mill, a gas house, an 18-horsepower steam engine and boiler, and an extensive area of open land used as tenter fields by the flax mill. The rent was £300 per year, and Yates named his collection of buildings, which he converted into a foundry, the **Effingham Works** (Figure 1), after the ground landlord, the Earl of Effingham.[20] Yates continued to use the name Kirk Kidgell until 1849, trading as 'Kirk & Kidgell the Rotherham Foundry', and also as 'James Yates, Effingham Works'. Indeed, the Rotherham Foundry name was used until well into the twentieth century for general cast products manufactured by the firm.

William Owen, an erstwhile apprentice of Sandford & Yates, had attempted to establish a small general foundry in Masbrough, but it was a short-lived investment, and by 1841 he was in partnership with Sandford and Son, at the Phoenix Works, making stove grates and also forgings, railway wheels, axles and tyres. The company exhibited examples of the latter at the Great Exhibition of 1851 and at the London International Exhibition of 1862.[21] At the latter event, William Owen (late Sandford & Owen) at the Phoenix Works, Rotherham, also exhibited an example of 'Bradley's patent kitchener' and stable fittings.[22] By 1865 Owen had removed from the Phoenix Works to the Wheathill Foundry. The Phoenix Works then became Owen's Patent Wheel, Tyre, & Axle Company Limited, specialising in these products until it went into liquidation in about 1872.[23]

In June, 1846, Yates took into partnership George Haywood and John Drabble, both employees of his: Haywood as a designer and pattern maker, and Drabble as a commercial man but one who also had technical skills. Drabble was not formally acknowledged in the reformed company until the 1860s when the name was registered as **Yates, Haywood & Drabble.**

George Haywood had been born in Rawmarsh in 1805. He served an apprenticeship to Longden, Walker & Co., stove grate makers of the Phoenix Foundry, Sheffield, and then, during the early 1830s, he joined Nicholson & Hoole at their Green Lane Works as their designer and model maker. He became employed by Yates during the 1840s, and, though he was often approached to join other firms, he stayed with Yates, and together they built up what was probably the largest establishment of its kind in Great Britain.[24]

At the Great Exhibition of 1851 Yates Haywood displayed a magnificent range of their products alongside, and in competition with, the Sheffield stove grate makers Nicholson & Hoole, Henry Longden, and Robertson Carr and Steel. The firm retained several of their exhibits which were available for display 100 years later during the Festival of Britain held in 1951!

Between 1852 and 1856 large new premises, retaining the name Effingham Works, were built on the Tenter Meadows in front of the old works. By the 1860s the company employed some 500 people and had opened a warehouse and showrooms on in London. Their products were being exported world wide, and included cottage grates at 2/6d each (12.5p) and drawing room grates at 400 guineas each (£420); fenders made from cast iron, wrought iron , steel and cast ormolu; warm air stoves suitable for a small shop for 7s (35p) to ones for ships' cabins, and for large public halls at up to 100 guineas each (£105). They also made kitchen ranges and cooking stoves, hall and drawing room tables, table ornaments, flower pot stands, hat stands, umbrella stands, garden sofas and chairs and tables, guttering, down pipes, drain covers, stable fittings, railings, structural cast ironwork, ornamental rails, balustrades, and cornices.[25]

John Drabble was forced to retire through ill-health in 1868, and he died the following year. Consequently, on 1 July, 1869, a new Memorandum of Association was drafted and signed, establishing a new company: **Yates, Haywood & Co, and the Rotherham Foundry Company**. The new partners were: James Yates, whose capital investment amounted to £32,000; George Haywood with a similar investment; Robert Bentley Shaw (£8,000); and George Harris Haywood (£8,000). George Haywood was designated manager in charge of design and manufacture at a salary of £1,000 per annum; Robert Bentley Shaw, the husband of Yates' only daughter, assisted Haywood and was responsible for all commercial matters at a salary of £500; and George Harris Haywood, George's son, managed the London warehouse and showrooms at a salary of £500. Robert Bentley Shaw changed his name to Shaw-Yates but he died at the early age of 30 in 1873. Further expansion of the company took place in 1873 with the opening of a warehouse in Liverpool to accommodate an extensive trade with the Americas.

In 1879 James Yates, by now 81 years old, and George Haywood, now 74, retired, and a new company was formed under the direction of Chairman and Managing Director, George Harris Haywood, of London; Joint Managing Directors, William Henry Haywood of Rotherham and Edward Drabble of Rotherham; and Directors, Rogers Haywood of Rotherham; George Haywood (to keep a watching brief it is suspected); Mary Drabble, wife of Edward; Ann Oxley, wife of William H. Oxley of Rotherham; and Thomas Wragby, a Rotherham bank manager.

James Yates died following a long illness on the 3 December, 1881, aged 83. George Haywood followed his friend 23 months later.

Other Rotherham stove grate manufacturers

Rogers & Knowles established the **Midland Foundry** on Masbrough Common some time before 1841, to make general cast products and stove grates. Their last appearance in a directory as stove grate makers was in 1862.

The **White Lees Foundry**, on White Lees Road, Swinton, was described in 1861 and in 1862 as a stove grate foundry, run by George Shaw. Thomas and Charles Hattersley, who operated a stove grate and fender making foundry on Kelham Island, Sheffield, transferred some of their manufacturing to a collection of sheds at the end of Queen Street, Swinton, following the Dale Dyke Dam disaster in March, 1864, which inundated the Sheffield foundry. By 1869 the brothers had taken over and renovated the White Lees Foundry and re-named it Queen's Foundry. In an advertisement dated 1887 (Figure 2) they were listed as manufacturers of stove grates, fenders, ashpans, kitchen and 'Leamington ranges', and plain and ornamental ironwork and castings.[26] By 1930 the Company included heavy duty catering appliances and the 'Swinton' electric

Figure 2. Hattersley Brothers & Co. advertisement of 1887 showing, a 'kitchener' with a slow oven and a roasting oven, and three boiling tops. *Author's collection*

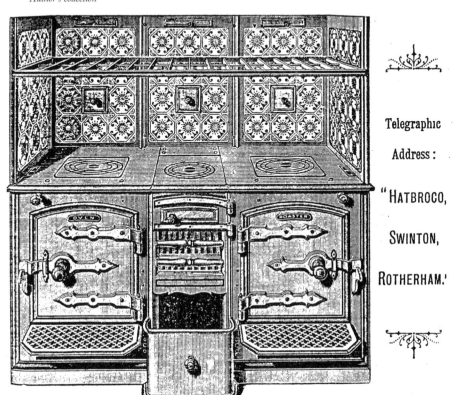

Telegraphic

Address :

"Hatbroco,

Swinton,

Rotherham.'

cooker and fire among its output. During the 1950s the firm
concentrated upon the design of gas central heating boilers, and their
'Vulcan Autostat' boiler gained national popularity. **Hattersley
Brothers Ltd.** was taken into the fold of the Stelrad Group, a
subsidiary of the Metal Box Company and in 1976 merged with the
group's Ideal Boiler Co. of Hull. The factory, now much modernised
and without its foundry, produces pressed steel central heating
radiators and is part of the Caradon Group of companies.

Another outlying stove grate foundry was one established at
Kilnhurst by **Messrs. Cook & Co.** in 1814, probably as a part of the
forge and furnace there. By 1872 **Messrs. Weir, Whittaker &
Sibrey,** were established as stove grate makers, and in 1881 **Thomas
William & Son**, stove grate makers, were the proprietors of the
Queen's Foundry in Kilnhurst. In 1889 the **Kilnhurst Foundry
Company Ltd**. of J. and C. H. Goodinson, on Wharf Road,
Kilnhurst, were listed as stove grate makers. Their last entry in a
directory was in 1890.

Messrs. Myers & Corbitt & Co. were stove makers in the
Masbro' Works, on the site of Walkers' Steel Works, in 1850. By
1860, **William Corbitt & Co**. were manufacturing stove grates,
fenders, ranges, and ornamental ironwork and general castings in the
Masbro' Works, and continued to do so until 1894. From a drawing
of about 1865 the Masbro' Works appears to have retained and
continued to operate the cementation furnace of the old Walker steel
works (Figure 3).

Figure 3. Masbro' Works, College Road, in about 1865 on the site of the
Walkers' Steel Cementation Furnace. In 1894 the Masbro' Works became
the Sheffield Grate Works of Skelton, Corbitt & Co. Ltd. *Rotherham Museum*

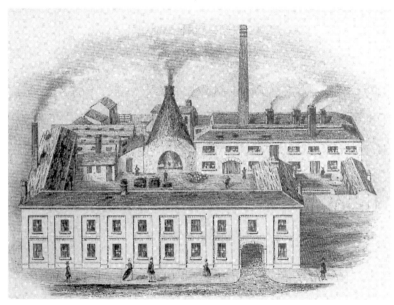

William G. Skelton & Co. was first recorded on Bridge Street, Sheffield, during 1880 where they made stove grates. By 1887 their premises were **The Sheffield Grate Works**. Skelton and Corbitt merged in 1894, becoming a limited liability company, and all work was transferred to the Masbro' Works, which they then called The Sheffield Grate Works. There **W. G. Skelton, Corbitt & Co. Ltd.** concentrated on the production of fine stove grates and fenders based upon classic Regency and Queen Anne styles. The company completely rejected the over ornate styles of Victoriana, and their products became immensely popular. Unfortunately, being under capitalised they could not introduce the capital expenditure necessary to keep pace with demand, and Yates, Haywood & Co. Ltd., with a discerning eye upon the fine products of the smaller firm, took them over in 1910, closing down the small Masbro' Works, transferring all production and the workforce to the Effingham Works. The names Skelton, Corbitt & Co., and Sheffield Grate Works, were retained and used by Yates, Haywood as a marketing company for the sale of quality reproduction grates and fenders.

George Wright had served his apprenticeship under George Haywood at Yates, Haywood and became a noted designer of stove grates, being largely responsible for the Yates, Haywood display at the 1851 Great Exhibition. Aided by the financial support of Henry Critchley, a Sheffield coal merchant, he commenced in business as a

Figure 4. Part of the title page of George Wright & Co. Catalogue of *c*.1880. The Burton Weir Works off Brinsworth Street, Masbrough, is shown, together with illustrations of the London office and the warehouse. Not all of the catalogued products were manufactured by George Wright; their London showrooms were factors for a wide range of architectural ironmongers wares. *Author's collection*

MANTELS, STOVES, RANGES, STABLE FITTINGS, BASEMENT LIGHTS.

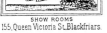

SHOW ROOMS
· 155, Queen Victoria St, Blackfriars.

WORKS, ROTHERHAM, YORKSHIRE.

WAREHOUSE
238, Upper Thames Street, E.C.
and 1, Upper Thames Street, E.C.

GEORGE WRIGHT & Co.,

IRONFOUNDERS.

Telegraphic Addresses—
" MAYPOLE, LONDON."
" MAYPOLE, ROTHERHAM."

ESTABLISHED 1854.

London
Telephone Exchange,
No. 1921.

stove grate manufacturer on Attercliffe Road, Sheffield, in 1854 at the **Burton Weir Works** close to the Burton Weir on the River Don. His partnership with Critchley broke up in 1862, after the firm had successfully exhibited at the 1862 Exhibition, and, in partnership with George Wilton Chambers, Wright moved into the Ferham Works on Midland Road, Masbrough, in 1864 although Chambers was never formally acknowledged as a partner in the company name, **George Wright & Co**. In 1870 the firm moved into a new **Burton Weir Works** at Rotherham, illustrated on the title page of their 1880 catalogue (Figure 4) which also shows that by 1880 G. Wright & Co. had also opened a London office and showrooms which became factors' agents for numerous stove grate and decorative cast iron manufacturers. The company exhibited at many British and International exhibitions during the latter decades of the nineteenth century and they won several awards.

George Wright died in 1904, and the company, now taken over by the sons of his financial partner, G. W. Chambers, was made into a limited liability company. Just before the First World War they took over the Manchester firm of E. H. Shorland & Brothers, the makers of 'Manchester Stoves'. In 1920 George Wright & Co. Ltd. was divided into two companies: G. Wright (London) Ltd., of Newman Street, W1, and **G. Wright (Rotherham) Ltd**. Masbrough Street, Rotherham, the latter being the address of the Burton Weir Works. In 1954, George Wright (Rotherham) Ltd. were listed with offices and showrooms on Masbrough Street, Rotherham, and works at the Wheathill Foundry, Rotherham, with their London company on Great Portland Street, W1. By 1965 George Wright (London) Ltd. were listed as architectural ironworkers, and George Wright (Rotherham) Ltd. were at The Crofts, Rotherham, operating as fireplace manufacturers.

The **Baths Foundry** was opened on the site of the old Rotherham Baths in Westgate by George Aizlewood prior to 1849, by which time William Aizlewood was the proprietor. In 1852 the firm was listed as Aizlewood & Co. During 1854 Joseph Aizlewood withdrew from a partnership running the Wheathill Foundry to take over the Baths Foundry and by 1856 the operating company was, once again, simply known as Aizlewood & Co. **Henry Tomlinson**, a grocer from Masbrough, was the next proprietor, probably taking over in 1860 although an article in the *Rotherham and Masbro' Advertiser* on 19 April, 1862, reporting upon the forthcoming 1862 International Exhibition, named Mr H. Thompson of the Baths Foundry. Upon the retirement of Henry Tomlinson, Messrs. Morgan, Macaulay, &

Waide, held a supper in the *Crown Hotel* at which about 90 workmen gathered to wish the ex-proprietor well. The event was reported in the *Rotherham and Masbro' Advertiser* on 18 March, 1865, and **Morgan, Macaulay, & Waide** became the new owners. They continued until 1872 with their successors, **Morgan & Waide** at the now renamed **Baths Works**, lasting until 1883 when they stopped manufacturing stove grates. The Baths Works was taken over by the Rotherham Steel Strip Co. in 1914.

The **Ferham Works**, on Foundry Street, just off Midland Road, Masbrough, to which George Wright had moved in 1864, had been established as a stove and grate foundry by the partnership of William Bagnall and Thomas A. Cockin sometime before 1860. After Wright had moved out in 1870, the Ferham Works appears to then have been unconnected with the industry until John and Richard Corker took it over in about 1880 to make stove grates and ranges. John Corker died in 1886 and from 1889, as Figure 5 shows, the firm was known as **J. & R. Corker**. Richard Corker, born in 1834, had been employed by Yates, Haywood for 26 years, and he carried on the firm until 1894, when it became J. & R. Corker Ltd. It ceased production shortly after the First World War.

The **Wheathill Foundry** on Sheffield Road, Rotherham, was commenced by Joseph Aizlewood to make stove grates, and by 1854 a partnership of Jackson, Redmayne & Aizlewood was the operator.

Figure 5. Part of the advertisement for J & R Corker, Ferham Works, of 1889. The 'Leamington' kitchener ranges were made to the design of Sidney Flavel & Co. of Leamington Spa who introduced this type of kitchen range during the 1790s. It was copied by many stove grate makers, as were the 'Yorkshire', the 'Lancashire', and the 'Lincolnshire' and 'Glendenning' ranges. *Author's collection*

J. & R. CORKER
Ferham Works, ROTHERHAM,
Makers of every description of

Tiled and other Register Stoves,
MANTEL REGISTERS & SHAMS, DOG GRATES,

Cast-Iron
CHIMNEY
PIECES
AND
OVER
MANTELS.

YORKSHIRE AND LEAMINGTON RANGES,
With Open and Close Fire, and Patent Lifting Fire Arrangements.

In the same year Joseph Aizlewood left to take over the Baths Foundry from William Aizlewood, and Messrs Watson, Redmayne & Co. manufactured stove grates at the Wheathill Foundry until 1860 when Thomas Redmayne & Co. took over. Watson joined Marshall & Moorwood's stove grate works in Sheffield during 1861. From 1861 to 1862 the company was known as Redmayne & Co. but, following Redmayne's removal to Sheffield in 1863, the foundry was then leased by William Owen (ex-Sandford and Owen of the Phoenix Works) to accommodate his expanding business. Owen remained there until he went into liquidation in 1883. **The Wheathill Foundry Co. Ltd.** then took over a company that existed until 1888 when Thomas Watson, the son of an earlier operator of the foundry, left Watson, Moorwood & Co. and returned to the Wheathill Foundry as **Thomas Watson & Sons.** Their last entry in a directory was in 1890. The Wheathill Foundry returned to stove grate manufacture when George Wright (Rotherham) Ltd. moved there in 1954.

George Neatby of the **Railway Foundry,** Rotherham, made an appearance in directories as a stove grate maker during the 1860s. His background and the later history of his firm is not known.

Harris Jarvis, of Westgate, Rotherham, are recorded as being ironfounders in a directory for 1823. They appeared in White's Directory for 1841 as being on Westgate and on Wellgate. In 1856 the firm was Harris, Robert & Jarvis, stove grate makers at the **Westgate Foundry** on Sheffield Road, Rotherham. A directory entry in 1860 recorded the name, Robert Harris & Jarvis – still on Sheffield Road;

Figure 6. Letter head of W. H. Micklethwait & Co., 1880s, showing the Clough Works on Clough Road, Rotherham. The two foundry cupola melting furnaces are clearly seen in the centre of the illustration. *Author's collection*

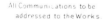

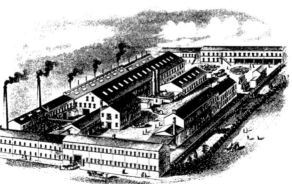

from 1861 the firm was known as **R. & J. Harris** until it made a final entry as stove grate makers in 1868 although it continued as a light castings foundry until well into the twentieth century.

The **Alma Works** on Chemist Lane, Masbrough, was established by Henry Watson in about 1860. In 1865 it was listed as the **Masboro Stove & Grate Co.** a name it retained until 1880.

In 1881 Messrs. Perrot, Clement, Hamil & Co. were at the Alma Works as stove grate makers and in 1883 the firm was listed as Perrot & Habershon, Clement having moved to Sheffield to partner Carr at the Chantry Works. By 1896 the **Masboro Foundry Co. Ltd.** was manufacturing stove grates at the Alma Works and continued there until 1920 when it withdrew from stove grate and allied casting.

William Henry Mickelthwait was an oil and waste merchant before he started ironfounding at a new site, the **Clough Works**, on Clough Road, Masbrough in 1880, an illustration of which is given on the firm's letterhead (Figure 6). In 1908 he installed a vitreous enamelling plant, purchased from Germany, probably the first Rotherham stove grate maker to carry out that process of finishing on cast iron and sheet metal parts. Their advertisement of 1935 (Figure 7) shows that they had recently renewed the plant. During the 1920s some 700 appliances a week were produced. The firm was taken over by Allied Ironfounders in December, 1964, and closed down at the end of March, 1967, making 80 men redundant. 'An old foundry without machinery' was the reason given to the *Rotherham Advertiser* and reported on 4 March, 1967.

Mathew William Henry Hale & Co. were listed as stove grate makers on Greasbrough Road in 1896 and in 1899, but no further information regarding this company has been found.

Figure 7. W. H. Micklethwait & Co. Ltd. advertisement of 1935 showing typical 'Combination' grates which replaced the old kitchen ranges. *Author's collection*

The **"ROTHER DE-LUXE"**

COMBINATION GRATE

Renowned for its handsome appearance, efficiency with simplicity of control & economy

W. H. Micklethwait
and Company Limited
CLOUGH WORKS

Telephone 1184–5 (2 lines) **Rotherham**

MANUFACTURERS OF THE FAMOUS

"Rother" Combination Grates
"Clough" Back-to-Back Ranges
"Heatwell" Oven Interior Grates
and Porcelain Enamelled Baths

Extensive and well appointed Showrooms contain every variety of Stoves and Grates to suit the most discriminating taste.

INSPECTION IS CORDIALLY INVITED

Our Grates are now available in Permanent Enamel finish (which will not burn off). Our recently installed plant for this process is one of the latest in the country.

The **"ROTHER MINOR"**

COMBINATION GRATE

A well-constructed and remarkably efficient grate, the cost of which is within the reach of everyone. Our sales speak of the great popularity this grate enjoys throughout the country.

The end of the stove grate industry in Rotherham

The year 1908 brought great changes to the ownership and management structure of Yates, Haywood & Co. Ltd. and the Rotherham Foundry Co. Ltd. – they went into voluntary liquidation. After limping along for almost three years with the liquidators asset stripping it, Messrs. O'Brien, Thomas & Co. a London builders' and iron goods merchants took a majority shareholding (bought for a song!) in the company and appointed Henry O'Brien as Chairman. It was an association that ,was to last until 1952. Yates, Haywood struggled on manufacturing solid fuel appliances in the face of stiff competition from oil and gas until 1967 when the capital of the company was taken over by William Heaton Holdings Ltd. an old established Rotherham business that had grown from William Heaton & Co. manufacturers of water works articles, hollowware, and baths. The firm survived for three more years and then, on 4 December, 1970, the *Rotherham Advertiser* reported the decision to close down Yates, Haywood & Co. Ltd. with effect from Christmas Eve, 1970. Yates, Haywood was the last of the Rotherham stove grate and decorative cast iron manufacturers, an industry that started with the Walkers and had lasted some 200 years.

The stove grate products

What were the products of the Rotherham stove grate makers? The following notes will provide part of the answer to that question, and, perhaps, also illustrate why the industry in Rotherham achieved such a national and international reputation.

One can appreciate the interest taken in the subject of heating and cooking by totalling the number of patents taken out connected with fireplaces, stoves, etc. Between 2 March, 1617, and 1 October, 1852, when the Patent Laws (Amendment) Act came into operation, some 169 were filed. Between October, 1852, and 31 December, 1863, some 348 were applied for! Obviously most of the patents were worthless, and many were taken out for the prestige they were thought to gain for a product, and as a selling point. From a Yates, Haywood catalogue of *c.*1869[27] there were three appliances that were claimed to have been patented: Steven's Patent Register Stove, George Wright's (of Rotherham) Patent Radiating Stove, and Yates' own Patent Single Valve Back Register. It was these, and others like them, that formed the bread and butter products for the stove grate makers.

The over-ornate design applied to the decorative light castings of the mid-nineteenth century can be imagined from a description of a visit to Yates, Haywood in 1850:

In ornamental castings they have some beautiful patterns of hall and drawing-room tables, table ornaments, flower pot stands, hat stands, umbrella stands, etc. During our inspection of this establishment we were particularly pleased with festoons of flowers, and scroll-work, executed in iron, with the apparent lightness of wood carving. We were also much gratified with some garden sofas and tables, constructed to represent rustic work, and treated in a very natural and characteristic manner, the rough stems of the trees apparently tied together by cords, and the whole painted very naturally exhibiting the apparent slenderness of wood with the enduring strength of metal.[28]

The Great Exhibition held in 1851 at the Crystal Palace in Hyde Park granted the first opportunity to inspect the various products, albeit in the main the most prestigious products, from the industry. From the catalogue one finds that Yates, Haywood represented Rotherham, exhibiting:

Specimen of drawing-room iron register stove grate and fender to match, in ormolu and burnished steel, combining the appliances of style to a modern English grate, and uniting some novelties with the palatial character of the middle ages; with mantel-piece executed by Mr. Hartley, Westminster Marble Works, London [Figure 8].

Pier table and flower-pot stand, in cast-iron gilt.

Dining-room register stove grate, in polished black, with burnished steel mountings, complete with hearth, and fender; with mantel-piece in Berlin Black.

Parlour, breakfast-room, and bedroom register stove grates, with fenders.

Cottage sham or full stove grate with iron mantle. Cottage elliptic stove grate.

Miniature model of a drawing-room grate and mantle, on Jeffrey's patent pneumatic principle.

Warm air and other stoves, for public buildings, etc.

Self-acting cooking stoves, with modern improvements.

Hall tables. Flower stands. Umbrella stands, and other ornamental castings.[29]

The 1862 International Exhibition, held in London, witnessed an increase in the representative exhibitors from the Rotherham stove grate industry. From the Catalogue, under Class XXXI, Iron and General Hardware, we find:

Page 67. *Owen, William (late Sandford & Owen), Phoenix Works, Rotherham.*
Page 73. *Redmayne & Co. Wheathill Foundry, Rotherham.*
Pages 94 & 95. *Yates, Haywood, & Drabble, Rotherham & London.*

I do not have the catalogue entry for Henry Tomlinson, of the Baths Foundry, but this is what the *Rotherham and Masbro'Advertiser* reported on 19 April, 1862:

A beautiful specimen of stove grate manufacture will be exhibited by

Figure 8. Drawing Room Register Stove Grate designed by George Wright and made and exhibited by Yates, Haywood & Co. at the 1851 Great Exhibition. The cast iron was decorated with burnished steel and ormolu clipped-on ornament for ease of cleaning. The marble surround and mantelpiece was carved by a Mr. Hartley of the Westminster Marble Works, London. *Author's collection*

Mr. H. Thompson [sic] of the Baths Foundry. It is of a peculiar make, and intended to illustrate the principle, and show the advantages of the 'Patent Pneumatic Movable Fire Grate' of which Mr. Thompson [sic] is the sole manufacturer, and from the simplicity of its construction it appears admirably adapted to answer the ends of the designer, namely to comprise in the most effectual manner, warmth, cleanliness, beauty, and economy. Apart from its merits simply as a fire grate, it presents a most chase and elegant appearance. The mantle and sides, which were designed by Mr. Green of Sheffield, are in electro bronze, and form a rich contrast to the bright steelwork of the interior*. The inside, which is very beautiful, was designed by Mr. W. Dodd of Rotherham. The arch over the fire is formed of two curves of bright steel, with scroll-work of ormolu in between. The fender to match is richly worked in bright steel, and adorned with human figures in ormolu.

* An interior is the frame that forms the front side and top corners of an opening into the chimney breast for a stove grate to sit into.

George Wright, although not then in Rotherham, exhibited:
Stoves, grates, fenders, kitcheners, umbrella stands, chairs, tables, etc.

The *Rotherham and Masbro' Advertiser* on 19 April, 1862, also reported upon Wright's exhibit, mentioning one item:

An extensive kitchen range 12'-0 long x 9'-0 high. 4 large roasting ovens, and smaller ones for other types of cooking. The boilers are at the back of the range. The ornamentation and general appearance of the front, exhibiting as it does, excellent taste, superior workmanship, and beautiful finish, is deserving of great praise, and reflects the highest credit on Messrs. Wright. It is formed partly by bright wrought iron and partly by 'Cumberland metal' whose polished surface is of a rather darker shade than steel.

Obviously, stove grates and kitchen ranges formed the principal products of the Rotherham foundries, but they also produced a host of general castings, too, and catalogues show drain gulleys and gratings, roof guttering, water collection troughs, and down pipes. There was also a large market in stable and cattle byre fittings, ornamental railings and gates for parks and gardens. Cast iron street lamps and other types of street furniture such as bollards and kerb edges, street nameplates, direction posts and fingers for the motoring age, fire hydrant indicators, and a host of other products adorning our streets were made by the light foundries. But, they were products that were subsidised to a large extent by the staple trade, and when demand for solid fuel fired appliances dwindled, so it became uneconomical to cast other things, and the death of Rotherham's stove grate industry became inevitable.

Notes and References

1. *Patterson's Road Book*, 1829 edition, pp. 367 & 368.
2. J. Guest, *Relics and Records of Men and Manufactures at or in the Neighbourhood of Rotherham, etc.* A paper read before the members of the Rotherham Literary & Scientific Society, 27 March, 1865, re-published by Rotherham MBC, 1980, p. 50.
3. Guest, *Relics and Records*, p. 72 *et seq.* It should be noted that Baker, in his lecture of 1945 - see note 4 – stated that the formal closure did not occur until 1833. See p. 4 of the published lecture.
4. H. G. Baker, *Samuel Walker & His Partners*, a published lecture given to the Society for the Preservation of Old Sheffield Tools, 16 October, 1945, p. 5.
5. C. Morley, *The Walkers of Masbrough – a re-examination*, unpublished typescript in Rotherham Central Library, Archives and Local Studies Section, p. 11.
6. Details of the progress made by the Walkers' enterprise may be seen in A. H. John (ed), *The Walker Family*, Council for the Preservation of Business Archives, 1951.
7. R. H. Campbell, *Carron Company*, Oliver & Boyd, Edinburgh and London, 1961, p. 7 *et seq.*
8. Campbell, *Carron Company*, p. 114.
9. William Glossop, *The Stove Grate Maker's Guide*, P. Taylor, London, 1771.
10. R. S. Fitton and A. P. Wadsworth, *The Strutts and the Arkwrights*, 1758-1830, Manchester University Press, 1958; Campbell, Carron Company.
11. J. Guest, *Historic Notices of Rotherham*, Robert White, Worksop, 1879.
12. V. Thornes, *Walker, A World Famous Firm*, Thornes Publications, Rotherham, 1991. Contains illustrations and locations of several Walker cannons.
13. Wentworth Woodhouse Muniments in Sheffield Archives, A 1099, Ledger No 1, 1765-1770, p. 128 'Messrs Clay & Co, Rotherham Foundry, "by goods"'.
14. Campbell, *Carron Company*, p. 114.
15. Campbell, *Carron Company*, p. 106.
16. M. H. Habershon, *Chapeltown Researches*, Pawson & Brailsford, Sheffield, 1893, p. 176.
17. Guest, *Relics and Records*, pp. 56-57.
18. Guest, *Historic Notices.*
19. On a rough tracing of a site plan of a proposed railway station for the Sheffield & Rotherham Railway Co. the site of Rotherham Foundry is shown during the time it was leased by Sandford & Yates. The tracing also carries a note to the effect that, 'Some of the 3rd class carriages (for the S & R Railway?) were made by Sandfords and Yates'. – See the Westgate Station File, Rotherham Central Library, Local Studies and Archives Section. Also Miss D. Green (Mrs D.G. Blundell) in unpublished MS in same records.
20. Lease in Beatson Clark's archives, Rotherham Central Library; D. Green, 'The Glassworks of Rotherham', unpublished MS, Rotherham Central Library.
21. For details of the railway products see Trevor Lodge, 'Rotherham's Railway Engineering Trades' in M. Jones (ed), *Aspects of Rotherham*, 1995, Wharncliffe Publishing, Barnsley, pp. 241-72.
22. Catalogue of the International Exhibition held in London, 1862, p. 67, Class XXXI - Iron & General Hardware.
23. *Aspects of Rotherham*, p. 248.
24. Haywood's obituary notice, in the *Rotherham Advertiser*, 1 December, 1893.
25. *Art Journal*, December, 1850. See also surviving garden benches at Kew gardens next to the great glass houses today (1995).
26. Slater's Directory, 1887 in Sheffield Archives.
27. Yates, Haywood Catalogue, *c.*1869, Rotherham Central Library, Archives and Local Studies Section.
28. Article in *Art Journal*, December, 1850, p. 386.
29. Great Exhibition, Official Descriptive & Illustrated Catalogue, Class XXII, General Hardware, pp. 640-41, Spicer Brothers, 1851.

Acknowledgements

My interest in the stove grate industry in South Yorkshire has been greatly assisted, over many years than I care to remember, by the excellent and most co-operative staff of Sheffield Local Studies Library and Rotherham Central Library's Archives and Local Studies Section, Sheffield Archives, the Victoria & Albert Museum, the Iron Bridge Gorge Archives, and many others. I am also indebted to numerous individuals, especially to members and friends in the South Yorkshire Industrial History Society, for their information and assistance, and to companies and individuals who have been connected with the Industry.

12. THE WATH WOOD VOLUNTEERS: A CHAPTER IN LOCAL MILITARY HISTORY

by John Goodchild M. Univ.

THE LONG CONTINUED WARS with revolutionary and (later) Napoleonic France extended almost uninterruptedly between 1793 and 1815, but in 1802 peace returned temporarily with the negotiations which led to the Peace of Amiens. It was subsequent to the resumption of war in 1803 that it appeared increasingly evident that Napoleon was intent upon an invasion of England, and the British Government took increasingly active – not to say frenetic – steps to raise and organise forces for home defence if the French armada, which was being prepared, actually landed. A whole spate of Acts of Parliament were passed in 1803 relating to British defence, and as the likelihood of invasion was popularly appreciated, great enthusiasm for home defence was aroused.

In October, 1803, a meeting was held in Leeds under the chairmanship of Bacon Frank of Campsall Hall, Vice Lieutenant of the West Riding (in Earl Fitzwilliam, the Lord Lieutenant's absence), to arrange for a system of beacons to give warning of invasion – we shall return to the beacon system later – and to organise the new volunteer regiments, or 'corps' as they were known, as the gravity of the situation had already led to the establishment of numerous local regiments of military volunteers, whose duties would extend geographically no further than the county in which the regiment was raised, and the local seaboard. Curiously the new regiments were also seen as support for the local maintenance of law and order, in case of local civil disturbance. In the West Riding, 35 such corps were established and their costs of formation covered by either public subscription or by a local landowner. Of these, 27 were infantry corps, seven cavalry corps, and one mixed. One of the infantry regiments was the Wath Wood Volunteer Infantry, whose interest to the historian stems from a bundle of papers which record in detail the deliberations of the regiment's officers. The diary of Thomas Asline Ward of Sheffield, who was active in the Sheffield volunteers, tells much of 'active service' as a volunteer, and numbers of volunteer regiments' papers survive, but perhaps the Wath Wood Volunteers' papers provide detail which is, in part at least, not available elsewhere.

The first West Riding local regiments of volunteers were 'accepted' by Earl Fitzwilliam (as Lord Lieutenant) for Government service in August, 1803, and in the following month the Wath Wood Volunteers were among a number of further approvals. This new regiment was to have as its commander Lieutenant Colonel F. S. Foljambe of Aldwarke Hall (1776-1805). Foljambe's father (born Moore) was of Osberton in Nottinghamshire and of Aldwarke in the West Riding, and was himself Lieutenant Colonel commanding the Southern Regiment of West Riding Yeomanry Cavalry; he had been one of the two Members of Parliament for Yorkshire, and High Sheriff for the County in 1787. The father outlived the son, and in fact before the Wath Wood Volunteers' commandant died in 1805 – and he was still under 30 – he had been succeeded in 1804 as commandant by Samuel Walker (1779-1851), an even younger man and of course one of the ironmaster family of Masbrough. It is unlikely that any of the young fellows who officered the new Wath Wood Volunteers had had any earlier military experience: such was the situation with T. A. Ward too. It is interesting that like most (at the least) of his junior officers, Walker was a Whig – he was to become himself an MP – and he and others of the officers were recorded as plumpers solely for Earl Fitzwilliam's eldest son, Lord Milton, at the great Yorkshire election of 1807, when he successfully stood as the sole Whig candidate for the representation of Yorkshire in Parliament. The Fitzwilliam interest as both resident landowner and potential customer was doubtless significant to the businessmen-officers in the new regiment as it was to the whole of the region round Wentworth Woodhouse; there was also evident a very real feeling of regional pride.

Below Lt. Col. F. S. Foljambe in the regiment's hierarchy were four captains, each in charge of one company. The companies were based upon Rawmarsh, Swinton, Wentworth and Wath, and bore their names; the Wentworth company encompassed Hoyland too. Perhaps the most active of the officers holding the rank of captain was William Blacksmith: he was apparently the one of that name of Rawmarsh who was a freeholder maltster at the time of the 1807 Yorkshire election; William Tofield was described in 1807 as of Wath, esquire, with his qualifying freehold in Wombwell township; William Brameld (1772-1813) was a master potter at Swinton at the famous Rockingham Works: of John Wheatley, I know at present nothing. The four company lieutenants were Samuel Thompson (in 1807 a cordwainer residing in and with a freehold at Wath?); William Green of the Don Pottery at Swinton; Thomas Brameld (1787-1850), younger brother of Capt. William Brameld and also in the Rockingham Pottery partnership; and Robert Wigfield, (a nail factor at and freeholder in Hoyland). Ensigns were Philip Hawley (d.1830) of Kilnhurst Old Pottery; John Milner of the Don Pottery and of Swinton; and William Stainton, a farmer of Hoyland Nether township. Of the total of 12 officers, five were pottery manufacturers, in an area where the overall significance of pottery manufacture in terms of employment and rating amounted to less than five-twelfths of the total.

The four captains and four lieutenants held minuted meetings to organise and regulate their concerns, at their colonels' request; their men were also consulted from time to time, and the men's view expressed by votes taken among them. In fact, the volunteer regiments were specifically less subject to military discipline than the older but parallel militia regiments, or, of course, the regular army, and a degree of what can only be described as democracy is observable in the Wath Wood Volunteers' papers. Officers' meetings minutes survive for six dates in 1804, and one in 1809, although other meetings are known to have been at least arranged for other occasions. The meetings were held at the *Star Inn* at Wath in 1804, and at the *Bull's Head* at Brampton in 1809; drills were held weekly in 1804, alternating between Wath Wood and Wood Nook.

The subscriptions for the raising and maintenance of the Wath Wood Volunteers totalled 562 guineas; this warranted a strength of 281 men (i.e., at two guineas each), but the total strength of volunteers in the whole West Riding, 14,301, was not at least initially reached: they were 273 short of the quota, based on six times the strength of the local militia regiments. In the case of the Wath Wood Volunteers, it seems that the total did reach 281: the numbers reported were:

September, 1803   160
October, 1803   260
1804   285
1807   289

The subscriptions for each company were roughly equal (varying from 134 to 148 guineas) and the total subscription allowed of

11 Officers
1 Sergeant Major
1 Paymaster's Clerk
14 Sergeants
12 Corporals
8 Drummers
234 Private Soldiers

There were in fact a number of other officials of the regiment: Surgeon Clarke of Wentworth became Surgeon; Lt. Thomas Brameld was Quarter Master and Paymaster; and there was a Drill Sergeant. The regiment also had a strong musical concern: the Rev. Mr. Trebeck raised a fund to support the band, which had instruments (including a double drum) and music books. It was led by the Master of the Band, who had a sword and sash like the sergeants, and a gold shoulder fringe like the Drum Major. When the Bandmaster was absent, the band was to be led by William Speight of Swinton; the Drum Major was to have 1s 6d a week, plus one guinea from each of the four companies, while the Bandmaster had 3s 6d a week for all his expenses starting from the 'Day we go to Wath Church' for some ceremony.

The weekly drills were each year accompanied by camps held for

various periods of up to 21 days, and after a volunteer regiment had thus been out twice, the Government paid a guinea a man, spent on the purchase of two sets of linen, two pairs of shoes and two shoe brushes, etc. and off the regiment went for its training to Wakefield for 21 days in May, 1804, where the officers' mess was to be established at the *Black Bull* or the *Strafford Arms*, and each officer was to have allowed a pint of wine with his dinner. Each company was to have an attached pioneer at this time, and allowances were to be daily for captains 9s 5d, lieutenants 4s 8d, ensign or second lieutenant 3s 8d plus one shilling, and privates one shilling. 280 knapsacks were to be bought for the regiment, marked with three letters (WWV?) and to cost a substantial 4s 9d each, while officers who wished to buy for themselves undress uniform, could buy such on the pattern of Capt. Blacksmith's. The privates wore scarlet jackets, pantaloons and gaiters, and caps with a feather.

Reference is made in 1804 to the Wath Wood Infantry and Cavalry and later in 1804, the regimental accounts were reported as 'deranged', and Earl Fitzwilliam's chaplain had to be asked to delicately enquire if money had been paid over by the colonel – or perhaps by his father, as they both bore that title. At this time too, Thomas Wilson was to be paid 25 shillings for teaching the fifers of the Swinton and Wath companies.

The military effectiveness of the regiment was overseen – as he oversaw that of others – by the Inspecting Officer of Group 11 of Infantry Corps, Lt. Col. Bell, stationed at Doncaster; whether he had any authority over the 'deranged' accounts of the Wath Wood Regiment of 1804, or whether they were kept from him or other authority, is not clear. Certainly, military exercises were held, as the arrangements for one to be held in June, 1804, when the regiment was still young, record that the officers met at the *Star* at Wath to organise the event:

Agreed that a Field Day of the Wath Wood Infantry & Cavalry be appointed for Thursday the 28th Instant at 10 o'Clock in the Morning

Agreed that the Legion be on that day divided for the purpose of skirmishing (viz) that the Second Troop be attached to the Right Wing & that they leave their Feathers at Home – And that the First Troop be attached to the Left Wing & appear with Feathers & yield the Victory to the Right Wing –

It is to be understood that the above Arrangement was decided by lot, without intending any preeminence to either Wing – the Feathers are to be left at Home that each Party may be better known by the other & to facilitate the operations of the Day

Perhaps the most memorable of the regiment's days on duty was when they took part in the famous alarm of invasion by Napoleonic forces, occasioned by the accidental lighting of a local 'invasion' beacon at Woolley Edge, between Wakefield and Barnsley, in August, 1805. The parson at Woolley, the Rev. Jeremiah Dixon, a local magistrate, 'having mistaken a brick kiln for a beacon', ordered the lighting of the Woolley Beacon, causing all the local regiments to turn out, as envisaged, for invasion defence. This was done with such efficiency, despite its being soon seen as unnecessary in fact, that there were congratulations all round, ornamental plate presented as a mark of appreciation, and – what must have seemed more real to the men involved – in the following month the Wath Wood regiment (doubtless as with others) received an order from the Treasury in London to pay two guineas per man:

> *to the Volunteers who marched in consequence of the Signal of Alarm lately made by the lighting up of the Beacons.*

The occasion of this event may appear to us almost farcical, but in the state of public concern at the time, it was immensely threatening, and the prompt action of the local regiments was doubtless something of a publicity coup for the authorities.

The collapse of the threat of Napoleonic invasion rendered the existence – not to mention the considerable public expense – of this

system of a kind of superior Home Guard unnecessary. In February, 1809, a meeting of the Captains of Companies of what now receives its full and long title, the Loyal Wath Wood Volunteer Light Infantry, was held at the *Bull's Head* at Brampton, 'pursuant to Directions from Lt Col: Hewett who has delegated his Powers to the Meeting' under the recent legislation in regard to volunteer organisations: it was *de facto* a winding-up meeting. It was decided that the clothing and equipment of the men should be considered as 'vested in the powers of the Commanding Officer': these interestingly were listed as being jackets, pantaloons, caps, tufts, stocks, knapsacks, kneecaps, brush and picker, sergeants' swords, sashes and halberts, drummers' swords, belts and drums, bandsmen's swords, music major's sash and sword '& every Article belonging to the Band', sergeant major's uniform, sword and sash complete.

The captains' meeting decided further that the property belonging to the Government which was liable to delivery up 'on a call from the Ordnance board' consisted of muskets, slings, bayonets, cross belts, pouches, haversacks, canteens and belts. It was decided that the sergeant major, sergeants, drummers, band, music major and privates should have their uniforms and (where applicable) their swords given to them, but not the Government properties of halbert and haversacks, canteens and belts. It was felt 'highly advisable' to immediately call in muskets and slings, cross belts, breast plates, pouches and bayonets, haversacks, canteens and belts, and sergeants' pikes – any man neglecting to bring these in 'proper order' to be brought before a magistrate by his captain. As 'one or more' muskets were 'out of Repair', they were to be repaired as necessary out of regimental funds.

And so ended this short-lived but potentially reasonably effective system of defence against European invasion. It was of course a system which spread across the whole country, although the eastern seaboard of England was the most likely locale of any invasive landing. Here we see something of how it was organised in the southern part of the West Riding.

References

This essay is based upon the original manuscripts of The Loyal Wath Wood Volunteer Light Infantry in The John Goodchild Collection at Wakefield . Some details are derived from the 1807 printed Poll Book, from the printed diaries of T. A. Ward of Sheffield, from the lists of accepted regiments in the Bacon Frank papers also in The John Goodchild Collection, and from the newspapers of the time, the *Leeds Mercury* and *Leeds Intelligencer.*

13. THE WATH GENERAL ELECTION RIOT OF 1865

by Alex Fleming

This trade of politics is a rascally business. It is a trade for a scoundrel, not for a gentleman. King George III

KING GEORGE MAY BE EXCUSED such a jaundiced view when the antics of his ministers in the late eighteenth and early nineteenth centuries are known. For example, Charles James Fox denied taking part in a riot in London in which Prime Minister Pitt was attacked. Fox said that at the time of the attack he was in bed with his mistress, Mrs Armistead, and she was quite prepared to swear to the fact on oath![1] This robust approach to distinguishing private from public morality eventually gave way to what we have come to regard as Victorian strait-laced behaviour. Consequently, by the middle of the nineteenth century Britain had become a more civilised country and the conduct of public and private affairs was more in keeping with her status as a great nation. There was, however, still much that was unacceptable by today's standards and, it must be said, increasingly unacceptable to people of that time as well.

One person who can be credited with helping to bring about a change in attitude to public office is Lord Palmerston, Liberal prime minister 1859-65. He brought stability because he was respected by all politicians. Not the least of his talents was his energy in working very hard at being prime minister, from 7 a.m. to midnight. He too, however, was touched by scandal arising from his private life, like so many politicians before him and since. As late as 1864 he was cited in the divorce case of O'Kane v O'Kane, as the lover of Mrs O'Kane. This affair gave rise to the following little riddle which alluded to Palmerston's advanced years (he was then aged 79):

> *She was certainly Kane*
> *But was he Able?* [2]

By now the reader will be wondering what this has to do with the Wath riot of 1865. First of all, it was Palmerston who called for a general election in July, 1865, because parliament was nearing the end of its term – the last election had been in 1859. Secondly, although there was an expectation of higher standards in politics and public life, there was much of the old days and the old ways which lingered on. Such ways are graphically illustrated by that classic account of an election campaign in the early nineteenth century – the Eatanswill Election in the *Pickwick Papers* by Charles Dickens, published in 1836-37:

> *Mr Pickwick had chosen a peculiarly desirable moment for his visit to the borough of Eatanswill. The Honourable Samuel Slumkey of Slumkey Hall as the Blue candidate and Horatio Fizkin of Fizkin Lodge, near Eatanswill, had been prevailed upon by his friends to stand as the Buff candidate.*

> *The stable-yard exhibited clear symptoms of the glory and strength of the Eatanswill Blues. There was a regular army of blue flags. There was a grand band of trumpets, bassoons and drums marshalled four abreast, and earning their money, if ever men did especially the drum beaters, who were very muscular. There were bodies of constables with blue staves, 20 committee-men with blue scarves, and a mob of voters with blue cockades. There were electors on horseback and electors afoot. There was an open carriage and four, for the honourable Samuel Slumkey; and there were four carriages and pair for his friends and supporters; and the flags were rustling, and the band was playing, and the constables were swearing and the 20 committee-men were squabbling, and the mob was shouting and the horses were backing, and the post-boys perspiring – all for the honourable Samuel Slumkey, one of the candidates for the representation of the Borough of Eatanswill.*

This brings us to the nature of elections in the mid-nineteenth century: they could be as violent and corrupt as they had long been, and at Wath on Friday, 21 July, 1865, the election certainly was violent. In brief, on polling day there was a riot in the centre of town. Some 200 to 400 people gathered on High Street, attacked voters, smashed windows and fought with the police. A total of 24 men were charged with rioting, nine of them were also charged with assaulting the police. After arrest they were bailed to appear before Rotherham magistrates on Saturday, 5 August. From there seventeen were sent for trial at the Quarter Sessions at Sheffield on Friday, 18 August (Figure 1). The action took place in a relatively confined area along High Street, between Moor Road and West Street. There were three focal points for the rioters: Polling Booth No. 2, somewhere to the east of the *Red Lion Hotel*; the *Red Lion* itself, containing the Conservative Committee Room, and the *Saracen's Head Inn*, containing the Liberal Committee Room (Figure 2).

For the 1865 general election the right to vote was still based on the Great Reform Act of 1832 and so only one in five adult males had the right to vote. In Wath, for example, only 44 men actually voted in the 1865 general election, a tiny 0.5 per cent of the total population of the town (Figure 3). Nonetheless 1865 opened a new chapter in the electoral history of our district, because for the first time the West Riding was separated into northern and southern areas, each area returning two MPs. Previously there had been only two MPs for the entire county of the West Riding, which in 1861 had a population of one and a half million. The new Southern Division contained nineteen polling districts, of which Wath was one of the smallest with 471 voters on the electoral register. Wath Polling District included Adwick, Barnburgh, Billingley, Bolton, Brampton, Darfield, Denaby, Houghton, Mexborough, Swinton, Thurnscoe and Wombwell.[3]

Doubling the parliamentary representation of the county was an acknowledgement that the growth of population in the West Riding

Figure 1. List of rioters to appear at Sheffield Quarter Sessions.

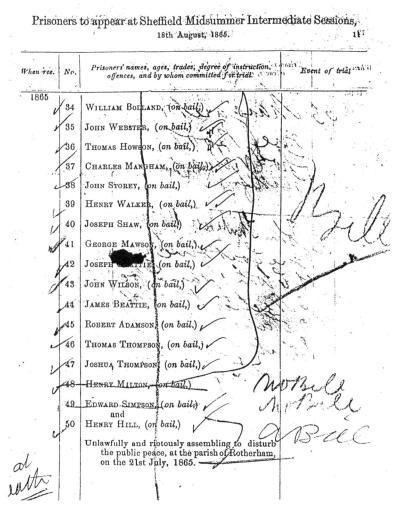

Prisoners to appear at Sheffield Midsummer Intermediate Sessions, 18th August, 1865.

When rec.	No.	Prisoners' names, ages, trades, degree of instruction, offences, and by whom committed for trial	Event of trial
1865	34	WILLIAM BOLLAND, (on bail,)	
	35	JOHN WEBSTER, (on bail,)	
	36	THOMAS HOWSON, (on bail,)	
	37	CHARLES MANSHAM, (on bail,)	
	38	JOHN STOREY, (on bail,)	
	39	HENRY WALKER, (on bail,)	
	40	JOSEPH SHAW, (on bail)	
	41	GEORGE MAWSON, (on bail,)	
	42	JOSEPH ..... (on bail,)	
	43	JOHN WILSON, (on bail,)	
	44	JAMES BEATTIE, (on bail,)	
	45	ROBERT ADAMSON, (on bail,)	
	46	THOMAS THOMPSON, (on bail,)	
	47	JOSHUA THOMPSON (on bail,)	
	48	HENRY MILTON, (on bail,)	
	49	EDWARD SIMPSON, (on bail,) and	
	50	HENRY HILL, (on bail,)	
		Unlawfully and riotously assembling to disturb the public peace, at the parish of Rotherham, on the 21st July, 1865.	

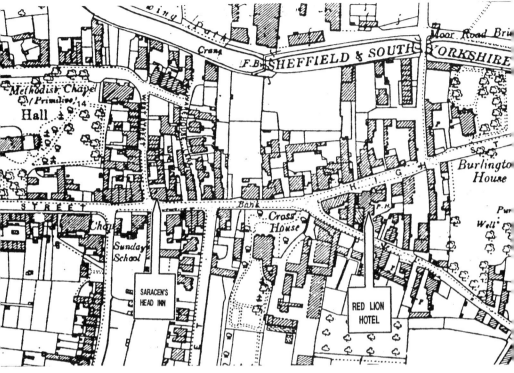

Figure 2. The centre of Wath. Although this O. S. Map extract is from 1903 little had changed since 1865.

had made the distribution of seats quite outdated. This is where we have the seeds of unrest, because the development of industry in South Yorkshire was producing an increasingly concentrated, disenfranchised body of labouring men who wanted their voice heard. The problem of course was that the electoral system encouraged popular participation without allowing legitimate expression through the ballot box, and that was a recipe for frustration. In spite of the limited number eligible to vote, enormous crowds turned out for the nominations for the constituencies and the subsequent poll declarations. For example, when nominations for the two representatives for Leeds were made on 12 July, 1865, on Woodhouse Moor, there was '... an immense concourse of spectators not less than 50,000'.[4]

The Liberal candidates for the Southern Division were Viscount Milton of Wentworth Woodhouse and Henry Beaumont from London, while the Conservative candidates were Christopher

1861 CENSUS	1865 POLL BOOK	
Adams, Charles, Corn Miller, 34 years, Doncaster Road, Wath Mill	Cons	
Adams, James, Quarry Hill, Darfield		Lib
Bamforth, John, Butcher/Farmer, 45, Church Street	Cons	
Blackburn, George, Butcher/Farmer, 52, West Street	Stanhope & Milton	
Brailsford, Isaac, Draper, 51, High Street	Cons	
Burman, James, Doctor, GP, 65, Chapel Street	Cons	
Burman, William M., Doctor, GP, 35, Chapel Street	Cons	
Cadman, William, Cross House	Cons	
Casely, George, School Master, 23, School Field, Grammar School	Cons	
Cheetham, John	Cons	
Clarke, Thomas		Lib
Cox, Joseph, South Parade		Lib
Dyson, Colin		Lib
Earnshaw, William A., Landed Proprietor, 36, Wath Hall	Cons	
Evers, George	Cons	
Finch, Thomas		Stanhope & Milton
Firth, Henry, Farmer, 47, Burlington Street (High St)		Lib
Green, Joseph, Wheelwright, 48, Sandygate	Cons	
Hague, Joh, Farmer, 39, Wath Wood, Swinton Stables		Lib
Harrison, Edward, Grocer, 58, Burlington Street	Lib	
Johnson, Charles H, Wine Merchant's clerk, 19, Sandygate, Woodside House	Cons	
Johnson, Samuel, Solicitor's Articled clerk, 21, Sandygate, Woodside House	Cons	
Johnson, William, Wine & Spirit Merchant, 51, Thornhill	Cons	
Law, John, Winterwell Field, Townend		Lib
Lister, John, Stone Mason, 33, Sandygate		Lib
Liversedge, Robert, Swinton		Lib
Mawson, John		Lib
Nash, William, Brick Manufacturer, 54, Chapel, Street		Lib
Nicholson, George P, Solicitor, 47, Burlington Street (High St)	Cons	
Otter, Henry, Swinton	Cons	
Otter, Robert W, Aisthorpe, Lincolnshire	Cons	
Oxley, Robert, Newhill		Lib
Pacy, Thomas, Boat Owner, 28, Doncaster Road		Lib
Palmer, George, Hill Foot Bridge, Sheffield		Lib
Pollard, George, Penrith, Cumberland		Lib
Reeder, Thomas, Solicitor's Managing Clerk, 38, Burlington Street (High St)	Cons	
Rodgers, Thomas, Innkeeper, 60, Red Lion Inn, High Street	Cons	
Saunders, George M, Solicitor, 33, Sandygate	Cons	
Thorpe, James, Innkeeper & Farmer, 45, Cross Keys Inn		Milton
Tilbury, Henry, Doncaster		Lib
Wade, Jonathan G, Surgeon, 50, High Street	Cons	
Wever, Frank, Wolstenholme Rd, Ecclesall		Lib
Whiteley, William, Farmer, 34, Well Lane, Town End House		Milton
Whitworth, Spedding, Brewer	Cons	

22 voted Conservative, 18 voted Liberal, 2 split their vote, 2 gave 1 vote to the Liberals
Thus: Conservatives 24 votes, Liberals 22 votes

Figure 3. Wath Voters. This table is based on the 1865 Poll Book and the 1861 Census.

Beckett Denison of Doncaster and Walter Spencer Stanhope of Cannon Hall, Barnsley. Lord Milton was typical of the aristocrats who felt more at home with the Liberals than the Conservatives and was part of that group known as Whigs, the forerunners of the Liberals. In his election address he declared his support for the abolition of Church rates, even though he was an Anglican, and he also supported the admission of Nonconformists to universities. More importantly, he was clear in wanting more men to be given the vote. Henry Beaumont, a latecomer to the lists when the original candidates withdrew, shared his lordship's views. They did not believe that giving the working man the vote would create some uncontrollable monster (Figure 4).

Christopher Denison, the senior of the two Conservative candidates, was the son of Edmund Denison who for 17 years had been one of the two West Riding MPs. Denison was very open about his stance on extending the right to vote:

> *On the great question of Electoral Reform I am opposed to any measure that has appeared for the mere lowering of the voting qualification in town or county.*

Likewise, his running mate, Walter Stanhope, made no bones about his stance when he declared in his election address:

> *On the question of Reform, I believe that the House of Commons as at present constituted fairly represents all classes and interests in the United Kingdom.*[5]

Given such views by the Conservative candidates it is no surprise that there was much hostility in the district towards them. Moreover, inefficiency in compiling electoral registers was matched by a failure to police effectively polling day itself. When the expectation is added of many electors being 'treated' and the absence of a secret ballot,

Figure 4. *Punch* cartoon, September, 1866. Votes for working men were seen as monstrous. An enormous public meeting was held in Birmingham to press for the vote.

THE BRUMMAGEM FRANKENSTEIN

JOHN BRIGHT. "*I have no fe—fe—fear of ma—manhood suffrage!*"

there is a volatile brew indeed. Within such a profoundly undemocratic system it is not surprising that working men who did not have the vote expressed their views forcibly, and so hostility towards the Conservatives boiled over in Wath on polling day.

Unlike modern times there were several days during which polling in a general election took place. In 1865 the process was that following the nomination of candidates a show of hands was called for to decide who was to represent the constituency; a poll would then be demanded on behalf of the other candidates. Thus, at the Wakefield nomination on Thursday, 18 July, the show of hands was judged to be in favour of Lord Milton and Walter Stanhope, with a poll being demanded and arranged for Friday, 21 July. Voting would take place between 8 a.m. and 5 p.m. A flavour of what was to come on that day was given by events at Scarborough a few days earlier:

Figure 5. Summary details of all those accused of riot.

Name and Address	Charge	Magistrates Court	Quarter Sessions
Robert Adamson, Mexborough	Riot		Not guilty
David Beevers, Mexborough	Riot	Discharged	
William Beevers senior, Mexborough	Riot	Discharged	
William Beevers junior, Mexborough	Riot	Discharged	
John Harrison, Mexborough	Riot	Discharged	
George Mawson, Mexborough	Riot		Not guilty
Henry Milton, Mexborough	Riot		No charges
Thomas Sayers, Mexborough	Riot	Discharged	
William White, Mexborough	Riot	Discharged	
John Wilson, Mexborough	Riot		Not guilty
Edward Simpson, Swinton	Riot		No charges
William Bolland, Wath	Riot		Not guilty
Thomas Howson, Wath	Riot		1 month hard labour
John Webster, Wath	Riot		Not guilty
James Beattie, Mexborough	Riot & Assaulting police		Bound over 1 year in £20
Joseph Shaw, Mexborough	Riot & Assaulting police		6 weeks hard labour
Joshua Thompson, Mexborough	Riot & Assaulting police		Bound over 1 year in £20
Thomas Thompson, Mexborough	Riot & Assaulting police		2 weeks hard labour
Henry Hill, Swinton	Riot & Assaulting police		Bound over 1 year in £20
Charles Mangham, Swinton	Riot & Assaulting police		1 month hard labour
John Storey, Wath	Riot & Assaulting police		6 weeks hard labour
Henry Walker, Wath	Riot & Assaulting police		6 weeks hard labour
Joseph Beattie, Mexborough	Riot & Assaulting police		2 months hard labour
William Herring, Mexborough	Riot & Assaulting police		Sailed to America before trial
23 men charged:	6 discharged,	1 emigrated,	17 for Quarter Sessions trial
17 at Quarter Sessions:	2 no charge,	5 not guilty,	10 guilty

1861 Census:
Thomas Howson, 17, coal miner, Mangham Lane (Cemetery Road), born Sheffield.
Henry Walker, 18, coal miner, Townend, born Wath.

There was immense excitement – the candidates were pelted with eggs and missiles by the mob. Bonnetting, hooting, and drunkenness in a few cases, led to heads being broken by the police. One man was much injured by a policeman's staff.[6]

The seriousness, however, of events at Wath is indicated very clearly by the wording of the indictment read out at the trial of the seventeen accused at the Quarter Sessions in Sheffield in August, 1865:

[the accused] *together with divers other persons to the number of two hundred and more with force and arms to wit with bludgeons sticks stones staves and other offensive weapons unlawfully riotously and tumultuously did assemble and gather together to break and disturb the peace of our lady the Queen and did then and there remain and continue armed as aforesaid for a long space of time to wit three hours and more to the great disturbance terror and alarm of all the liege subjects of our said lady the Queen.*[7] (See Figure 5)

The Riot

Among the 26 witnesses who gave evidence, or made statements there was agreement that the day began peacefully enough. Police Sergeant Horne had prepared for the day and said:

I was at Wath on the election-day, and had command of the police there. I paraded my men at about 7.30 in the morning. I placed men at each polling booth, whilst the others were ordered to patrol the streets in twos.

John Makin was a party activist who had been canvassing for Walter Stanhope and Christopher Denison. When he began the day, with a peaceful visit to the Conservative Committee Room at the *Red Lion* (see Figures 6 and 7), he could not have known how traumatic the polling was to become:

I received the canvassing book from Mr. Nicholson and I brought voters up to the poll first between nine and ten o'clock. The voters mostly wore rosettes. I wore a blue rosette.

William Cadman was Chairman of the Committee for promoting the election of Stanhope and Denison. He lived in Cross House (Church House), a few yards from the *Red Lion* and he said:

Up to about noon the proceedings of the Election were harmless enough, there being nothing but shouting by the crowd of young lads.

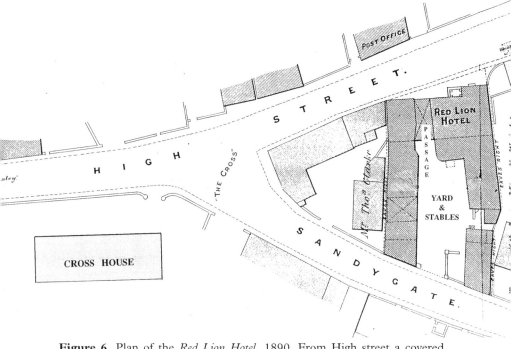

Figure 6. Plan of the *Red Lion Hotel*, 1890. From High street a covered passageway for coaches led through to the yard and stables on Sandygate.

Figure 7. Wath High Street, looking east. This photograph shows the *Saracen's Head Inn* on the left, with the road dipping down towards the *Red Lion* in the distance.

From midday onwards the good-natured party rivalry quickly degenerated into vicious assaults. As Sergeant Horne testified:

Between twelve and one o'clock I saw the mob attack a gentleman near the Saracen's Head. They pulled him about by the hair of the head. Police-constable Hobson tried to recover his hat, but was struck several times by the crowd. I went to his assistance and got him behind me and two other constables near an opening. The prisoner Joseph Shaw struck me and called out, "Go into the bugger." I stood up above the others, and a man in the crowd shouted out that the constable had struck some one. I told them that I had not seen it, and I hoped they would not be indiscreet. I told them I was in charge of the police, and intended to keep quiet without blows, if possible. Mr. Henry Barker, of the Don Pottery, pulled out a yellow card and held it up to the crowd to encourage them to hurrah! And he asked them not to resort to violence of any kind. There were more than 200 of the mob present, and they then fell back.

Henry Barker's plea to the crowd was an interesting one because in the polling booth he split his two votes between Milton and Denison! Despite the attempt by Mr. Barker to channel the energy of the crowd, William Cadman became increasingly concerned about the ugly mood which was developing along High Street:

Hats began to be knocked off and the people passing to and from the polling booth No. 2 were hustled about by the crowd. The excitement gradually rose until it was quite unsafe for respectable dressed people, especially if he was known or suspected to be a blue, to pass the crowd. Towards middle day I went home and locked up my watch so that I had no means of subsequently telling the time.

Cadman had gauged the mood of the mob correctly, for as John Makin recalled when giving evidence at Rotherham Magistrates' Court:

About noon there was a very great uproar in the streets from a mob of men and women parading opposite the Conservative Committee Room. There were from 200 to 300 people assembled, and the number afterwards increased. They were hooting and shouting, and I was kicked about when I was before the Committee Room. I saw several persons knocked down and their hats knocked off. There were many sticks and stones thrown at the police, and several missiles were thrown through the Committee Room windows before the shutters were closed. Many of the other windows of the Red Lion Inn were broken. The mob

got inside the house and some of them went upstairs, but were forced
out by Mr. Rodgers and the police, who afterwards closed the doors.
There was a band of musicians on a dray and the mob followed it.

Mr. Rodgers was probably Thomas Rodgers, owner of the *Red Lion*
and understandably anxious to protect his property. The reference to
the role of a band provides an interesting comparison with the
'Eatanswill' extract from *Pickwick Papers*.

Another Rodgers who became involved in events was James
Rodgers, butler in the service of Mr Montague of Melton Hall. From
his statement it is obvious that elections in Wath were usually rowdy
affairs, for in evidence he said:

I did not carry any colours. I have had experience in electioneering at
Wath, some six or seven years ago, and learned not to carry colours.

The absence from his coat of a blue rosette was, however, no guar-
antee of safety, for as he related:

I took two electors to Wath to vote last Friday, arriving there about 2
p.m. I saw a large mob rioting in the street, some of the men seized me
and others threw stones at me and the two electors I had. We were
prevented from going to the Polling Booth by the mob and I heard
Edward Simpson, of Swinton, say something about 'Here's a Blue
from Melton', and immediately the mob surrounded the dog-cart, and
the gentleman who was riding behind was struck on the head. We had
to seek refuge in the Red Lion Inn. After reaching the Red Lion about
a dozen of the men then got upon my cart and tried to break it up.

Also employed by Mr Montague, of Melton Hall, was Thomas Cundy,
his land agent. He was a marked man in two ways, for as agent the
colour of his politics was clear and he had canvassed for Stanhope and
Denison. Consequently, as he related:

I was in the streets of Wath on the polling-day, having been to call on
Mr. Wade. I had my hat knocked off and stones were thrown at me.
There was a great noise and disturbance. I saw Mr. Reed hustled
about. I can only recognise Joseph Beattie, who was one who made a
rush at me.

John Reed, who was a manufacturer from Swinton, confirmed the
butler's account:

I was with Mr. Cundy on the day named, and I was hustled and
pushed about, and a man attempted to throw me down. I saw Mr.
Stenton's hat knocked off and destroyed. My hat was also knocked off

and I received a severe blow at the back of my ear which caused me great pain for several days. I saw a gentleman's coat and waistcoat torn off his back and thrown into the air and torn into pieces. The mob then commenced throwing stones through the windows of the Red Lion. A woman came from amongst them and spat upon the window of the Committee Room. They then forced their way into the Red Lion and took possession of the house, doing considerable damage.

Thus, by mid-afternoon the *Red Lion* had become the focal point of the riot and William Cadman was in its midst:

I saw a great many stones thrown at the windows of the Red Lion Inn, both at the Committee Room windows and at the other rooms. I saw large stones as big as a man's foot thrown through the windows. They all came from the crowd in front and round the house. The Committee Room window shutters were obliged to be closed. Several attempts were made to get into the Red Lion Inn and on one of the attempts my hat was knocked off and I was struck and very much hustled about. The police were quite powerless to quell the riot, or oppose much resistance to the mob. I saw many acts of violence committed upon several people. Owing to the violence of the mob the doors of the Red Lion Inn were obliged to be closed to keep out the mob and it was with difficulty we could do so. (Figure 8)

John Makin's evidence continued to portray an ever increasing storm of violence at and near to the *Red Lion*:

In going to No. 2 Booth from the Committee Room I was knocked about by the mob and several of them called out "Into him, kill the bugger". I remained in the Booth about ten minutes and then attempted to come out. I should have returned directly to the Committee Room, but was prevented by the mob who threatened if I came out to kill me. There were some 300 to 400 people hooting, yelling, and knocking hats off, and threatening violence. Joseph Beattie called upon the others to break into the Booth and fetch me out forcibly. In a few minutes I was called out and seeing the mob a little way up the street I went towards the Red Lion Inn. I left the Booth about three o'clock, but when about thirty yards from the Committee Room, some of the crowd said, "He's here". When they came running Joseph Beattie struck me over the temple, cutting my head and knocking off my hat, after which he struck me several blows. The mob tried to force me down upon the ground and I was struck by several persons, so that I did not know what I was doing for some time. I was rescued by some friends who got me into the Red Lion, and

*a female followed me and struck me on the face. The mob then forced
their way through and drove us before them in great disorder. One of
them threatened to stick me, and my cravat and gold pin were stolen.
I saw the man steal them, but dare not resist. I also lost my 'favour'
and my hat. When I entered the Committee Room again I found
several squares of glass broken in the window. Whilst there several
larger stones were thrown through the window at me and others in the
room and we had to shelter ourselves by closing the window shutters
inside.*

What were the police doing while the mob ran amuck? According to
the evidence of Sergeant Horne:

*I saw several gentlemen in the streets have their hats knocked off, and
they were otherwise ill-treated. I saw a great many of the mob armed
with sticks. Between two pm and three pm, I saw three panes broken
in the Red Lion. I then called the constables and placed them in the
doorways. I again saw several gentlemen in front have their hats
taken, and their clothes torn. The police partly succeeded in keeping
them back, but some of the mob got in and assaulted some gentlemen*

Figure 8. *Red Lion Hotel* on the left, with coach entrance. This photograph
was taken in High Street looking west. The trees in the background are in the
grounds of Cross House.

Figure 9. Wath High Street, looking west from the junction with Sandygate. Although this photograph dates from many years after the riot, the line of buildings had not altered and emphasises how the riot was channelled along the High Street.

> *in the passage. I saw Captain Day, of Wombwell, attacked. His hat and riding whip were taken, and his clothes were torn. I went to his assistance and was struck by Henry Walker, John Storey, and a man named William Herring. I spoke to Walker and Storey first and requested them not to be guilty of taking anything from any person. In the course of twenty minutes I recovered the whip and gave it to the owner. Shortly afterwards there was a great rush to get into the house, and again I spoke to the mob and asked them to desist. I spoke to Joseph Beattie who was one of the mob. I saw police-constable Molesbury struck many times, and Joshua Thompson was one of his assailants. There was a great deal of fighting at that time.*

Although the *Red Lion* was still the focus of the riot, there were still serious attacks happening further west along High Street. Thus, Edward Pashley of Mexborough, labourer, said in his statement:

> *I went to Wath last Friday and there I saw a mob composed of colliers, glassblowers and etc. attack Mr. Benjamin Wales of Harlington. They knocked his hat off then kicked him several times, it was about three o'clock and opposite the Saracen's Head, his coat was very much torn. I went to his rescue when one of the Manghams of Wath*

assaulted me and said "This is one of the Blue buggers, go into him".
I got a black-eye in rescuing Wales. I also saw George Shaw's and
William Dyson's hats destroyed. Joseph Beattie of Mexborough was a
ringleader of the mob, the whole of which were exceedingly riotous.
(Figure 9)

Obviously the police were under enormous pressure and Sergeant
Horne must have felt his prayers had been answered when reinforcements arrived. In evidence the sergeant said:

When Colonel Cobbe and about forty fresh policemen came into the
Red Lion Yard, the mob began to throw at them, and the police were
ordered to charge on the mob in Sandygate. They drove the crowd
back for a moment or two. Afterwards the policemen returned to the
yard. At that time a man named Hicks was injured on the head, and
as I and police-constable Williamson were taking him to get medical
assistance, we were both knocked down by the mob, who kicked us and
trampled on us. I got up and tried to get Williamson up. A great many
were kicking him, and some of them held him by the hair of the head.
The mob then ran to the front of the Red Lion and scores of stones
were thrown at the windows and the police and other gentlemen.

Despite the arrival of Colonel Cobbe, the size and violence of the mob
were proving too great and so when Sergeant Horne saw that his force
was insufficient, he sent a note to Superintendent Gillett at
Rotherham. He did so because his men were overpowered. The
answer from Rotherham was that he could have no help from there.
Superintendent Gillett had his own election mayhem to deal with! It
is possible, however, that poor riot control tactics by the police in Wath
were to blame for their failure to regain the upper hand. For example,
William Cadman made a statement that

Had Colonel Cobbe remained in the Red Lion Inn yard and in the
street, instead of drawing off his force after he had charged the mob,
the riot would have been quelled much sooner than it was.

Although the height of the riot was in the mid-afternoon, it is clear
that violence continued for some time afterwards. Constable
Molesbury had been attacked by Joshua Thompson, who held him
while the crowd beat him. Consequently, the constable would have
more than sympathised with the incident he witnessed about six
o'clock when he saw a gentleman knocked down, kicked and pulled
about the *Red Lion* yard by his hair and whiskers. Constable
Molesbury testified that the poor man was completely covered with

blood and his clothes were partly torn from his back. With the assistance of other officers he rescued the man. Later he saw Mr. Nicholson's hat knocked off whilst that gentleman was in the street opposite No. 2 Booth. Sergeant Horne's testimony also makes clear that violence continued for some hours:

> *I saw Mangham pushing the police and other gentlemen amongst the mob until about five o'clock. I saw Henry Hill amongst the crowd assisting in taking and destroying hats and pushing the police when they interfered. Between six and seven o'clock I saw him throw several stones at persons and windows.*

Not until sunset on that summer's day did events calm down sufficiently to allow people to feel safe. Combining the testimonies of William Cadman, John Reed and John Makin we know that they felt they had been kept as prisoners in the Conservative Committee Room in the *Red Lion* until 9 pm. They had not dared to look outside because they were afraid of being attacked again, the mob having sworn they would kill them or any other Conservatives they could get hold of. William Cadman's emotions must have been very mixed: anger at the treatment so prominent a citizen of Wath had been subjected to, relief that his mansion so close to the *Red Lion* had not been attacked, observing that 'The violence of the mob was more directed against persons than property.'

The Reckoning

The machinery of justice moved quickly to gather evidence against the rioters and on Saturday, 5 August, charges against 24 men were presented to the bench of magistrates at Rotherham Court House. On the bench were the Hon and Rev W. Howard (Chairman), F. J. S. Foljambe, Esq., M.P., and H. Otter, Esq. The case for the prosecution was conducted by Mr Whitfield, with Mr Hirst and Mr Branson acting for the defence. One defendant did not appear, William Herring having sailed for America a few days previously!

Sergeant Horne's testimony was crucial to the prosecution and after detailing the events as he experienced them, he walked round the court and said:

> *I saw the prisoner John Webster in the crowd when they were throwing stones at the windows and the police. I saw Storey taking part the whole of the day in the throwing of stones at the police, other persons and windows. I saw Howson with a short stick in his hand taking hats, throwing stones and knocking about. I saw Thompson taking*

part in the disturbance. He was knocking hats off and was very active amongst the crowd. I saw him go up to several constables and use threats if they interfered. He was afterwards injured and was taken away in the cart. I saw Henry Walker amongst them from about noon, and he was one who attacked Captain Day: and when I went to the rescue, he struck me. I saw Walker hold the riding whip and I asked him several times to give it up.

The ability of the Sergeant to be so positive and the fact that he wrongly identified one of the accused in court, raises some doubts about his evidence. Indeed, as Mr Branson for the defence said:

All witnesses not in police uniform qualified their evidence, but all the policemen were strong 'down upon these men' and they appear to have very much exaggerated the facts.

John Pitt Makin, however, proved to be credible because his various roles as auctioneer, farmer, assistant overseer of the poor and collector of taxes brought him into contact with many people in the Mexborough district. Consequently, he was believable when he said in court that he had known several of the prisoners by sight for some time, having seen them in Mexborough, Swinton and Wath. He identified: Mawson, Milton, Adamson, Bolland, T. Thompson, Mangham, James Beattie, J. Thompson and Joseph Beattie. He recognised James Beattie as the man who stole his pin and cravat.

Further evidence against the accused was provided by William Waring of Mexborough, a Conservative elector, whose statement declared:

When at the Red Lion Hotel I saw Henry Milton of Mexborough amongst a mob of colliers rushing about and saying in great excitement "go into them". I observed David Beevers and William Beevers junior, both of Mexborough, also inciting the mob to acts of violence. I also saw George Mawson of Mexborough taking a leading part in the riot and threatening the Conservative electors. I saw the hat of the inspector of No. 2 Booth knocked off and destroyed.

A summary of the men accused and their sentences has been given in Figure 5. What is interesting is the low conviction rate, with less than half the men accused being found guilty. Of the fourteen who were accused of riot only, Thomas Hewson was alone in being convicted. Each of the eight additionally charged with assaulting the police was found guilty, but even then only five were imprisoned. Of course part of the problem with the case for the prosecution, both at the magis-

THE SHERIFF'S DECLARATION OF THE POLL.

Polling Districts.	Voters on the Register.	Voters Polled.	Milton.	Beaumont	Denison.	Stanhope.
1 Barnsley	1098	908	512	480	391	426
2 Dewsbury	1946	1606	1059	1009	561	537
3 Dobcross	743	605	333	324	271	271
4 Doncaster	1280	1017	465	433	564	528
5 Goole	329	268	55	56	206	210
6 Holmfirth	636	511	284	279	225	222
7 Huddersfield	1913	1617	873	852	742	718
8 Penistone	346	268	90	86	172	180
9 Pontefract............	936	719	334	308	425	408
10 Rotherham	971	771	572	538	204	210
11 Scissett	439	358	241	247	121	127
12 Selby	604	468	142	136	333	327
13 Sheffield............	3015	2151	1301	1280	837	851
14 Sherburn	290	238	18	18	220	215
15 Snaith................	324	251	22	20	229	229
16 Tadcaster	285	223	59	57	164	156
17 Thorne	589	438	205	195	243	236
18 Wakefield	1688	1293	496	487	788	785
19 Wath-upon-Dearne	471	379	197	170	188	183
Total............	17903	14089	7258	6975	6884	6819

Majority of Lord Milton over Mr. Denison....................................... 374
Majority of Lord Milton over Mr. Stanhope 439
Majority of Mr. Beaumont over Mr. Denison.............................. 91
Majority of Mr. Beaumont over Mr. Stanhope 156

Figure 10. Voting results for the Southern Division, by Polling Districts. The turnout was nearly 80 per cent.

trates' court and at the Quarter Sessions, was that witnesses were either policemen or Conservative electors! At the Rotherham hearing even the prosecution acknowledged there was no case against William Beevers senior and John Harrison. The Chairman of the bench said he did not think there was anything much against William White, T. Sayers or William Beevers junior. The seventeen who were committed for trial at the Quarter Sessions were not considered to be a danger to the public and they were released on bail at £20 for each prisoner, in their own recognizance.

There is a contrast with the experience of the 23 men tried at Leeds for the Rotherham election riot which prevented Superintendent Gillett sending reinforcements to Wath. All but one of the Rotherham rioters were found guilty and they received much

longer prison sentences, ranging from one month to six months.[8]
That of course is another story.

What then was the result of the election which had generated so
much interest and violence? At Wakefield on Monday, 21 July, in
front of a crowd of about 10,000, the Under-Sheriff declared the poll
to be:

Lord Milton	Liberal	7258
Mr Beaumont	Liberal	6975
Mr Denison	Conservative	6884
Mr Stanhope	Conservative	6819

(see Figure 10)

Although the new constituency marked a point of departure for the
West Riding, the national picture was little changed. The 1865 general
election, like that of 1857, was a vote for Palmerston and it left the
state of the parties virtually unaltered. The great pity, from
Palmerston's view, is that he died on 18 October, 1865, two days
before his eighty-first birthday.

Notes and References

Detailed evidence relating to the riot and individuals involved is taken from documents in
Rotherham Central Library's Local Studies and Archives Section, as well as from contemporary
newspaper accounts. The witness statements were part of the papers of Nicholson & Co. of Wath,
solicitors, subsequently deposited by Bridge, Sanderson and Munro, solicitors.

1. P. Johnson, *The Oxford Book of Political Anecdotes*, OUP, 1986.
2. L.C.B. Seaman, *Victorian England*, Routledge, 1984.
3. Poll Book for the Southern Division of the West Riding, 1865 election, published 1866.
4. *Annals of Yorkshire*, vol 2, published 1866.
5. Poll Book 1865 election.
6. *Annals of Yorkshire,* vol 2.
7. Regina v Mawson, West Riding Intermediate Sessions Sheffield, 18 August, 1865.
8. *Annals of Yorkshire*, vol 2.

Acknowledgements

I am particularly indebted to the staff of the Local Studies and Archives Section of Rotherham
Central Library. I also wish to thank the staff of Sheffield Local Studies Library and the West
Yorkshire Archives Service at Wakefield.

CONTRIBUTORS

1. DEER PARKS IN THE MALTBY AREA

Alice Rodgers was born and brought up in Burton-on-Trent. She came to South Yorkshire in the late sixties after qualifying as a teacher and, for ten years, lived and worked in Sheffield. In 1978 she and her family moved to Maltby where, in her spare time, she has been able to pursue her life-long interest in local history. In 1981 she co-founded Maltby Local History Society whose regular monthly meetings now draw people from the wider Rotherham area and beyond. She is now employed part-time as a lecturer and community outreach worker at Rother Valley College at Dinnington. She contributed an article on water-powered sites in the Maltby area to *Aspects of Rotherham 1* and another on archaeological excavations at Roche Abbey, 1857-1935, to *Aspects of Rotherham 2*.

2. ANCIENT HIGHWAYS THROUGH ROTHERHAM

Howard Smith was born and bred in Sheffield, and spent all his professional career as a schoolmaster and further education lecturer in the city. His interest in the Rotherham area began when he lived in Maltby for a time, where he helped to found its local history society to which he still belongs. Immediately following early retirement he studied for an MA in Local History under the tutelage of David Hey. His thesis was converted into his first book *A History of Rotherham's Roads and Transport* (1992). He has also produced six 'Turnpike Trails' designed to make local history accessible to the layman. His specific research area of roads was triggered by his being invited to write a script on the history of local roads for Radio Sheffield in its early days. Guide stoops caught his eye whilst researching old packhorse ways and he produced *The Guide Stoops of Derbyshire* in 1996. Howard enjoys the countryside, especially whilst undertaking fieldwork for his research, photography (much of it for archival purposes) and giving illustrated lectures to a wide variety of groups and societies.

3. CORN WINDMILLS OF ROTHERHAM AND DISTRICT

Alan Whitworth trained at Bradford College of Art and, after a number of years in the world of printing and graphic design, in 1977 he predominantly turned his attention to promoting the preservation of English parish churches, founding and running a charity to that end, writing and lecturing on the subject, mounting many exhibitions and organising the first national conference dealing with churches and tourism; and yet his interests are wider, and his regard for old buildings and history has led to the founding of the British Dovecote Society and the Yorkshire Dovecote Society. He now writes and lectures about local history subjects and his books include *Yorkshire Windmills* (MTD Rigg Publications, 1991); *Village Tales: A History of Scalby* (Alan Sutton, 1993); and *Exploring Churches* (Lion Publishing, 1993).

4. 'REMEMBERED IN STONE': CHURCH MONUMENTS IN THE ROTHERHAM AREA

Brought up on the Derbyshire/Staffordshire border, **Simeon Bennett** attended Hatton Comprehensive School where he developed an enthusiasm for medieval history and architecture. Currently working in a high street bank, he is married with a baby son and lives on the outskirts of Derby. He is an active member of the Church Monuments Society through which he met his fellow author Tony Dodsworth.

Tony Dodsworth was born in Crystal Palace and grew up in south London. He attended St Joseph's College, Beulah Hill, before studying for a combined Geography and History degree at Birmingham University. He began teaching in London but moved north in 1974 and has now taught for more than twenty years at Pope Pius X School, Wath upon Dearne, where he is Head of Humanities. It was under the influence of Professor Harry Thorpe at Birmingham University that he developed a keen interest in the historical geography of England and learned to recognise ridge and furrow at more than twenty paces! This interest has continued to grow through membership of English Heritage and the National Trust and he is an enthusiastic visitor of churches, particularly as a member of the Church Monuments Society.

5. THE EXPANSION OF A GREAT LANDED ESTATE: THE WATSON-WENTWORTH SOUTH YORKSHIRE ESTATE, 1695-1782

Melvyn Jones, who edited *Aspects of Rotherham* and *Aspects of Rotherham 2,* and who is also the editor of the *Aspects of Sheffield* series, was born in Barnsley and educated at the Holgate Grammar School and the universities of Nottingham and Leeds. He taught for seven years at Myers Grove, Sheffield's first comprehensive school, and then for nine years at Sheffield City College of Education before its amalgamation into Sheffield City Polytechnic in 1976. He has recently retired from the post of Head of Academic Resources in the School of Leisure and Food Management at Sheffield Hallam University, but continues an association with the university as an Associate Research Fellow at the Leisure Industries Research Centre. He has written extensively on the economic, social and environmental history of South Yorkshire, including more than twenty articles on its woodland history. Books on local subjects include *A Most Enterprising Thing* (1991) (an illustrated history of Newton Chambers at Thorncliffe); the widely acclaimed *Sheffield's Woodland Heritage* (1989; 2nd edition, 1993); and *Rotherham's Woodland Heritage* (1995). He is also co-author of *Chapeltown and High Green* (1996) and *Chapeltown, High Green, Grenoside and Ecclesfield* (1998) both in Chalford Publishing's Archive Photographs series. He is currently working on a book on the history of South Yorkshire's countryside. He is BBC Radio Sheffield's 'History Man' with a 25 minute weekly 'Local History Spot'.

6. THE TROUBLE WITH SERVANTS…DOMESTIC LIFE AT WENTWORTH WOODHOUSE IN THE EIGHTEENTH CENTURY

Marjorie Bloy (née Williamson) was born in Rotherham and was educated at the Girls' High School and Alnwick College of Education. She obtained graduate and postgraduate qualifications on a part-time basis from the University of London and the University of Sheffield. Since 1968 she has taught History in schools and further and higher educational establishments in South Yorkshire (sometimes concurrently). A more recent venture has been publishing academic materials on the Internet.

7. ARCHITECTS OF NO SLENDER MERIT: PLATT OF ROTHERHAM, 1700-1810

Brian Elliott was born and educated in the Barnsley area. After an undistinguished spell as an apprentice professional footballer he obtained a proper job, working for Barnsley Corporation in a Dickensian office next to the Public Cleansing Department. Whilst Head of Geography at Royston Comprehensive School he also tutored adult education courses for the WEA and University of Sheffield and published short histories of Royston parish. He researched his own town for an MPhil, awarded by the University of Sheffield in 1990. His popular book *The Making of Barnsley* (1988) was the first published history of the town since 1858. He founded the acclaimed *Aspects of Local History* series, edits *Aspects of Barnsley* and *Aspects of Doncaster* and advises Wharncliffe on local books. His recent publications include *Barnsley's History From the Air, 1926-1939* (1994) , *Barnsley's Sporting Heroes* (as editor, 1997) and *Discovering South Yorkshire's History* (1998). Brian works at Rother Valley College where he is Head of the School of General and Community Education.

8. COAL MINING ON THE WENTWORTH ESTATE, 1740-1840

Ian Medlicott was born in Doncaster where he spent his early years before moving to Sheffield. He was educated at High Green Secondary Modern School, Barnsley College of Technology and Ecclesfield Grammar School. After qualifying as a school teacher, he taught in primary and secondary schools in Sheffield and Barnsley. He gained a BA (Hons) and an MPhil with the Open University. He has been interested in local history for many years, especially early coal mining in South Yorkshire, about which he has published articles in archaeological journals.

9. COLLIERY TRAMROADS OF NORTH-WEST ROTHERHAM

Graham Hague was born in Sheffield where he has always lived. All his recent forbears however were born in Rotherham. It was school holidays spent exploring the canals and railways of the Masbrough and Holmes areas that developed a lifetime's interest in transport and industrial archaeology generally. His technical education was at

Salmon Pastures (Attercliffe) Technical College. He spent most of his career working for Sheffield Corporation, first in the Architects Department and latterly as a conservation officer within the Planning Department. He is a co-author of *Industrial History of South Yorkshire* published by the South Yorkshire Industrial History Society in 1995 and of *Sheffield Trams Remembered.*

10. COAL FOR COMMERCE: SUSTAINING A MANUFACTURING ECONOMY

Sheffield born and bred, **Trevor Lodge** was educated at Abbeydale Grammar School and Manchester and Sheffield universities. An industrial chemist by training, he had an early career which comprised spells of teaching interspersed by a memorable but brief period as a research chemist with Newton Chambers & Co. Ltd. at Chapeltown. He eventually found his feet in South Yorkshire's special steels industry, retraining as a metallurgist in the early 1970s, largely through developmental work at British Steel's Templeborough Steelworks. He currently works as an Information Officer in the region's special steels industry. He has carried out research since the mid-1960s into the UK's heavy industries and the railways that served them. His most notable published works - the histories of the Park Gate Iron & Steel Co. Ltd., Steel Peech and Tozer Ltd., and Samuel Fox & Co. Ltd. - appeared in serialised form in British Steel's *Steel News* and United Engineering Steels' Journal, *Stocksbridge Gazette*, between 1981 and 1993. He is a regular contributor to the *Aspects* series.

11. THE STOVE GRATE, RANGE, AND DECORATIVE CAST IRON INDUSTRY OF ROTHERHAM

Chris Morley was born in Manchester but served his apprenticeship as a design draughtsman with the Light Castings Division of Newton Chambers & Co. Ltd. (Redfyre). Until his early retirement he worked as a designer for several domestic appliance manufacturers, designing everything from solid fuel cookers and fires, hairdryers and irons, gas fires, cookers, electric cookers and washing machines, and, for the last fifteen years of his employment, large-scale catering equipment. He qualified as a mechanical engineer, and went on to study industrial design, and the utilisation of gas. He is a chartered engineer. He has studied social and economic history as an extra-mural student, specialising in the history of the stove grate and domestic appliance industries. He and his long-suffering wife have travelled widely in the UK and abroad, following leads into early ironmaking and casting. When they have not been spending 'Casting' holidays, they have been 'Gattying', researching the biography of the family of the Rev. Alfred Gatty, erstwhile vicar of Ecclesfield. Chris is also an expert on the Walkers of Grenoside and Masbrough and his *The Walkers of Masbrough: a re-examination* was privately published in 1996.

12. The Wath Wood Volunteers: A Chapter in Local Military History

John Goodchild, M. Univ., is a native of Wakefield and was educated at the Grammar School there. He has been active in local historical research since about the age of thirteen, and he is the author of some 130 books and published essays on aspects of the history of the West Riding. He was the founder-Curator of Cusworth Hall Museum near Doncaster, and subsequently Archivist to Wakefield MDC. In his retirement, he runs a Local History Study Centre at Wakefield which houses his immense collections of manuscripts and research materials, and which is open for all to use, free of charge by appointment. John also holds an honorary Masters degree from the Open University, awarded for academic and scholarly distinction and for public services. Outside historical research, his interests lie in Freemasonry and Unitarianism - and his dog.

13. The Wath General Election Riot of 1865

Alex Fleming was born and educated in Liverpool. After obtaining graduate and postgraduate qualifications from London, Newcastle and Keele universities, he joined the staff of Wath Comprehensive School in 1972, where he is now Head of History. As secretary of Wath History Group since its inception in 1979, he has given many illustrated talks at its quarterly meetings and organised several local history exhibitions at Wath Library. His publications include a Wath town trail, a photographic history of the town (jointly with Steve Hird) and commentaries on reprints of old Ordnance Survey maps of the area. A long-term project is the creation of an oral history archive for Wath. He contributed articles on Wath to *Aspects of Rotherham 1* and *Aspects of Rotherham 2*. For many years a long-distance runner, Alex tries to spend as much time as possible walking, climbing and cross-country skiing with his wife Susan in Scotland and the Alps.